The Blackwell Handbook of Education

Michael Farrell, Trevor Kerry
and Carolle Kerry

BLACKWELL
Oxford UK & Cambridge USA

The right of Michael Farrell, Trevor Kerry and Carolle Kerry to be identified
as authors of this work has been asserted in accordance with the Copyright,
Designs and Patents Act 1988.

First published 1995

Blackwell Publishers, the publishing imprint of
Basil Blackwell Ltd
108 Cowley Road
Oxford OX4 1JF
UK

Basil Blackwell Inc.
238 Main Street
Cambridge, Massachusetts 02142
USA

British Library Cataloguing in Publication Data
A CIP catalogue record for this book is available from the British Library.

Library of Congress Cataloging-in-Publication Data
Farrell, Michael
    The Blackwell handbook of education / Michael Farrell, Trevor
Kerry, and Carolle Kerry.
    p.   cm.
    ISBN 0–631–19279–4. — ISBN 0–631–19281–6 (pbk.)
    1. Education—Great Britain—Handbooks, manuals, etc.
2. Education—Great Britain—Terminology. 3. Education—Great
Britain—Directories. I. Kerry, Trevor. II. Kerry, Carolle.
III. Title.
LA632.F37 1995
370'.941—dc20   94-27461
                                                     CIP

Typeset in 10 on 12pt Ehrhardt by Photoprint, Torquay
Printed in Great Britain by Hartnolls Ltd, Bodmin, Cornwall

This book is printed on acid-free paper

Contents

Acknowledgements

In attempting to cover such a broad area as education, it has been inevitable that we needed to turn to others for advice and help and we have been most fortunate in the response we have received.

In particular we would like to thank Tony Millns, Assistant Chief Executive of the School Curriculum and Assessment Authority (SCAA) and professional officers of SCAA for helpful comments on the entries concerned with the National Curriculum. Elizabeth Wallis of the Advisory Centre for Education generously gave advice on Section 4, 'Legislation'. Representatives of the various bodies covered in Section 3, 'Organizations', were helpful in providing necessary information. We are also grateful to the Diocesan Schools Adviser for Religious Education, Diocese of Lincoln; the Cathedral School, Lincoln; and the National Association of Governors and Managers.

We felt that it was important that the Handbook should be 'trialled' on a range of potential readers and we are grateful to all who helped in this. In particular we would like to thank Professor David Reid, Professor of Education at Manchester University, his colleagues and students at the University; Tony Pannell, Consultant at Surrey LEA, and his colleagues; and Hugh Senior and Christine Shadbolt of Glebelands School in Surrey.

Alison Mudditt and staff at Blackwell Publishing gave generous support and practical help throughout and we are most grateful to them.

Introduction

Our Readers

It is particularly important to publish a book of this kind now, for more people than ever before are taking an interest in education.

We envisage that this Handbook will be used in schools, colleges, universities, libraries, and in homes too. Readers will include professionals and parents. Among professionals, we particularly have in mind teachers (experienced practitioners, returning teachers and trainee teachers), head-teachers, and school governors. We hope also that the book will be helpful for administrators, civil servants, politicians, researchers, academics, educational psychologists, inspectors and advisors.

The Handbook will serve two broad purposes: as a work of reference and as a vehicle for more sustained study. This latter will be achieved through its system of cross-referencing (see below).

In compiling this book we have standardized on certain conventions. We have made personal choices about which topics should, and should not, be included (though we are happy to receive comments and suggestions to guide future revisions). Our aim has been to present factual information, recent data and significant research in a readable style. We have given references to important material which you may wish to follow up in detail. Where appropriate we have not been afraid to make comments which are value-laden; the authorship of each entry is indicated by initials since we may not all share identical views!

The following sections of this introduction are intended to help you get the most from the Handbook.

The Changing Face of Education

Education is not an area of knowledge like mathematics or physics where it is fairly easy to agree on the content of the topic and the methods associated with it. On the contrary, it is a wide and complex sphere to which many people from various disciplines have made contributions. Philosophy, sociology, history, psychology, politics, pedagogy and comparative studies have all laid claim to aspects of education.

At the same time, and quite rightly, various groups within our society today have their own interpretations of, and views about, education. Parents, pupils and students, teachers, politicians, administrators, civil servants, HMI, academics, journalists, school governors, headteachers, business people, industrialists and others all have their own perspectives.

A shared perspective is not always easy to find; indeed, even shared understanding of issues is sometimes elusive. In England and Wales, the great changes brought about by education legislation in the 1980s and 1990s have made it even harder to find common ground with others as whatever ground is occupied seems to change quickly.

What we have tried to do in this Handbook is therefore to map out aspects of education with particular reference to England and Wales, and with particular emphasis on primary and secondary school education. Underlying our approach and choice of entries were several broad and equally important aspects of education.

The Underlying Structure of the Handbook

Although the main body of this Handbook presents items in an A to Z format, it has an underlying structure and rationale reflected in the eight broad areas which the book covers. (These areas also form the structure of the classified list of A to Z entries.)

1. **Education: Concepts, Issues, Disciplines, Types and Phases**
   Recognizing the importance of educational concepts and issues, and their relationship with other ideas and issues is an essential aspect of understanding education itself.

   For example, what do we mean by the terms 'knowledge' and 'understanding' and a host of others?

   Entries under this broad heading include not only educational concepts and issues but also an outline of the disciplines associated with education (e.g. psychology).

2. **Schools and Other Institutions and their Organization**
   Our emphasis is on institutions in England and Wales, particularly schools.

   We cover the various types of schools and units; school organization; and educational (and other) institutions and their organization.

3. Roles (Duties and Responsibilities) and People

The roles, duties and responsibilities of teachers in various settings are covered as are roles of associated professionals and roles within associated organizations.

We cover roles, duties and responsibilities in (or relating to) schools, tertiary education and other areas.

Mention is made of a few key educationalists, such as Rousseau and Montessori.

4. Rules, Regulations and Conditions

An area of potential confusion for many people new to the world of education is rules and regulations. These include admission to schools, complaints, exclusion and parental choice of school.

In this area, we have concentrated mainly on schools and on procedures likely to be of shared interest to parents and education professionals.

5. Individual Differences (Among Learners)

Pupils and students can attract study and attention for a variety of reasons. For example their ability may be considered, as with average ability or gifted pupils. Gender, age and behaviour are other characteristics with educational implications. We cover issues related to individual differences.

6. Curriculum and Assessment

The curriculum has been the focus of much recent Government attention. The curriculum followed by any organization, institution or individual involves making choices and, indeed, value-judgements about the content, what is being learned and how the knowledge or skill is structured.

The main focus is on schools and on England and Wales because of the curricular changes in schools brought about by such influences as the National Curriculum. But alternative ways of mapping knowledge and skills, such as humanities, are also represented.

In tertiary education, similar decisions are made which colour the way knowledge is understood, and these too are included – for example, vocational perspectives. In all phases of education, the 'hidden curriculum' is considered.

Parallel with any curriculum or syllabus or course is the way in which learning is assessed. Assessments associated with the National Curriculum, and awards and qualifications in tertiary education are explained.

We cover the school curriculum, school-related assessment and examinations, post-school courses and qualifications, and teacher training/education.

Entries concerning the National Curriculum and related topics were made as up to date as possible and it is proposed to incorporate any subsequent changes in a second edition.

7. Pedagogy

The essence of what goes on in the classroom is the way in which the content of education, whether it is knowledge, skills or attitudes, is learned by the pupil and taught or facilitated by the teacher.

Consequently, entries include such items as lesson planning, questioning techniques, communication in the classroom and discovery learning.

We cover teaching methods relating to the whole class and groups, to approaches through audio-visual media or information technology, or through individual subject disciplines and integration. These issues stand at the heart of the whole process of education from birth to death.

8. Resources

Entries concerning resources include such topics as computers and information technology.

These eight broad areas comprise the underlying structure of the Handbook and are compiled and presented in A to Z format.

Following the alphabetical entries in Section 1, the Handbook comprises three further sections.

Section 2 is 'Acronyms and Abbreviations', of which there is an increasingly bewildering array.

Section 3 is a 'Directory of Organizations' of particular concern to teachers. This includes a selection of education bodies and organizations, unions, professional associations, subject associations and research bodies and projects in the UK.

Section 4 is 'Legislation', which focuses on England, Wales and Scotland, and aims to provide both concise data on individual topics and a broad historical overview.

Using the Handbook for Systematic Study

One use of the Handbook is as a means of systematically, yet flexibly developing an understanding of UK education. The classified list of A to Z entries can be used as an aid. We recommend that any systematic reading begins with the broad area 'Education: Concepts, Issues and Disciplines'. A system of cross-referencing (by printing in small capitals, entries which supplement the topic consulted) leads the reader to pursue individual issues to greater depth and aims to provide a broader context. In appropriate cases, references to other books and articles will take the reader to a more specialist understanding.

Using the Handbook for Reference

Of course, systematic reading is not the only use of the Handbook. Used in the way that reference books are generally used, it is a source of information and clarification.

Suggestions

We have tried to cover areas and topics in this Handbook that our 'trialling' of the book indicated that our potential readers would find most useful. We hope that we have included entries which readers will find most helpful and excluded others which are less necessary. However, we would be pleased to hear from any readers and organizations with suggestions for any amendments so that later editions of the Handbook will continue to be as informative as possible. Please write to Michael Farrell via the publishers as follows:

Michael Farrell
The Blackwell Handbook of Education
Blackwell Publishers
108 Cowley Road
Oxford OX4 1JF
United Kingdom

Section 1 – A to Z Entries

Michael Farrell, Trevor Kerry, Carolle Kerry

ABILITY GROUPING

Grouping by ability refers to the formation of classes of pupils that are composed of pupils of similar general or specific abilities. There are various kinds of grouping by ability, described in more detail under the topics STREAMING, SETTING and BANDING. Grouping by ability contrasts with MIXED ABILITY ORGANIZATION. Recent government pressure has tried to move even primary schools towards more use of ability groups. The arguments for and against ability groups include the following:

Arguments for:

Ability grouping allows pupils to advance at their own rate.

It challenges the pupil to do his/her best in the group to which he/she is assigned.

Pupils may still associate with others of different abilities in games, assemblies, clubs and other joint activities.

Methods and materials used with homogenous ability groups are directly applicable to the entire group of pupils because of the pupils' similarity.

This form of organization makes it easier for the teacher to make the class feel an entity; so there are better opportunities, e.g. for whole class discussions.

Pupils of less ability are able to receive more individual attention from the teacher when they are placed together in class.

Providing for individual differences within the mixed ability classroom becomes complex and time-consuming with such a great variation of individual differences.

When mixed ability grouping is used, the teacher tends to teach to the average or below.

Arguments against:

A stigma may be attached to the pupil if he/she is placed in a slower group; in a fast group he/she may develop snobbishness and an exaggerated view of him/herself.

Mixed ability classes provide personal contacts similar to those the pupil will encounter as an adult.

Pupils need the social experience of working with others of different abilities.

Less able pupils benefit from learning experiences in association with those of more ability.

True ability grouping is impossible, since any particular factor used for such grouping may be the only point of similarity in the class.

In ability grouping, teachers may neglect pupils' differences. Since individuals have different patterns of ability, mixed ability grouping allows various levels of ability to show themselves among pupils of the same age.

Pupils do not develop at the same rate. Mixed ability classes help pupils cope with different maturation rates.

TLK

ABLE PUPILS – CHARACTERISTICS

Research into the characteristics of able pupils has been conducted throughout this century on both sides of the Atlantic. Definitions of ability and INTELLIGENCE are useful in defining which pupils are classed as ABLE; and some workers make fine distinctions between GIFTED, talented, very able and able. This entry seeks only to define the general characteristics commonly found in the ablest segment of the school/college population – though individuals differ widely in whether and to what extent they exhibit these characteristics. Able pupils exhibit extensive general and/or specialized knowledge: often they have 'passions' for particular themes on which they become incredibly expert. They have good recall, understand difficult concepts easily, and ask many – usually unanswerable or provocative – questions. Behaviour may appear obsessive and they may become absorbed (failing to respond while engrossed in a task, for example). These youngsters often have an eye for detail, and reach the end of a train of thought long before the teacher or other speaker has finished. They often show enormous CREATIVITY, imaginativeness and inventiveness. They appreciate verbal puns and tricks of language; often they argue rather than take even adult wisdom at face value. They may read quickly, but often rush intellectual processes and are bored by slow, manual activities like writing, often becoming extremely untidy or attempting to avoid the chore. Able youngsters are talkative, with large vocabularies, and may seek out adults and older students for company rather than 'average' peers. They may be interested in 'adult' issues such as world news, but may not always distinguish fact from imaginative construction when young. While usually well integrated with peers, showing leadership characteristics, some able youngsters become socially withdrawn (see UNDERACHIEVEMENT, and may develop difficulties in integrating socially in class. The vast majority of able pupils are conformist to school DISCIPLINE and codes of behaviour. Only a tiny minority use their ability to become inventively disruptive. Teachers who suspect the presence of able pupils in the class would do well to use the techniques of INDIVIDUALIZED LEARNING and QUESTIONING to maximize their involvement (see also: ABLE PUPILS – MANAGING THE LEARNING OF). Specialist information and advice can be sought in the journal *Gifted Education International* and through the NATIONAL ASSOCIATION FOR GIFTED CHILDREN.

TLK

ABLE PUPILS: MANAGING THE LEARNING OF
Professional wisdom suggests that teachers can adopt a number of strategies which will help to keep the most able pupils in classrooms purposefully engaged in school work. These strategies include:

1. Prepare material to extend, stretch or stimulate bright pupils.
2. Have plenty of (additional) work prepared.
3. Keep them fully (and meaningfully) occupied.
4. Encourage their abilities and potential.
5. Admit one's own areas of weakness or lack of knowledge.
6. Set them extra work over and above the rest of the class.
7. Treat them as equals and respect their abilities.
8. Keep them integrated and free of peer-group social pressures.
9. Give individual help as required.
10. Sustain their interest.
11. Do not allow them to become isolated.
12. Demand work of quality not quantity.
13. Explain your own standards and values and stick to them.
14. Be versatile in approach to them.
15. Give them time; don't just leave them to get on.
16. Encourage freedom and independence in learning.
17. Listen to them and hold conversations in depth with them.
18. Keep them challenged.
19. Do not allow complacency in work or attitudes.
20. Keep contacts with teacher as frequent as possible.
21. Discuss their work with them.
22. Answer their questions with honesty.
23. Provide as many open-ended situations as possible.
24. Have supplementary resource materials available.
25. Treat them the same as others.

26. Encourage depth of thinking.
27. Prepare lessons thoroughly.
28. Make them research and report back.
29. Give them responsibilities to others.
30. Set them plenty of goals beyond the class level.

By contrast, teachers advise as follows:

DONT
dismiss their questions with 'find out for the next lesson';
shut them up;
ask only the bright pupils in the class for answers to questions;
talk down to them;
make them feel they are different from the rest;
show favouritism towards them;
use them as 'odd jobbers';
use them as pupil teachers;
be overprotective to them;
push them too hard;
allow them to dominate the class;
give them too much attention;
set repetitive tasks;
assume they always understand work set.

TLK

ABLE PUPILS: NEEDS OF

Just as ABLE PUPILS exhibit specific CHARACTERISTICS which help teachers recognize them so they have specific learning needs which need to be met through appropriate SKILLS and TEACHING METHODS. These needs do not necessarily differ substantially from the needs of AVERAGE PUPILS or those with LEARNING DIFFICULTIES (see also SPECIAL EDUCATIONAL NEEDS): but they may need putting into a specific context relative to the able pupil's experience. These needs include:

- a sound psychological climate;
- opportunities for competition;
- learning co-operation;
- stimulus of work at the higher cognitive levels;
- developing skills of problem-solving and problem-devising;
- security to ask difficult questions of the teacher;
- independence in learning;
- their ideas and suggestions valued;
- encouragement to speculate;

- experience of failure;
- becoming self-critical;
- the ability to accept criticism;
- social skills (tolerance, humour);
- peer-group friendships;
- being steered away from unhelpful traits, e.g. perfectionism, non-conformity, attention-seeking;
- broadening their interests beyond those of their specific skills.

TLK

ABUSED CHILDREN

When Lord Justice Elisabeth Butler-Sloss chaired the Cleveland Judicial Inquiry into child sex abuse, the committee pointed out important basic facts about such abuse. It occurs with children of all ages, of both sexes, in all classes of society and often within the privacy of the family.

Child abuse is a term also used more broadly to include such ill treatment as emotional neglect and physical injury. Where it is known that children have been abused or are endangered, they are entered on a local social service department's 'at risk' register. Teachers are well placed with regard to protecting children from abuse as they are often the first adults outside the home to suspect that a child is being abused. However, great care and sensitivity is needed and good working relationships between the education service and the social services is important.

(See also: BULLYING)

Addresses

Kidscape, 152 Buckingham Palace Road, London SW1W 9TR
tel: 071 730 3300   fax: 071 730 7081
National Society for the Prevention of Cruelty to Children (NSPCC)
67 Saffron Hill, London EC1N 8RS
tel: 071 242 1626

MF

ACADEMIC AWARDS

The collective description given to specific levels of achievement for examinations and assessments validated by recognized bodies such as universities. Lower levels of award are exemplified by GCSE and GCE passes and by the vocational awards such as GNVQ and NVQ and CITY AND GUILDS qualifications. Higher level awards would include some BTEC courses (HNC/HND) and BACHELOR'S, MASTER'S and DOCTOR'S DEGREES given by universities. The PGCE and similar awards given as a result of IN-SERVICE EDUCATION would also fall into this category.

TLK

ACADEMIC DRESS

Academic dress has a long history going back to medieval times in the ancient universities. The black gown worn as a contemporary item of clothing by scholars was hooded against the cold. Scholars who graduated to the degree of BACHELOR were allowed to line or edge the hood with fur; while graduates who obtained master of arts status were allowed a silk lining of a regulation colour. This pattern of academic dress survived to form the basis of today's system. The hoods for the degrees of BA and MA in the oldest universities follow this pattern, the hood shape (described as full or simple) varying from one university to another. Thus academic dress for bachelors of arts at Oxford is a simple black hood half-lined and edged with white fur; at Cambridge University BAs wear a full-shaped hood half-lined with fur; and at Durham the full-shape with fur lining and edging is retained also. These hoods are worn over a black gown with pointed sleeves; masters of arts' gowns have a distinctive sleeve pattern. At Oxford University hoods for MAs are lined with red silk, in Cambridge with white, and in Durham with Palatinate purple (a shade of lilac).

This system was generally adopted in the early days by the emergent British universities; but as the number of degrees proliferated and the number of universities increased, it has tended to break down. To the degree of BA first degrees such as B.Sc., B.Ch. (Bachelor of Surgery), B.Ed. and LLB were added and these required to be distinguished in dress. A few 'bachelors' degrees' were created which were postgraduate – most BD (Bachelor of Divinity) and B.Phil. qualifications were actually 'higher' degrees and the style of academic dress tends to reflect this by the use of conventions such as use of silk or fuller linings usually reserved for masters. Masters' degrees proliferated similarly and fresh conventions had to be sought, such as edging hoods with a ribbon of the faculty colour. Thus Nottingham University graduates wear black hoods lined with the University blue, each faculty being distinguished by the ribbon binding the cowl (cherry for Arts, lilac for Education, maroon for Law, etc.). There are, however, many exceptions to these systems and the newer universities have introduced new shapes to the garments and new ground colours (e.g. Exeter hoods are dove grey).

In academic dress bachelors and masters wear 'mortar-boards'. Doctors' gowns usually feature claret, red or the University's distinctive colour; and the hoods are similar and usually fully lined with a regulation colour. Thus, at London University, bachelors' and masters' gowns and hoods are black; Doctor of Philosophy (Ph.D.) robes are claret, and those of the higher doctorates (e.g. D.Litt., D.Sc., DCL) are scarlet. Head-wear for doctors varies but is often a soft round cap resembling those worn in Tudor times. Academic dress is now often reserved for use on formal occasions, for example at graduation ceremonies. Its use by staff at school functions such as speech days tended to diminish in the egalitarian climate of the 1960s and has not revived, though it is still worn by Protestant clergy when they are officiating, usually at services other than Communion. Academic dress is, however, another part of our rich heritage of ceremonial and tradition; and perhaps its survival should be nurtured in recognition of its deep cultural roots.

TLK

ACADEMIC (ROLE)
The term 'academic' when applied to a person usually refers to a university lecturer, senior lecturer, principal lecturer, reader, professor or researcher who is involved in teaching and/or research of a high academic standard.

MF

ACCESS TO INFORMATION
Many documents are available for inspection at schools. These should include:

- in the case of an LEA school, the County Council's Statement of Curriculum Policy;
- the governing body's statement of curriculum aims;
- all statutory instruments, circulars and administrative memoranda sent by the Department for Education to the headteacher or governing body;
- all syllabuses followed by pupils;
- the agreed syllabus for religious education;
- the school brochure;
- examination and National Curriculum test results.

In addition to the above documents, the school must keep full records of pupils' academic achievement, skills, abilities and progress. Parents of pupils under sixteen years of age may ask to see and discuss these records. Pupils aged sixteen and seventeen may ask to see records in conjunction with parents, and pupils aged eighteen and over have the right to ask to see their own academic records.

A charge may be made by schools for copies produced for the personal use of parents.

CAK

ACCOUNTABILITY

Accountability in education implies that policies and aims are made explicit and that criteria are agreed to enable an assessment to be made about the extent to which policies have worked (or have been followed) and the degree to which aims have been achieved.

An example arises from the Education Reform Act (ERA) 1988 which requires headteachers and teachers to deliver the national curriculum and to be accountable for so doing. One way of assessing the success or otherwise of the implementation of this policy and the achievement of NC aims is the testing of pupils at various stages of their school career as required by the ERA 1988.

Further reading

Sallis, J. (1991) *Schools, Parents and Governors: a New Approach to Accountability* (Routledge).

MF

ACCREDITATION OF PRIOR ACHIEVEMENT (APA)

Skilled persons do not have to attend courses of training for the achievement of NVQs in their chosen area. Through the APA and ACCREDITATION OF PRIOR LEARNING method, skills already possessed can be assessed against the units of competence required for the level of award sought.

CAK

ACCREDITATION OF PRIOR LEARNING (APL)

Skilled persons do not have to attend courses of training for the achievement of NVQs in areas where they are already competent. Through the ACCREDITATION OF PRIOR ACHIEVEMENT and APL method, skills already possessed can be assessed against the units of competence required for the level of the award sought. This accreditation of prior learning:

- recognizes past achievement;
- encourages further learning;
- benefits adult learners and those without formal training.

Further reading

Field, M. (1993) *A.P.L.: Developing More Flexible Colleges* (Routledge).

CAK

ACQUIRED IMMUNE DEFICIENCY SYNDROME (AIDS)

AIDS is a consequence of being infected by the human immunodeficiency virus (HIV). HIV affects the normal immune defences of the body so that someone with AIDS is susceptible to being affected by a wide range of potentially fatal diseases. Despite massive investment and extensive research, AIDS is at present incurable although drugs have been developed which appear to delay the onset of AIDS and slow down its development.

The HIV may be passed from an infected person in blood, semen, or vaginal fluids. It can be passed through:

(a)   unprotected sexual intercourse (either vaginal or anal or through oral sex);
(b)   sharing unsterilized drug injecting equipment;
(c)   receiving transfusions of infected blood;
(d)   an infected pregnant mother contaminating her child.

Schools and their respective umbrella authorities (e.g. Grant Maintained Schools Trust, LEAs) should have a policy on AIDS encompassing health education, AIDS prevention and the management of situations in which a teacher or pupil is found to be HIV positive. Under the Education (No. 2) Act 1986 sex education was made the responsibility of school governors. AIDS education falls under this remit, Personal Social Education can also include education about AIDS.

The Terence Higgins Trust, a charity set up to offer help for AIDS and HIV sufferers and their families, provides leaflets, videos and posters relating to AIDS. For details of these, and courses run by the Trust, contact:

Terence Higgins Trust, 52–54 Grays Inn Road, London WC1 8JU
tel: 071 831 0330

Further reading

Harris, D. and Haigh, R. (1990) (Eds) *AIDS: A Guide to the Law*
(Routledge).

MF

ACTION RESEARCH

Most people asked to describe research into classroom process would talk
in terms of an independent observer or detached investigator looking
objectively at the behaviour of a teacher and/or pupils. Action research
differs significantly from this objective model because a significant actor in
the scenario (sometimes a researcher, sometimes the teacher him/herself)
becomes actively involved in the classroom process as an agent of change –
PARTICIPANT OBSERVER.

At its simplest a piece of action research would involve a teacher trying a
new way of delivering a piece of curriculum content and monitoring the
result compared with previous practice. But action research can be carried
out on a much larger scale, as when a team of researchers collaborates with
groups of teachers to adapt and experiment with teaching methods and/or
curriculum materials and then monitor the results in systematic ways.
Action research of this kind has the advantage that the subjects of the
research can be very responsive, bringing a whole series of changes to bear
on a situation in the light of immediate and changing circumstances. This
kind of research is popular with teachers because it is collaborative, retains
their autonomy for adaptive action, and is related to real practice. In this
way action research has become associated with self-analytical practice as a
means to more reflective and continuous PROFESSIONAL DEVELOPMENT. The
methodology contrasts with views of IN-SERVICE EDUCATION which depend on
'experts' giving 'received answers' for teachers to emulate. The values of
action research are sometimes listed as:

- its democratic approach (with researcher/teacher as equal partners);
- its problem-solving nature;
- its flexibility;
- its ability to achieve rapid change without sacrificing empiricism.

Criticism of action research centres around its alleged lack of rigour:
control of the experiment is sacrificed to adaptiveness; the observer is less

objective; its samples are often unrepresentative; and there is little control of independent variables.

TLK

ACTIVE LEARNING
Active learning is an approach which has epitomized work in the primary sector, at least since the PLOWDEN REPORT. It is a way of teaching which holds that children are more likely to make knowledge their own when they are involved in it, e.g. through PLAYING, making, doing or ROLE-PLAYING.

(See also: EXPERIENTIAL LEARNING)

TLK

ADMISSION TO SCHOOLS
Under law, full-time compulsory education of children extends from the age of 5 to 16 years and children must be admitted to school at the start of the term which follows their fifth birthday.

Details of admission to independent (preparatory) schools and Grant Maintained primary schools may be obtained from the particular school. Similarly at secondary level, details of admission to independent (including public) schools, Grant Maintained secondary schools, and City Technology Colleges can be obtained from the school concerned.

In the case of LEA schools, under 'open enrolment', a parent may choose a school for their child other than that allocated by the LEA. The school of choice must have a place available, the parent must be prepared to transport the child to and from the school at their own expense, and the director of education must consent.

In the case of LEA schools where demand for a place in a school is greater than supply, the Association of Metropolitan Authorities suggests that LEAs take account of four criteria:

1. historical family links;
2. priority based on proximity to the school (not for example the boundary of the LEA in which the school operates);
3. catchment areas giving equal priority to children on either side of a boundary;
4. well-established feeder primary schools and links already existing between the primary and secondary sectors.

Under the Education Act 1986 (section 33), LEAs responsible for admission arrangements must consult governors about these at least annually. Where governors are responsible for admissions, they must consult with the LEA. The LEA has to publish admission criteria and each school has to publish a brochure of information including its admission criteria.

Under the Education Act 1980, parents who do not get the school of their choice for their child may appeal through a procedure administered by the LEA. The parent may have grounds to believe that the LEA or governors have acted unreasonably and not according to statutory duties with respect to:

• general admission arrangements;
• the constitution of the appeals committee;
• the presentation of the parents' case to the appeals committee.

In such cases, the parent may complain to the Secretary of State for Education.

Further reading

(1990) *Schools Choice and Appeals* (Advisory Centre for Education).

MF

ADOLESCENCE

Adolescence in western society is characterized as a time of physical, psychological and social change which young people experience as they grow into adults.

Rapid physical changes, physical growth and the emergence of sexual characteristics can lead to clumsiness and over self-consciousness. As children may be increasingly influenced by peers and decreasingly influenced by family and school, they can present difficulties at home and school. At the same time the adolescent may feel emotionally and socially confused as he or she searches for an identity.

Educational implications of adolescence include the following:

• at a time of confusion and change, learners tend to appreciate consistency and stability in the way they are treated;
• a teacher's sensitivity to pupils' possible swings between feelings of maturity and feelings of inadequacy can be helpful.
• activities which develop physical skills and grace can help with clumsiness and improve feelings of self worth;
• group discussion on personal and social issues can be very rewarding as

can drama and other creative work which helps learners explore their changing identity;
- peer influence can be positively channelled in group work on team activities.

Further reading

Kutnick, P. (1994) 'Development and Learning' in the series Farrell, M. (Ed.), *Education for Teaching* (HMSO).

MF

ADULT EDUCATION
Adult education, sometimes known as continuing education, is a broad term encompassing education beyond the minimum school-leaving age. Venues include evening classes in local schools and courses in Colleges of Further and Higher Education. Areas of study include academic and vocational courses varying from basic skills learning to degree courses. They are often part-time.

The Education (Adult Education Centres Funding Schemes) Regulations 1989 form the statutory foundation for adult education in further education. Under DES circular 19/89, local authorities have discretion on the running of adult education courses. The Education Reform Act 1988 imposes a duty on LEAs to secure the provision of 'adequate' facilities for further education in their area. However, the term 'adequate' is open to different interpretations and there is a worry that the present variety of adult education courses may be slimmed down to predominantly vocational courses.

Under the FURTHER AND HIGHER EDUCATION ACT 1992 (see Section 4, 'Legislation') two types of adult education course were established. The first was generally non-vocational courses which do not lead to an examination or qualification. These remained the responsibility of LEAs. The second type of course was broadly vocational courses funded by the Further Education Funding Council.

Details of local courses can be obtained from particular institutions or from the LEA.

Addresses

National Institute for Adult and Continuing Education, 19B De Montfort Street, Leicester LE1 7GE
tel: 0533 551451

Scottish Institute of Adult and Continuing Education, 30 Rutland Square, Edinburgh EHl 2BW
tel: 031 229 0311
Northern Ireland Adult Education Association, c/o 42 Northland Road, Londonderry, BT48 7ND Northern Ireland
tel: 0504 265007
Workers' Educational Association, 17 Victoria Park Square, London E2 9PB
tel: 081 983 1515

MF

ADVANCED LEVELS (A LEVELS)

Advanced levels (A levels) are academic qualifications gained by examination usually taken at the age of 18 by sixth-form students and others. University degree courses normally require A levels as entry qualifications.

While three or four A levels are usually studied in England and Wales over a two-year course, in Scotland the closest comparable qualification is the Higher Grade of the Scottish Certificate of Education, which normally encompasses five subjects and takes one year.

Attempts to broaden the academic requirements of A levels have included the introduction of ADVANCED SUPPLEMENTARY LEVEL examinations (AS levels) and modular courses which contain units which could be put together to contribute to an A level or alternatively could form part of a vocational qualification.

MF

ADVANCED SUPPLEMENTARY LEVELS (AS LEVELS)

Advanced Supplementary levels (AS levels) are qualifications gained by examination and introduced as an alternative to A LEVELS in order to broaden the academic foundations normally provided by A levels.

AS levels enable students to study more subjects up to A level standard to ensure that a wider range of education and career choices remain open. Universities and institutions of higher education accept a combination of two A levels and two AS levels as equivalent to three A levels.

MF

ADVISERS

During the 1960s LEAs were encouraged to appoint advisers/INSPECTORS to support the role of teachers. Some LEAs distinguished between these two roles: using the term adviser in a training context and the word inspector in an evaluative one. In a few LEAs the personnel were actually different. Since the 1988 EDUCATION ACT the roles have changed (see: OFSTED and INSPECTION).

TLK

ADVISORY TEACHER

A senior teacher appointed by an LEA to carry out curriculum innovation and classroom support usually to subject teachers in a group of schools.

TLK

AFFECTIVE EDUCATION

Benjamin Bloom divided learning into domains: the COGNITIVE (see: COGNITION), which deals with intellectual abilities; the psycho-motor, which deals with physical development and adjustment to the environment; and the affective. The affective domain is about the growth of the individual as a social being and about adjustment to the social environment. The person has to develop a personal awareness and does this through building a consciousness of situations, phenomena and objects through the senses. The affective domain looks at the individual's growing awareness of colour, arrangement, form and design and at increasing perceptiveness about people, situations and symbolic representation (of which road signs and abstract art might be seen as simple and more complex examples).

Affective learning examines the individual's ability to receive messages from others and from society: to listen, to be tolerant of religious, political or natural differences; to develop sensitivity to human need or social issues. Discrimination of meaning and mood are part of the affective domain, and in schools pupils and teachers might explore these through art, drama, literature or music. Learning in the affective domain means that pupils come to accept basic safety rules, discipline and responsibility. Co-operation and competition, and the balance between them, are important here. As affective learning progresses the individual begins to internalize social values and adopt personal ones – a process often conspicuous in teenagers, who may espouse 'causes' readily and with passion.

The pupil who is affectively educated will value honesty, and will be able to discriminate between liberty and licence. Gradually the immediate and emotional appeal of 'causes' becomes reasoned into social responsibility and personal conviction. At its highest levels affective education leads to a personal philosophy based on an appreciation of abstract values: truth, beauty. It educates choice and leads to discrimination, e.g. the ability to evaluate a new invention or to debate a difficult issue such as euthanasia. It leads to the formation of a balanced personality characterized by mature judgement informed by an understanding of reasons and consequences and a respect for the views of others.

The affective domain is the theoretical base on which many other educational processes are based: RELIGIOUS EDUCATION, MORAL EDUCATION, SOCIAL EDUCATION see: PERSONAL SOCIAL EDUCATION) and life skills. As such it underpins appropriate themes in the NATIONAL CURRICULUM. As well as informing curriculum practice, affective education is built into much teacher behaviour and school practice: e.g. the setting of norms of behaviour in the classroom, school rules, and the standards that underpin the school ETHOS which is signalled by the headteacher and staff together. Thus the maturation of the pupil's affective skills forms an important and continuing strand throughout pre-school and school life and is critically placed alongside intellectual development and physical growth.

Further reading:

Bloom, B. S. (1956) *Taxonomy on Educational Objectives* (New York: Longman).

TLK

AIDED SCHOOLS – ADMISSIONS TO

In Aided schools, i.e. schools provided by the Church of England or Roman Catholic Church, the governors are responsible for admissions by setting the school's admission limit after consulting with the Local Authority Education Officer, and agreeing the criteria to be used in the allocation of places where there are more applications than vacancies.

In the event of the governors not offering a place, parents have the RIGHT OF APPEAL and an Independent Appeals Committee considers each case; the decision of the committee is binding on the school's governors.

CAK

ALCOHOL ABUSE

(See: DRUG ABUSE)

ALTERNATIVE EDUCATION

The Education Act 1944 made it a parent's duty to ensure that their school age children were educated full-time in school 'or otherwise'.

One alternative to conventional schools is home education, for which the LEA has to give permission. If a parent is educating a child at home one of the considerations (apart from having the time and skills) is to weigh the individual attention possible at home against the social skills developed in school. Free home tuition is provided by LEAs in certain circumstances, such as for children with profound and multiple learning difficulties.

Other alternatives are offered by various types of 'progressive' schools. (See also: FREE SCHOOLS, MONTESSORI SCHOOLS or STEINER SCHOOLS)

Addresses

Education Otherwise, 25 Common Lane, Hemmingford Abbots, Cambridgeshire PE9 AN.
World-Wide Education Service, Barleymow Passage, London W4 4PH.

MF

ANNUAL MAINTENANCE GRANT (AMG)
The Annual Maintenance Grant is the principal grant paid by the DFE to a Grant Maintained school, and is expected to cover the school's every-day running costs, such as salaries, books, materials, etc.

CAK

ANNUAL REPORT TO PARENTS
The governing body of each school must publish an annual report to parents, which is then available for discussion by parents with the governors at the annual meeting. The GOVERNORS' annual report to parents relates to the work of the governing body and is not intended to be a full report on the school. It should contain the following information:

- date, time, place and agenda of the meeting;
- a description of the purpose of the meeting;
- names of all governors and their terms of office, and name and address of the chairperson and clerk;
- information relating to the election of parent governors;
- examination and National Curriculum test results for the whole school;
- rates of truancy (unauthorized absence);
- the governors' conclusions on whether to ballot parents about applying for the school to become Grant Maintained;
- financial details, including expenditure of moneys allocated to the school by the LEA in the case of schools within the LEA system, or the DFE for Grant Maintained schools, and details of donations, gifts, etc., and the use to which they have been put;

- notification of changes to the school brochure;
- a report on the results of any resolutions passed at the previous meeting.

The report must be distributed to parents of all pupils registered at the school, and to all staff employed at the school, at least two weeks before the date of the meeting, and where parents have separated, the school should try to ensure that each parent receives a copy of the report. The report may be sent home via the pupil.

CAK

APPOINTED GOVERNORS

The LEA nominates a number of GOVERNORS to all governing bodies of maintained, voluntary-aided and special agreement schools, who may be appointed according to the political party distribution on the council. Whilst it is legal for the LEA to give all the places to the ruling political party, this is discouraged by the Local Government and Housing Act 1989.

(See also: FIRST GOVERNORS and FOUNDATION GOVERNORS)

CAK

APPRAISAL

(See: TEACHER APPRAISAL)

APPRENTICESHIP

Apprenticeship has traditionally referred to a system of training whereby a young person (often a school-leaver) would be 'bound' to a master craftsman for up to five years to learn by example on-the-job the skills of a specific trade. While historically this was usually a one-to-one relationship, in more modern industrial times large firms – especially in fields like engineering – took on apprentices as routes into workshop skills. With increasing economic recession such opportunities have diminished, and would-be trainees are now more likely to attend training courses, e.g. in COLLEGES OF FURTHER EDUCATION as a route to a career. A scheme to create a 'modern apprenticeship' for all 16 and 17-year-old school leavers and which, it is hoped, will encourage employers to train young people to NVQ level 3, was announced in 1993. The money for the scheme will be channelled through the TRAINING AND ENTERPRISE COUNCILS, and the scheme is expected to be on offer to up to 150,000 people at any one time.

The concept of apprenticeship has applications, e.g. in the INITIAL TRAINING

OF TEACHERS where the master craftsman idea is replaced by that of the MENTOR. The concept is of limited value in the concept of MENTORING.

TLK

ART (IN THE NATIONAL CURRICULUM)
If you are not familiar with National Curriculum terminology, before reading this subject entry, you may find it helpful to first
read the entries on:

Attainment Targets
National Curriculum
Programmes of Study
Standard Assessment Tasks

There are two Attainment targets (ATs) for art:

AT1	Investigating and making	The development of visual perception and the skills associated with investigating and making in art, craft and design.
AT2	Knowledge and understanding	The development of visual literacy, understanding of art, craft and design including the history of art, our diverse artistic heritage and a variety of other artistic traditions, together with the ability to make practical connections betwen this and pupils' own work.

Each end of the key stage attainment relates to a 'STRAND' of progression, as indicated below.
AT1:

* recording what has been seen, imagined or remembered: visual perception;
* gathering and using resources and materials;
* using different materials and techniques in practical work;
* reviewing and modifying work.

AT2:

* knowledge of different kinds of art and the development of visual literacy;

- knowledge of different periods, cultures and traditions in art, and the work of influential artists;
- applying knowledge of work of other artists to their own work.

There is not a statutory ten-level framework for art. For Key Stage (KS) 1–3, end of key stage statements define the knowledge, skills and understanding which pupils of different abilities and maturities can be expected to achieve by the end of each key stage. Programmes of study at KS4 are non-statutory.

There are two parts of the Programmes of Study (PoS):

1. specific key stage requirements;
2. more general requirements which apply throughout the three key stages.

The latter establish ground rules on the importance of:

- balance between art, craft and design;
- planning, taking into account previous achievement;
- varied methods of working, individually, in groups, and as a whole class;
- working in two and three dimensions on a variety of scales;
- appropriate use of information technology;
- pupil evaluation of their own and others' work;
- art from a variety of cultures, western and non-western.

The specific requirements for each key stage are set out in relation to each AT. Each Programme of Study statement relates to an end of key stage statement and is illustrated by non-statutory examples.

The timetable for ATs and PoS applying to art is as follows:

	KS1	KS2	KS3	KS4
ATs and PoS first apply (August)	1992	1992	1992	1995*
First statutory assessment (Summer)	1994	1996	1995	1997*

*KS4 is non-statutory. In England the great majority of schools are expected to offer art to pupils who wish to continue their study of the subject after the age of 14.

Further reading

DES/WO (1992) *Art in the National Curriculum* (HMSO).

MF

ARTICLED TEACHERS

The TASC (Teaching as a Career) organization produced the following description of the articled teacher scheme in an information leaflet dated 1989:

> The articled teacher scheme is a new form of Post-Graduate Certificate in Education (PGCE). The first courses started in September 1990 and further courses from September 1991. Articled teachers spend two years on their PGCE course and will be based in schools for 80 per cent of this time, i.e. 40 per cent equivalent of one year is not in school.
>
> The entry requirements are the same for any PGCE course – normally a good degree in a subject relevant to the school curriculum. In addition, all entrants to teacher training must have GCSE Grade C or above (or the equivalent) in mathematics and English Language – or have reached the equivalent standard. Articled teachers recruit through the GRADUATE TEACHER TRAINING REGISTRY.
>
> Articled teachers are paid a special bursary rather than a grant. The bursary is not means tested and is tax-free, and articled teachers who undertake their training in London will receive a higher rate of bursary than elsewhere in the country. Articled teachers who teach in shortage subjects (i.e. mathematics, physics, technology, CDT, chemistry, modern foreign languages, Welsh, biology and combined/balanced science in the secondary school sector) are eligible for the additional shortage subject bursary.
>
> Articled teacher courses are available for both primary (early years or junior) and a variety of secondary subjects. Courses have been developed by partnerships of teacher training institutions, local education authorities and schools. They consist of on-the-job training, with experienced teachers acting as trainers or MENTORS, combined with an institution-based course of training. Qualifications gained are identical to the PGCE and will give QUALIFIED TEACHER STATUS which will enable successful students to work in maintained schools.

TLK

ARTICLES OF GOVERNMENT

The Articles of Government are rules of management for schools. They set out the responsibilities of the governing body, the head and the LEA in the running of maintained schools, and LEAs must consult with the head and governing body over the Articles of Government. All staff and GOVERNORS will be given a copy of the Articles of Government, together with the Instrument of Government.

The Secretary of State for Education is responsible for drawing up the Articles of Government for schools which achieve Grant Maintained status. The Articles lay down the rules by which the Secretary of State and the governors operate; the powers are wide, and the governors can do 'anything which appears to them to be necessary or expedient for the purpose of, or in connection with, the conduct of the school'.

CAK

ASSESSMENT (IN THE NATIONAL CURRICULUM)

In the NATIONAL CURRICULUM, assessments are made to establish what each pupil has achieved in relation to the relevant attainment target for a certain age group. In this way standards are nationally monitored.

The assessments comprise teacher assessment and STANDARD TESTS OR TASKS. Teacher assessments for each pupil are measured against attainment targets and moderated. Standard tests are taken when pupils are aged 7, 11 and 14 years, that is, at the end of each Key Stage.

Two terms often used in relation to assessment are 'formative' and 'summative', and the National Curriculum has adopted these terms. Formative assessment yields information which helps the teacher decide how the pupil's learning should progress. It gives the pupil targets for learning and feedback about what has been achieved. Also it indicates the need for other diagnostic assessments with certain pupils. Summative assessment gives an overview of a pupil's achievements, understanding and skills. The assessments at 7, 11 and 14 and at 16 (GCSE) are summative.

To report a child's results (for example, to parents) on attainment targets for each subject would be too cumbersome. Consequently, in each subject, attainment targets are grouped into clusters. In English for instance, the clusters are: reading; writing; and speaking and listening. These are called profile components.

The achievements of pupils at 16 plus are frequently summarized on a document known as a RECORD OF ACHIEVEMENT, although this procedure is not universal. Similar documents are used to report achievements at earlier ages.

MF

ASSISTED PLACES SCHEME

The Assisted Places Scheme was set up by the Government following the 1980 Education Act and is designed to help some academically able children to receive an education suited to their needs at independent secondary schools in England and Wales which have been designated for this purpose. A different Assisted Places Scheme operates in Scotland.

The Scheme is open to both boys and girls and age of entry is usually 11 or 13. The Scheme enables families who could not otherwise afford the tuition fees charged by independent schools to receive financial help so that places are available free or at reduced cost. The amount paid by parents will depend on wages and income, with a review of the scale of charges each spring. All children, whether they attend schools maintained by the LEA, those having Grant Maintained status, independent schools or schools run by the Services overseas, are eligible to apply for 'assisted places'. Children admitted under the Scheme will be selected by the schools and entry requirements therefore vary. The Scheme provides help only with day or tuition fees, not with boarding fees, but an assisted place may be given to a child to attend boarding school where the boarding fee is being paid partly or wholly from another source. Some independent schools may be able to help with boarding fees in the form of a bursary.

Full details of the Scheme may be obtained from:
The Department for Education, Mowden Hall, Staindrop Road, Darlington, County Durham DL3 9BG.

CAK

ATTAINMENT TARGET (AT) (IN THE NATIONAL CURRICULUM)

The content of each subject of the NATIONAL CURRICULUM is divided into a set of attainment targets. These are statements specifying what children are expected to know and understand or what they are expected to do at each key stage. An example of an attainment target from the English National Curriculum is AT2, which is concerned with reading:

> The development of the ability to read, understand and respond to all types of writing, as well as the development of information retrieval strategies for the purposes of study.

MF

AUDIO-VISUAL AIDS

Teaching is greatly enhanced in variety and interest if teachers are fluent in the use of a range of AV aids. These would include: posters, pictures, 35 mm slides, OHP transparencies, cassette audio and videotape. Such aids enhance learning by providing concrete support to illustrate TEACHER TALK.

TLK

AUTHORITY

The concept of authority is extremely important in teaching and a distinction is often made between the two facets of authority needed; being an authority and being in authority. Being an authority means being well informed and up-to-date in teaching itself including the content area taught and pedagogy. Being in authority relates to the role of the teacher in relation to the learner. At its most basic it involves the teacher being able to keep order in a classroom and relates to DISCIPLINE. Other important aspects are a school teacher's skills in CLASSROOM MANAGEMENT, which can involve pupils taking positions of authority, say as group leaders in a group task, without the authority of the teacher being diminished. Indeed in such situations the authority of the pupil rests on the acceptance of the class group that the pupil acts within the overall framework of authority engendered by the teacher.

Headteachers and teachers stand 'in loco parentis' to pupils and hold authority inherent in this special relationship.

MF

AUTONOMY

Personal autonomy is an aim of education. Rational autonomy implies independence. Independence involves self-determined behaviour and implies freedom to choose. (This excludes coercion and physical craving for drugs for example.)

In the case of educating children, it is necessary that a sense of selfhood develops before we can sensibly speak of a learner's self-determination. Also a child's freedom to choose has to be curtailed by parents and teachers in cases where unacceptable choices may be made (e.g. choices which would be harmful to themselves or others). Such freedom is also in practice limited by the teacher's view of education. If education is initiating learners into worthwhile activities, a learner's potential freedom may be curtailed to the extent that it runs counter to educational aims.

In general, a teacher aiming to encourage self-determination in learners should eschew indoctrination and encourage questioning. Combining the encouragement of self-determination with that of rationality leads to the aim of educating the learner for autonomy, self-determination based on reason.

MF

AVERAGE PUPILS

Sometimes called 'middle band' pupils, these are the pupils who fall, in ability, to the centre of a class/year group or who test at around an IQ score of 100. Research suggests that in MIXED ABILITY CLASSES teachers tend to view them positively because they are often quite conformist in behaviour;

but teachers tend to distinguish them by largely negative characteristics, e.g. as pupils who do not work very quickly or do not ask insightful questions.

TLK

BACCALAUREATE

The Baccalaureate is an examination qualification determining entrance to higher education in most European countries. It is comparable with A level or, in Scotland, with the Higher Grade of the Scottish Certificate of Education.

The broadly-based examination requires acceptable grades in a wide range of subjects such as mathematics, literature, a foreign language, sciences, history and religious or ethical education.

Different countries have their own form of the Baccalaureate. Also the European School movement awards the European Baccalaureate. In certain schools across the globe an International Baccalaureate Diploma is offered.

Address

International Baccalaureate Office (UK), 18 Woburn Square, London WC1H ONS
tel: 071 637 1682/1861

MF

BACHELOR OF EDUCATION

Up until the 1960s, entrants to the teaching profession came by one of two routes. The student either took a first degree (BA, B.Sc.) in a university, topping this up by a one-year POSTGRADUATE CERTIFICATE or Diploma in Education at a university department of education, or he/she attended two or three years at a College of Education and gained a Teachers' Certificate or a Certificate in Education. The former route was favoured by secondary subject specialists, the latter by would-be primary teachers.

In the 1960s, as a result of the James Report, it was decided to turn teaching into an all-graduate profession, and a new three-year (ordinary level) or four-year (honours level) bachelor's degree was devised. This combined subject studies, a study of the main disciplines of education, and periods of practical teaching. Known as the B.Ed., this became a regular qualification for primary staff and even for many secondary teachers through the 1970s and 1980s. Since many existing teachers were not graduates, however, provision was made in many Institutes of Higher Education for courses which enabled qualified teachers to top up their existing qualifications by part-time study to achieve the degree: the Inservice B.Ed. The degree has always been controversial in that some have maintained it was not as rigorous as a 'subject' degree. Many accept, however, that it is an excellent vocational degree; but it still can be asked whether it is as transferable as a BA/B.Sc. should the holder wish to have a career change. There can be little doubt that the institution of the B.Ed. was beneficial in raising standards in the profession and in increasing the morale of teachers. Its essentially practical nature also ensured its popularity.

TLK

BACHELOR'S DEGREE

The lowest level of graduate qualification awarded by a university below MASTER's and DOCTOR's. Normally the bachelor's degree is awarded after three years of post-school study. Courses may be assessed by (a combination of) examination, project work and continuous assessment through written and/or practical assignments. For example, a bachelor's degree in modern languages may require the student to be resident abroad for a year in the relevant country. The degree is awarded in the Faculty of study e.g. Art (BA), Science (B.Sc.), EDUCATION (B.ED.), Law (LLB), etc. Bachelor's degrees may be awarded without honours (a Pass degree) or with honours i.e. with an indication of the level of attainment. The normal classification system is First, 2i, 2ii, and Third (though Oxford uses the levels First, Second, Third and Fourth). Work for a first-class honours degree would require the student to be consistently of a high standard across all aspects of the course and to produce work of originality. The 2ii classification represents the 'norm' of the university population. Graduates normally have to achieve a first or second-class honours if they wish to proceed to a master's degree.

Holders of the degree are entitled to wear appropriate ACADEMIC DRESS of their university. In the older universities certain bachelor's degrees were accorded 'post-graduate' status, i.e. they could be awarded only after the candidate had studied Arts to MA level. These degrees were usually the BD (bachelor of divinity) and B.Litt. (bachelor of letters) degrees and are unclassified – though some universities (London, Lampeter) award a BD as a first degree in theology, which is classified on the BA pattern.

TLK

BANDING

A system of organizing children into classes of broadly similar ability. Thus, in a nine-form entry school, three classes may consist of the ablest one-third of pupils but randomly assigned to classes within the band; three classes may be similarly of 'middle band' pupils; and three of the least able. Less refined than STREAMING, a system often favoured in the run up to KS 4.

TLK

BASIC CURRICULUM
(See: NATIONAL CURRICULUM)

BASIC SKILLS
Basic skills are the ability to read, write and speak in English and use mathematics at a level necessary to function at work and in society in general. The Further and Higher Education Act 1992 established Further Education Funding Councils for England and for Wales. Schedule 2 of the Act included basic skills for the first time making them a statutory requirement in further education. However, basic skills is no longer the sole preserve of education. Many organizations that never previously offered basic skills training are now undertaking basic skills work with their employees and clients. This includes companies, training organizations, schools and sixth-form colleges, prisons and other penal establishments, voluntary organizations, health authorities, housing associations and social service departments.

ALBSU – The Basic Skills Unit – is the central organization in England and in Wales for basic skills. It provides consultancy and advisory services to providers of basic skills, sponsors projects, produces and publishes teaching and learning materials and initiates research. Further details of ALBSU may be obtained from:
Adult Literacy and Basic Skills Unit (ALBSU), Commonwealth House, 1–19 New Oxford Street, London WC1A INU
tel: 071 405 4017   fax: 071 404 5038

MF

BEHAVIOUR MODIFICATION
This is a discipline process based on the behaviourist LEARNING THEORY of B. F. Skinner. Its basic approach rests on two tenets: first, that student behaviour which is reinforced by an immediate reward or recognition is more likely to recur; second, that behaviour which is ignored is not likely to be repeated. Often the method begins with a contract between teacher and students about what is desirable behaviour based on actual classroom events. The outcome of the contract should, ideally, be a relatively small number of agreed 'rules', all stated in positive terms. Then, when pupils obey the rules, teachers reinforce behaviour using praise, while breaches of the rules are ignored. The result should be a reduction in undesirable

behaviours in favour of the reinforced, desirable ones. Behaviour modification is, some teachers believe, rather contrived in its approach; though it does have quite a good track record in the SPECIAL EDUCATIONAL NEEDS sector, where it can be effective, for example, with disruptive youngsters. It is only one possible approach to CLASS MANAGEMENT and should be considered as a possible method among many.

TLK

BILINGUAL PUPILS

Bilingualism should be seen not as a difficulty but rather as an asset and bilingual pupils can enhance a school community by enabling others to recognise the place of diverse languages in the world.

In Wales, some 15 per cent of schools either serve communities in which Welsh is the main language or are designated Welsh-speaking schools. In Welsh-speaking schools, Welsh is a core subject of the National Curriculum. In schools where English is the language of teaching then Welsh is a foundation subject of the National Curriculum.

In Scotland, the Scottish Office Education Department supports the Gaelic language through special grants. Gaelic is the language of primary education in some areas such as the Western Isles and there are Gaelic courses at Standard Grade and Higher Grade.

MF

BODY LANGUAGE

Also called non-verbal communication, this is described under COMMUNICATION IN THE CLASSROOM.

TLK

BOOKS

Even in the age of information technology, books remain the mainstay of information for pupils. With the changes brought about by the National Curriculum, it has been necessary for schools to change many of the books they use to ensure that they reflect curriculum needs. This has placed a burden on some schools particularly where National Curriculum requirements have been modified more than once and books which appeared suitable no longer meet needs.

The carefully planned use of a school library can make the optimum use of available books and the Schools Library Service can also be of great value particularly where school budgeting is tight.

Addresses

The Children's Book Foundation, Book House, 45 East Hill,
London SW18 2QZ
tel: 081 870 9055
Book Trust (same address as Children's Book Foundation)
Book Trust (Scotland), 15a Lynedoch Street, Glasgow G3 6EF
tel: 041 332 0391
Welsh Books Council (Cyngor Llyfrau Cymraeg), Castell Brychan,
Aberystwyth, Dyfed SY23 2JB
tel: 0970 624 151

MF

BUILDINGS

The Department for Education (DFE) and the Scottish Education
Department produce recommendations and regulations regarding the
building, safety, design and maintenance of schools and other educational
institutions.

The 1981 School Premises Regulations set out requirements. Further
School Premises Regulations are due in 1995 and will set out minimum
standards for school facilities.

The need for improving the upkeep of state schools is widely accepted
and one indication of this is that in 1989 the Department of Education and
Science estimated that there was a backlist of £3 billion of repairs in state
schools.

Capital spending on schools is controlled by the DFE. Each school with
more than 200 pupils must maintain buildings within a budget allocated by
the LEA. In Grant Maintained schools, governors are responsible for the
care of school buildings.

The Architects and Building Group (ABG) is responsible for educational
building policy. It deals with approval of building projects, handles issues of
standards and costs and maintains statistics on educational building.

Through its publications (free list) ABG offers information and guidance
on design techniques. Further information may be obtained from:
Architects and Building Group, Department For Education, Sanctuary
Building, Great Smith Street, London SW1P 3BT
tel: 071 925 5000

MF

BULLYING

Bullying involves psychological and physical intimidation and can
encompass such behaviour as excluding victims from a group and physical

violence or threats of violence. Its detection is hampered by the victim's fear of telling and sometimes by the bully's 'hold' over other pupils at school. Preventing bullying needs a whole school policy supported by governors, the headteacher and all staff as well as by pupils. Appropriate values and attitudes need to be encouraged as well as appropriate behaviour.

The charity Kidscape offers help both to parents of bullied children and to the youngsters themselves. As well as organizing a telephone helpline, Kidscape holds national conferences for parents, teachers and other professionals. Kidscape will also conduct in-school training courses for teachers.

Further information and a publications list is obtainable from:
Kidscape, 152 Buckingham Palace Road, London SW1W 9TR
tel: 071 730 3300   fax: 071 730 7081

MF

BUSINESS AND TECHNOLOGY EDUCATION COUNCIL (BTEC)

The Business and Technology Education Council was previously known as the Business and Technician Education Council. It is an awarding body which approves work-related programmes of study run by schools, colleges, universities and other training organizations in a wide range of subjects throughout England, Wales and Northern Ireland. It awards qualifications (other than degrees) to students who successfully complete these programmes, which are recognized by employers, educationalists and professional bodies throughout the United Kingdom.

BTEC is working with NVCQ (The National Council for Vocational Qualifications) to develop a framework of vocational qualifications. BTEC qualifications give entry to over 100 professional bodies and in many cases give exemption to some of their examinations.

The areas covered include the following main occupational fields: agriculture, business and finance, caring, computing and information systems, construction, design, distribution, engineering, horticulture, hotel and catering, housing, information technology, leisure services, management, public administration, and science.

The main awards are as follows:

- First Certificate or Diploma: (broadly equivalent to four or more GCSEs);
- National Certificate or Diploma: (broadly equivalent to A-LEVELS and accepted for university entrance in the relevant sphere);
- Higher National Certificate or Diploma: (approaching the pass standard of a university degree).

Both Diploma and Certificate qualifications are of the same standard but the Diploma courses offer a wider range of subjects than Certificate courses. Also, Diploma courses are usually full-time while Certificate courses are normally part-time.

For address and further information, see Section 3, 'Directory of Organizations'.

MF

BUSINESS EDUCATION
(See: NATIONAL VOCATIONAL QUALIFICATIONS)

CALCULATORS
The use of calculators in the classroom is a much debated issue with opponents arguing that they may dissuade children from developing mental calculation skills and proponents claiming that they enrich learning and take the drudgery out of calculation. A balance needs to be found in which the pupils develop skills and understanding in number and use the calculator as a tool. In general calculators are motivating, they can encourage understanding rather than cloud it, and they can be used as an aid to learning tables.

Graphic calculators and statistical calculators are increasingly used in schools.

MF

CAMCORDER
As the relative cost of camera-video recorders or camcorders has dropped in recent years they have been increasingly used in schools and in further and higher education.

Among their uses are the following:

• to record plays, dance and other performing arts for future analysis so that the performers and others can learn from strengths and weaknesses;
• to record aspects of the local environment that may be undergoing change for reference in environmental studies and humanities;
• to record and learn from mock careers interviews;
• to record sporting activities for later freeze-frame analysis.

In brief, the camcorder can be used educationally to aid pupils in reviewing their own and other people's skills (e.g. sports, interviews) and learning from strengths and weaknesses and to record material of historical, cultural or other interest.

MF

CAPITAL GRANT

Grant Maintained schools are eligible to make a bid to the DFE for capital (capital grant) for building work or equipment. For the years 1993–94 capital grants took two forms – FORMULA ALLOCATION and NAMED PROJECTS. The formula allocation is for use on small-scale capital projects; under the grant for named projects schools are invited annually to bid for allocations of capital grant for specific projects in the following year. In the past, priority has been given to urgent work based on health and safety criteria and for projects relating to science and technology. With each invitation to bid, Ministers' priorities for future allocations are outlined.

CAK

CAREERS EDUCATION AND GUIDANCE

The term 'career' describes occupational roles which we fulfil and can be seen in terms of paid and self employment, various occupations, and unpaid occupations (e.g. parent). Each of these roles is connected with acquiring qualifications, skills and experience.

Careers guidance in school involves helping young people consider and carry out their plans for what they propose to do when they leave school. Careers education and guidance (sometimes called careers counselling) gives pupils a structured series of activities concerning choices and changes affecting their future training, education, employment and citizenship (see HMI, 1988).

Careers education and guidance is the responsibility of all teachers. 'The School Teachers Pay and Conditions Document' (1989 Part 10, para. 35 (2) (b)) states that all teachers may be required to provide 'guidance and advice to pupils . . . on their future education and future careers, including information and sources of more expert advice on specific questions'. It is recognized that particularly in Years 10 and 11, pupils will need individual careers guidance from careers officers working with careers teachers and form tutors.

Under the Employment and Training Act 1973, LEAs in England and Wales are responsible for the careers service. The Department of Employment's Careers' Service Branch is responsible for inspecting and guiding local careers departments.

Useful Addresses

Addresses of Careers Services in England and Wales are listed in M. Evans (Ed.), *Education Year Book* (Longman).
Association of Graduate Careers Advisory Services, Careers Advisory Service, University of Sheffield, Sheffield S10 2TN

tel: 0742 738406
Careers and Occupational Information Centre, Moorfoot,
Sheffield S1 4PQ
tel: 0742 594563
(provides information on jobs and careers for job seekers and careers
advisers)
Northern Ireland Training and Employment Agency, Employment
Services Division, Clarendon House, 9–21 Adelaide Street,
Belfast BT2 8DJ
tel: 0232 239944
Scottish Office Education Department, Careers Service Branch,
New St Andrews House, St James's Centre, Edinburgh EH1 3SY
tel: 031 244 4442

Further reading

Barnes, A. (1994) 'Beyond School' in the series Farrell, M. (Ed.), *Education for Teaching* (HMSO).
HMI (1988) *Careers Education and Guidance from 5 to 16, Curriculum Matters 10* (HMSO).

MF

CATCHMENT AREA
Each school has an area that it traditionally serves, often called the 'catchment area'. However, under the EDUCATION ACT (1980) parents have the right to express a preference for the school they wish their child to attend, and whilst many are quite happy for this to be the local school, the Education Officer and governors have a duty to meet this preference insofar as the chosen alternative school is appropriate for the child and that there are places available. In the case of the chosen alternative school being outside the statutory walking distance for the child, it is the parent's duty to ensure the child's attendance at school, and the charge for transporting the child rests with the parent or guardian.

(See also: SCHOOL TRANSPORT)

CAK

CATHEDRAL (CHOIR) SCHOOLS
Historically Cathedral Schools date back to pre-Reformation days when each bishop had to provide for the education of clergy in areas without

schools. Then, boys and young men were taught within the household of the Bishop either by the Bishop himself or through a priest. Certain bishops' schools achieved eminence and became centres of excellence for both Christian and classical education.

Today Cathedral Schools provide education for both choristers and others. At present there are 39 schools attached to Cathedrals, churches and college chapels throughout the country. They educate in excess of 800 choristers as well as more than 14,000 other youngsters. The majority of choir schools are attached to Church of England cathedrals, but St Edward's College, Liverpool, St John's College, Cardiff and Westminster College are Roman Catholic. The majority of schools are independent, but for choristers, parents on average pay less than half fees.

Places for choristers at Cathedral schools are usually available from the age of 7–9, though some places are available at 10. Voice trials take place, and those youngsters accepted can expect to receive a first-class musical training at the same time as enjoying an excellent academic education. The CHOIR SCHOOLS ASSOCIATION publishes a short leaflet giving details of its membership, and this may be obtained from:

The Secretary, CSA, The Cathedral Choir School, Whitcliffe Lane, Ripon, North Yorkshire HG4 2LA

CAK

CATHOLIC SCHOOLS

There are some 2,227 state maintained Catholic schools (primary, middle and secondary) which include voluntary aided, special agreement and Grant Maintained schools. In addition there are 206 independent Catholic day and boarding schools. All are listed in the Catholic Education Handbook published bi-annually by the Catholic Education Service (address below) at £7 including postage. Copies may be obtained from the CES.

Address

Catholic Education Service, 41 Cromwell Road, London SW7 2DJ
tel: 071 584 7491　　　fax: 071 823 7545

MF

CHARGES FOR SCHOOL ACTIVITIES

The fundamental principle of the Education Reform Act 1988 is that education provided by any maintained school should be free of charge, and that activities offered wholly or mainly during normal teaching time should be available to all pupils regardless of their parents' ability or willingness to help meet the cost. This applies to activities such as school visits and journeys. However, LEAs and schools are not prohibited from inviting contributions towards the costs of such activities. LEAs and schools are required to draw up, and keep under review, their own policies relating to charging and remission arrangements; in the case of schools, the charging policy must be described in the SCHOOL BROCHURE. LEAs charging and remission policies across the country are generally similar, and activities within the school day that are generally charged include:

- music tuition, where the playing of the instrument is neither part of the syllabus for an approved public examination, nor part of the National Curriculum;
- ingredients and materials for practical subjects where parents have indicated in advance that they wish to receive the finished product;
- entry to a public examination for which the pupil has not been prepared by the school.

Charges are usually made for the full costs of any trip outside school time, except trips leading to a public examination or forming part of the National Curriculum. Remission of some charges is available to those parents on Income Support or Family Credit; full details of a school's charging policy may be obtained from the headteacher.

CAK

CHIEF EDUCATION OFFICER
The most senior person in a LOCAL EDUCATION AUTHORITY, who has a statutory responsibility for the delivery of education services in that Authority. He/she would normally work in close association with the EDUCATION COMMITTEE as the senior professional responsible to elected members. In shire counties, that individual is known as the County Education Officer.

TLK

CHILD-CENTRED EDUCATION
In contrast to TRADITIONALIST EDUCATION, child-centred education advocates allowing the learner freedom to develop his 'natural' personality, respecting the child's viewpoint and recognizing his right to determine the scope and direction of his education. In this approach, the teacher gives consideration to a child in his own right. The child is treated as a child, with the teacher taking into account developmental psychology. Each child

is recognized as a unique individual and treated as such, not regarded as merely an incipient adult.

A child-centred curriculum aims to meet the child's NEEDS and INTERESTS taking into account READINESS and learning is based on EXPERIENCE and DISCOVERY.

MF

CHILD DEVELOPMENT
(See: ADOLESCENCE)

CHOICE OF SCHOOL
The options open to most parents when considering a school place for a child fall into the following categories:

- LEA Schools: these schools are owned and provided by the County Council;
- Voluntary Schools: these schools are provided by a voluntary body and not the County Council. Most usually these schools are provided by the Church of England, the Roman Catholic Church, other churches and educational trusts. The two main types of voluntary schools are:
  (a) Voluntary Controlled schools where the full cost of replacing, improving or enlarging the schools rests with the Council, and
  (b) Voluntary Aided schools where these cost are the responsibility of the governors but they are eligible to ask for a contribution from the Secretary of State.
- Grant Maintained Schools: Grant Maintained schools have opted out of the control of the local authority, and receive their funding direct from Central Government. The governors of these schools have full responsibility for its day-to-day running.
- City Technology Colleges: these schools are run in partnership between the Department for Education and local industry. The full national curriculum is followed, with strong emphasis placed on science, technology and information technology.
- Boarding Schools: some authorities provide boarding places at certain schools (usually secondary) and may operate an assisted boarding scheme for those children whose home circumstances are seriously prejudicial to their normal development. Initial enquiries should be made to the local education authority.

(See also: STATE BOARDING INFORMATION SERVICE - STABIS)

CAK

CHOIR SCHOOLS
(See: CATHEDRAL SCHOOLS)

CHRISTIAN EDUCATION
Under amendments to the Education Act 1944 by the Education Reform Act 1988 (sections 2 and 6 to 13) all schools must arrange an act of collective worship each day although not necessarily for the whole school at once. A broadly undenominational Christian act of worship is required in county schools. In voluntary schools it will vary according to denomination.

If pupils' family background indicates, schools can apply for total or partial exemption from the Christian requirements. Such exemptions are granted by the Standing Advisory Committee on Religious Education. Parents may withdraw their child from worship or religious education. They may also arrange for their child to receive teaching reflecting their own faith at the beginning or end of school sessions.

(See also: CHURCH OF ENGLAND SCHOOLS; CATHOLIC SCHOOLS; RELIGIOUS EDUCATION (and the basic curriculum); QUAKER SCHOOLS, CATHEDRAL-CHOIR SCHOOLS; VOLUNTARY CONTROLLED SCHOOLS; VOLUNTARY AIDED SCHOOLS).

'Christians in Education' is an organization which aims to further the involvement in education of Christian teachers, parents and churches, and may be contacted at:

Christians in Education, 16 Maids Causeway, Cambridge CB5 8DA tel: 0223 66225

MF

CHURCH OF ENGLAND SCHOOLS
Since before the Norman Conquest the church in England has been involved in the field of education, and until the seventeenth century almost all schools had their origins in, and were run by, the church. Limited partnership with the state began with the first government grant to aided schools in 1833. However, it was not until the 1870 Education Act was passed and local board schools established to provide elementary schooling that all church schools received grant aid and thus a direct partnership between state and church began. It was during the Second World War that the question of Church Schools again came to the fore; at this time the Church of England and Catholics between them provided more than half the elementary schools in the country, many of which were in a poor state structurally. Re-organizing along the lines of the 1944 Act, coupled with the devastation caused by bomb-damage would have been beyond the means of most sections of the voluntary community and thus a carefully constructed compromise was reached in which state funding was offered in

return for extension of state control of church schools. In January 1990 (the most recent date for DFE statistics), there were 807,000 children and young people in 4,716 Church of England primary schools and 151 secondary schools. At national level the General Synod Board of Education and the National Society share the task of supporting and advising dioceses and Church schools, and whilst neither the Board or the Society has any powers of direction, close co-operation is maintained with the Government. The Church of England seeks to promote good quality education for children and young people through its support for teachers, parents and governors and through its involvement in curricular issues, particularly those associated with Religious Education.

(See also: VOLUNTARY AIDED and VOLUNTARY CONTROLLED schools)

                                                                              CAK

CITIZENSHIP

In western democracies, educating for citizenship implies initiating learners into understanding and participating in a democracy. Education for citizenship is a cross curricular theme in the National Curriculum and is therefore accepted as an integral part of every pupil's education. It includes issues such as the law, constitution and public services.

                                                                              MF

CITY TECHNOLOGY COLLEGES

The Education Reform Act 1988 allowed for the provision of a new category of school, the City Technology College, and initially fifteen CTCs were provided. The Secretary of State for Education enters into an agreement with persons (usually a consortium of local business people) who are prepared to provide partial funding and assist in setting up the city technology college. CTCs must be in an urban area, and their purpose is to provide a broadly based secondary education in accordance with the National Curriculum with special emphasis on science and technology. Education must be provided free for pupils of all abilities between the ages of 11 and 19.

The school day is usually extended over and above a 'normal' school day, with facilities available for post-school private study and community activities. Computer-assisted learning is a feature of the CTC, with technological equipment available to all students. As well as a longer school day, the school year may be lengthened slightly.

Over and above the sponsorship obtained from the local community, further funding is provided by the DFE and is subject to DFE rules.

In February 1994 the Secretary of State announced plans for the provision of a further twelve colleges to be known as Technical Colleges. Schools that are GRANT MAINTAINED may apply for the new status; financial conditions were imposed upon schools seeking Technology status i.e. they must provide evidence of funding by local businesses to £100,000 which will be matched by the Department for Education. Emphasis is to be placed upon science and technology, and evidence will be sought that standards in these subjects show improvement.

(See also: CITY TECHNOLOGY COLLEGES TRUST)

CAK

CLASS CONTROL
(See: CLASS MANAGEMENT)

CLASS MANAGEMENT
Perhaps the key TEACHING SKILL essential for all teachers, embracing CLASSROOM ORGANIZATION and DISCIPLINE, but going beyond both. Class management is 'what teachers do to ensure that children engage in the task in hand' (Wragg). How this is achieved is a matter of style. Some teachers adopt an authoritarian stance, some are more permissive; yet others use positive teaching methods and BEHAVIOUR MODIFICATION. Insights from sociology and social psychology may help teachers to use peer norms to achieve an agreed behaviour pattern. Certainly, teacher student and student–student relationships are important in creating a classroom ethos in which good class management can flourish. But while class management relates to being well organized, establishing good relations, keeping effective discipline and ensuring students engage in the task – nevertheless, there are many other sub-skills which feed into it: for example, curriculum planning, good lesson preparation (see: LESSON PLANNING), good voice control, and vigilance using a variety of TEACHING METHODS AND MODES, and applying the principles of sound TEACHING METHODS AND MODES in practice. Good class management also stems from personality factors such as constructive use of humour, and fundamentally on articulating and adhering to identified standards of classroom behaviour. Good class managers learn how to deal with critical events in classroom life such as interruptions with maximum PROFESSIONALISM and minimum disruption.

Further reading

Wragg, E. C. (1982) *Class Management and Control* (Basingstoke: Macmillan).

TLK

CLASS SIZE

One prevalent belief among teachers is that EFFECTIVE TEACHING is achieved more easily in smaller classes than in larger ones. Many lay people attribute the success of selective, public or independent schools to their (usually) small class size compared with the state sector. It is, of course, necessary to define effective teaching; but in this context one should take the definition of 'measured achievement' by pupils. The Centre for the Assessment of Educational Progress in the USA makes annual tests of school children in twenty countries. These tests cover a variety of subjects and several age ranges. In 1992 younger children tested in science were England's best performers – behind South Korea, Taiwan, Italy and the USA. The average Korean class size for 13-year-olds is 49 while in England it is more typically 27. In English primary schools class sizes might be in the low thirties, but are rarely at the Korean level. Thus it seems probable that class size is not a very significant factor in determining effective teaching/ learning, though logic demands it may well be just one of a cluster of issues – such as good SCHOOL ETHOS, EFFECTIVE MANAGEMENT and TEACHING SKILLS – which contribute to an overall qualitative improvement in pupils' performance. Larger classes are, of course, hard to manage and may cause more DISCIPLINE PROBLEMS; and they will require modification to TEACHING STYLE to suit the particular situation.

TLK

CLASSROOM CLIMATE

The ethos created by the teacher in his or her classes, and strongly related to the issue of the overall ETHOS OF THE SCHOOL. It seems probable that successful classroom climate is a blend of factors which would include: the variety and interest of LESSONS, the TEACHING SKILLS exhibited, the smoothness of the teacher's CLASS MANAGEMENT SKILLS and the effectiveness of the teacher in creating positive interpersonal relations in the classroom.

TLK

CLASSROOM LANGUAGE

(See: COMMUNICATION IN THE CLASSROOM)

CLASSROOM ORGANIZATION

The description is sometimes used synonymously with CLASS MANAGEMENT but should best be seen as a sub-set of management. Organization of the classroom includes such fundamental issues as the teacher's practice in gaining orderly entrance and exit OF students, classroom layout, the storage and effective use of resources and similar matters concerned with the physical and administrative life of the student group. All of these factors have an effect on creating a positive LEARNING ENVIRONMENT and in promoting good DISCIPLINE.

TLK

CLASSROOM TASKS
(See: TASKS)

COGNITION
Just as Bloom used the term 'AFFECTIVE domain' for social learning, so the description cognitive learning is applied to the process of thought. Put simply, cognition can operate at three levels:

- acquisition of simple information or data: (The Battle of Hastings was fought in 1066);
- reason giving, explanation or concept understanding: (The Battle was fought because);
- the abstract level: (Is war ever right?).

The art of the teacher is to move pupils through the hierarchy of THINKING SKILLS; though much research suggests that this is not always done very effectively.

TLK

COLLEGES AND INSTITUTES OF HIGHER EDUCATION
These provide:

(a)   degree courses validated by a local university;
(b)   various non-degree courses.

Many Colleges of Higher Education previously specialized in the education of teachers but have now widened the range of courses offered.

MF

COLLEGES OF FURTHER EDUCATION
(See: FURTHER EDUCATION COLLEGES)

COMBINED/BALANCED SCIENCE
Up to and including GCSE level there has been a move away from the traditional division of SCIENCE (physics, chemistry, and biology) and towards

an approach combining all three. Combined science aims to give a broad foundation and to discourage specialization too early.

MF

COMMON ENTRANCE EXAMINATION
The qualifying examination for independent secondary schools, the common entrance examination assesses traditional academic subjects. It is regulated by the headteachers of preparatory and independent secondary schools, set by a managing board and marked by each school.

Pupils sit the examination at age 13 and it is taken by nearly all independent boys' schools and over a third of girls' schools.

Address

Common Entrance Examination to Independent Schools (Boys),
Orax House, Tilstead, Salisbury, Wiltshire SP3 4SJ
tel: 0980 620473
Common Entrance Examination for Girls' Schools (address and telephone as above).

MF

COMMON FUNDING FORMULA (CFF)
Started in April 1994, the Common Funding Formula (CFF) was piloted in the secondary sector in areas where local authorities have a substantial number of GRANT MAINTAINED (GM) schools, and will later be extended to all councils with opted out schools. CFF will be based on the authority's standard spending assessment (SSA) – the government's estimate of the authority's requirements – and pupil numbers. Other factors, such as special educational needs, split-site schools, and pupils whose first language is not English may be taken into account.

CAK

COMMUNICATION IN THE CLASSROOM
The interpersonal process between teachers and pupils. Communication can be verbal or non-verbal. Verbal communication itself is a complicated phenomenon since language can perform many functions. It can be a way of getting things done (instrumental); it may control behaviour (regulatory); it will sustain relationships (interactional). Language can be investigative (heuristic); convey information and ideas (representational) or express feeling (personal). All of these kinds of language exist in classroom settings. Teachers use language in DIDACTIC ways. Fundamental to the teacher are

the skills of EXPLAINING and QUESTIONING. Pupils use language as a response; but also in DISCUSSION with one another. Some classroom language is overtly technical language. Language failure of one kind or another is a feature of many pupils with SPECIAL EDUCATIONAL NEEDS. Language, used in the wrong way or at the wrong time, can be associated with poor classroom DISCIPLINE. But communication is more subtle than just verbal; it can also be non-verbal. Meaning is conveyed by a look, a gesture, a posture, a facial movement and so on. Non-verbal signals include four types of major significance. Emblems are conventional signals like nodding the head or shaking a fist. Illustrators are non-verbal acts designed to reinforce speech: waving a hand to emphasize, pausing to make a point. Some non-verbal signals are regulators, as when we use 'mm' to signal another person to keep talking without interruption. Others, adapters, signal states of mind – such as scratching our heads when we have a problem. Teachers need to be able to read these non-verbal signals effectively in order to interpret the mood and life of the classroom. But teachers also give out such non-verbal cues which are read in turn by pupils – so understanding how to give out warm signals rather than cold ones will have an effect on CLASSROOM CLIMATE and TEACHING EFFECTIVENESS. Some psychologists have made detailed studies of this non-verbal communication in classrooms and there can be little doubt of its importance in overall communication. Other factors, too, affect the flow of communication in classrooms. For example, teachers who are good at CLASSROOM MANAGE-MENT will know that the seating plan can affect both pupil attitudes and task efficiency. Thus, while sitting pupils in rows will suit a DIDACTIC mode of teaching, a GROUP WORK task will need pupils to sit in smaller units facing one another; a DISCUSSION may be best when chairs are in a horseshoe without a barrier of tables between participants. So communication depends on a number of contextual as well as process factors of which teachers need to be constantly aware.

Further reading

Reid, D. (1994) 'Communicating in the Classroom' in the series, Farrell, M. (Ed.), *Education for Teaching* (HMSO).

TLK

COMPACT SCHEMES

Run by the London Education Business Partnership, Compact brings together secondary schools and industry to improve job prospects for pupils when they leave school. Inner city compacts are funded by the Department of Employment.

MF

COMPARATIVE EDUCATION

The importance of comparative education arises from several sources. Firstly, it is intrinsically interesting to consider the ways in which education systems and practices operate abroad and the extent to which they are similar or different. Secondly, such a review can provide ideas and approaches which may have relevance and usefulness in one's own country. The extent to which systems and approaches are transferable or the degree to which they are culture-bound is a useful area to explore giving us valuable insights into our own and others' capacity for change. Thirdly, there is always the danger that the status quo, whatever it might be, can come to be regarded as the right and only way to operate. The study of comparative education reminds us that there are many interpretations of education. Different answers to the questions, who is to be educated, by whom, how and for what purpose, arise from culture to culture.

MF

COMPETENCE

A criterion or measure by which a student can demonstrate that he/she is able to perform a learned task both effectively and with understanding.

(See also: COMPETENCY MODEL)

TLK

COMPETENCY MODEL

Recent emphasis on vocational training has pushed educationists to adopt a model of COMPETENCE as the basis for learning and course design. A competency model identifies those operations which a student must be able to carry out (in a hairdressing course, for example, operations like 'back-combing', washing, perming) and then sets out to assess the student's abilities against the competences. Competences cannot stand alone, but require knowledge and understanding. These three elements form the basis NVQs and of newly-developed PGCE courses.

TLK

COMPETITION IN SCHOOL

As a motivator, competition is used in many schools to encourage pupils to perform better. The competition may be between pupils in a class group or between house groups where points are awarded for academic, sporting or personal achievement. If the competition compares the performance of pupils against other pupils, there is the danger that certain pupils may 'fail' in many areas of school life while making their best efforts, because those efforts are not sufficient to lift them above the performance level of others. To mitigate against this, some schools encourage competition against personal targets individual to a particular pupil, thus giving the opportunity of reward and recognition for improvements in personal performance.

MF

COMPLAINTS PROCEDURE – CURRICULUM
Given that a school is unable to resolve a complaint by a parent on an amicable basis, there are procedures laid down by the Education Reform Act which must be followed. The procedures cover complaints about all aspects of the curriculum including religious education and collective worship. They also cover the operation of arrangements to exempt certain pupils from some aspects of the National Curriculum. If a parent of a child attending an LEA school wishes to express dissatisfaction, he or she should, in the first instance, make a formal written approach to the governing body for its consideration. If satisfaction is not gained at this stage, the parent can ask the LEA to consider the grievance and if still dissatisfied, can contact the Secretary of State for Education, who will consider whether the governing body or the LEA has acted unreasonably with respect to the complaint. In Grant Maintained schools, each governing body has to draw up a complaints procedure for approval by the Secretary of State. If a parent remains dissatisfied with the governors' decision, then contact is made at this stage with the Secretary of State.

CAK

COMPUTER-ASSISTED LEARNING
More and more schools and colleges are being equipped with computers, and increasingly learning materials are being put onto computer disks. This means students can access learning when they wish to, at their own pace, and with some control over sequence. Computer-assisted learning adds a dimension to FLEXIBLE LEARNING.

Further reading

Kerry, T and Price, P. (1994) 'The Classroom Organization, Effectiveness and Resources' in the series Farrell, M. (Ed.), *Education for Teaching* (HMSO).

TLK

COMPUTERS

The use of computers in the primary and secondary classroom has been encouraged by EDUCATION SUPPORT GRANTS. Information technology has wide applications in many aspects of the curriculum from historical and geographical databases, to computer-aided design, from scientific modelling to the shaping of reading skills.

Addresses

Association for Computers and Information Technology in Teaching, Educational Computing Centre, Tring Gardens, Harold Hill, Romford, Essex RM3 9QX
tel: 04023 49115

- supports the teaching of information technology in schools.

National Council for Educational Technology, Milburn Hill Road, Coventry CV4 7JJ
tel: 0203 416994
Also:
3 Devonshire Street, London W1N 2BA
tel: 071 636 4186

- directory of information (yearly subscription) includes coverage of information technology for schools and colleges, special educational needs and new developments in learning technologies;
- promotes the effective application of proven technologies and monitors and evaluates new technologies and systems.

Microelectronic Education Unit, Welsh Joint Education Committee, 245 Western Avenue, Cardiff CF5 2YX
tel: 0222 561231 ext. 260

- gives information on IT in education;
- publishes software and curriculum materials in Welsh and English.

Scottish Council for Educational Technology, Dowanhill, 74 Victoria Crescent Road, Glasgow G12 9JJ
tel: 041 334 9314

- focuses on education and training;
- promotes good practice;
- special needs database.

MF

CONDUCTIVE EDUCATION

Andras Peto, working in Hungary, developed an educational approach for people with motor disorders. The Peto Institute in Budapest continues the late founder's work. Specially trained staff ('conductors') aim to help the child become 'orthofunctional', that is to function as independently as possible.

Further reading

Hari, M. and Akos, K. (1988) *Conductive Education* (Routledge).
   Further information about Conductive Education and the Foundation for Conductive Education's aim to establish Conductive Education in England may be obtained from:
Foundation for Conductive Education (FCE), University of Birmingham, PO Box 363, Birmingham B15 2TT
tel: 021 414 4947/8

MF

CONTINUING EDUCATION
(See: ADULT EDUCATION)

CONTINUOUS ASSESSMENT

Continuous assessment assesses performance throughout a course of study by monitoring work. It may be used as well as an end of course examination or may replace an examination as the preferred form of assessment. Continuous assessment is a feature of the National Curriculum.
   Among the advantages of continuous assessment are the following:

- it requires continued, sustained work from the learner rather than allowing the temptation to rely on last-minute revision for an end of course examination;
- it reduces the possibility of getting an unfair impression of a learner's capability in an examination in which anxiety or illness might affect performance on the crucial day.

The disadvantages of continuous assessment include the points below:

- if there was a total reliance on continuous assessment, it would be necessary to monitor the continuous assessment itself in order to ensure that standards were maintained over a period of time;
- teachers are required to handle more paperwork in keeping pupil records up to date and in general administration;
- children from homes where education is not valued and in which insufficient support and facilities exist to enable course homework to be completed can be disadvantaged. However, these disadvantages can affect systematic long-term study and revision for examinations too.

MF

CO-OPTED GOVERNORS
In county and controlled schools co-opted governors are chosen by the LEA, parent and teacher governors, with at least three-quarters of the elected and appointed governors present before co-option can take place. Under the Education (No. 2) Act 1986, co-opted governors should represent some of the interests of the local business community if these interests are not already present on the governing body. Co-opted governors serve for a term of four years from the date of their co-option, and may seek re-election at the end of their term of office. In certain circumstances particular categories of governor may have to be co-opted.

In Grant Maintained schools FIRST or FOUNDATION governors fulfil the function of co-opted governors in county and controlled schools.

CAK

COPYRIGHT
Infringement of copyright occurs if a person copies or authorizes another person to copy work or written material without the consent of the copyright owner. Copyright laws cover original written material, sound recordings, films, broadcasts or cable programmes. Within the area of school/college use, the photocopier poses the greatest problem. The Copyright Designs and Patents Act 1988 led to the creation of the Copyright Licensing Agency (CLA). The CLA represents authors and publishers; it issues photocopy licences upon payment of the appropriate fee, and will give advice to a licensee regarding the scope of the licence (there are two types available).

Further information may be obtained from:
The Copyright Licensing Agency, 90 Tottenham Court Road,
London W1P 9HE
tel: 071 436 5931   fax: 071 436 3986

CAK

CORE SUBJECTS
(See: NATIONAL CURRICULUM)

COUNSELLING

The intentions behind the introduction of counselling into schools were benign, though the effect is subject to debate. The PASTORAL CARE of pupils was originally seen as inseparable from the teacher's overall ROLE: all teachers were also TUTORS in a pastoral sense. In the late 1960s the practice of counselling became progressively the role of a specialist teacher, who was often sent on appropriate IN-SERVICE TRAINING. Subsequently, the organization of schools often set up dichotomies between teachers and academic activity on the one hand, and counsellors/tutors and pastoral affairs on the other. Many secondary schools still have both academic structures (e.g. departments) and pastoral ones (e.g. tutor-groups, houses, etc.). The root of the problem lies in the fact that much theoretical training in counselling has its origins in the mental health movement. This tends to stress pupils' problems and to make them the centre of focus for the school. It may also, it is argued, highlight problem pupils.

The situation in FE colleges is similar, though these are even more likely to have a free standing counselling service whose personnel are not necessarily involved with, and thus share, the academic work of their colleagues. A significant development has been, therefore, to emphasize the confidentiality and separateness of counsellors and their services, and to throw into relief the ability of pupils to get a more sympathetic hearing from them than from teachers especially in matters of discipline. A balanced approach to in-school counselling should probably include a number of factors: the re-emphasis of the pastoral role of every teacher, the access to the specialist resource of a trained and experienced counsellor for some pupils/situations, the integration of pastoral and academic structures, and the existence of school policies to underpin these principles. Confusion about the counsellor's place in the hierarchy of the school or college, and his/her obligations to and independence from it, need to be clarified.

TLK

COUNSELLOR
The role of counsellor in a school may be undertaken by:

• all teachers;
• teachers considered particularly good in basic counselling skills;
• teachers who, by virtue of their position, are expected to carry out some counselling (e.g. head of house);

58 CREATIVITY

- occasionally, by a trained and qualified counsellor fulfilling a separate role.

Address

British Association for Counselling, 37a Sheep Street, Rugby, Warwickshire CV21 3BX
tel: 0788 78328/9

MF

CREATIVITY
Necessary aspects of creativity and the ways in which they might be encouraged through education are as follows:

1. Creativity involves a person producing something in a particular sphere (e.g. mathematics) which reflects their personal way of looking at things. It represents their reasoning, planning and development in a self-expressive way. A teacher might encourage a learner to follow the learner's own distinctive way of seeing things rather than giving the impression that there is only one correct way to do things.
2. Creativity implies that an original, distinctive product is made. A teacher might therefore foster activities which encourage imagination and may use discovery methods of learning and problem-solving activities.
3. Creativity suggests that a product is consciously produced to a high quality judged against critical, aesthetic standards. It is necessary then that a teacher promotes in learners skill, understanding and knowledge of the sphere in question so that creativity can emerge from this.

MF

CROSS CURRICULAR ISSUES (IN THE NATIONAL CURRICULUM)
Important aspects of the NATIONAL CURRICULUM are certain cross curricular competencies: literacy, numeracy and information technology skills. Themes or elements which form part of the whole curriculum are:

- careers education and guidance;
- health education;
- other aspects of personal and social education;
- cross curricular coverage of gender and multi-cultural issues.

Much learning related to these themes will be covered in the context of foundation subjects. Some elements will be contained in attainment targets and programmes of study.

The same can be said for other themes which can be taught in a cross curricular way such as:

- environmental education;
- economic awareness;
- political and international understanding.

MF

CURIOSITY
A natural characteristic of young people (and animals), and something which teachers should aim to encourage by the use of open-ended QUESTIONS and TASKS.

TLK

CURRICULUM
The 'curriculum' is a course of study followed by students at school or college, and for those students at school, it must contain religious education, a daily act of worship, and adherence to the NATIONAL CURRICULUM. Local authorities are required to produce their statement on the curriculum, and whilst governors of county or voluntary controlled schools may modify it, they may not replace it; they must meet the requirements of the National Curriculum. Governors in voluntary aided schools decide the format of the curriculum but they, too, must provide the National Curriculum. It is the responsibility of the headteacher to ensure that the curriculum is taught according to the governing body's agreed school curriculum policy.

CAK

DANCE
Dance is one of the named activities in the National Curriculum for physical education.

Three- or four-year university courses in which dance is a major part lead to diploma or degree qualifications. Public sector dance teachers also need a teaching diploma. Private sector teachers are likely to have a teaching qualification from a recognized association of teachers of dance

which would be a member of either the Council for Dance Education and Training or the British Council of Ballroom Dancing.

The Council for Dance Education and Training, which aims to maintain and raise standards of dance education, offers information on vocational dance training and may be contacted at:

Council for Dance Education and Training, 5 Tavistock Place, London WC1H 9SS
tel: 071 388 5770

MF

DAY NURSERY

A privately-run nursery facility accepting children of pre-school age, usually from families where both parents work. Such facilities may or may not employ qualified staff, but have to be registered with the Local Authority.

TLK

DAY RELEASE

Employees who are granted a day or two per week from work with pay to study at a College of Further Education are studying by 'day release'. The areas of study are usually closely related to the student's occupation.

MF

DEMOCRACY AND SCHOOLS

The degree of democracy, in schools and in education generally, relates to the ability of interested parties to exert influence and to freedom of information. Attempts have been made to involve parents more in decisions about the education of their children, for example, by providing for parent governors to be included on school governing bodies under the Education Act 1980. Under the Education (No. 2) Act 1986, school governing bodies in England and Wales must present an ANNUAL REPORT TO PARENTS followed by a meeting to enable parents to discuss issues raised in the report. Such examples indicate attempts to bring democratic forces to bear on schools although, at the same time, centralizing trends are at work in such developments as the National Curriculum. Also, when a school is being inspected, inspectors are required to hold a meeting with parents.

Democracy within schools has to be balanced against such forces as the accountability of teachers in their role 'in loco parentis' particularly where young children are concerned. The more democratic a school is, the greater will be the participation of pupils in decision-making which affects the community. Schools' councils are one way in which elected pupils can represent the views of other pupils.

Further reading

Jensen, K. and Walker, S. (Eds) (1989) 'Towards Democratic Schooling: European Experiences' *Innovations in Education Series* (Open University Press).

MF

DEPARTMENT FOR EDUCATION (BACKGROUND FROM 1833)

The seeds of the modern Department for Education (DFE) were sown in 1833 when the first government grant for education was made in order to help the National Society and the British and Foreign Schools Society to found voluntary provided schools. In order to administer the grants which followed, a Committee of the privy Council on Education was formed in 1839. This developed into the Board of Education in 1899, the Ministry of Education in 1944, the Department of Education and Science twenty years later and the Department for Education in 1992.

MF

DEPENDENT LEARNER

A pupil/student who, for a variety of reasons, cannot get on without very frequent attention from the teacher. Common reasons are: a lack of STUDY SKILLS, SPECIAL LEARNING NEEDS, a poor INTELLECTUAL CLIMATE in the class, failure to understand the teacher's instructions or EXPLAINING, a hiatus in understanding caused, e.g. by recent absence from school, or attention-seeking behaviour associated with poor CLASS CONTROL.

TLK

DESCHOOLING

In the 1970s the writings of such radical thinkers as Ivan Illich (1973) were adopted by a deschooling movement. Illich criticized existing schooling as being useless and corrupt. Pupils were persuaded that schooling was valuable of itself. A 'knowledge capitalism' was at work in which learning became not a worthwhile activity but a commodity. The failure of school, reflected in truancy and indiscipline, stemmed from the lack of respect of pupils for the whole authoritarian system. It had proved impossible to change schools from within because of vested interests. The educational establishment for example found true comprehensive education unpalatable and so it had never been really tried. Consequently, in Illich's view, 'the disestablishment of the school has become inevitable . . .'.

The deschooling movement proposed getting rid of schools and giving parents the responsibility for arranging the education of their children. Young people would manage their own education. Modern technology would be used to bring education directly to the individual.

Whereas Illich was writing initially with Third World countries in mind, his views and those of others were adopted by certain educators in the West who were discontented with the capitalist system. Its weakness in this context was that it offered no practical alternative to schooling beyond such notions as encouraging children to learn from adults doing their regular jobs.

Further reading

Illich, I. (1973) *Deschooling Society* (Penguin).

MF

DETENTION
The requirement for a student to stay behind during breaks or after school ends, as a PUNISHMENT for misbehaviour.

TLK

DEWEY, JOHN (1859–1952)
Dewey, the American philosopher, educationalist and psychologist taught in high school and later held university posts including that of professor of philosophy at Colombia. Developing the pragmatism of William James (1842–1910) and C. S. Peirce (1839–1914), Dewey formulated a theory of 'instrumentalism'. It concerned the nature of thought, logic and knowledge acquisition.

Particularly relevant to education, is Dewey's view that ideas and practice work together as 'instruments'.

MF

DIDACTIC TEACHING
Sometimes known as chalk-and-talk: the process of imparting information to a fairly large group by means of teacher-dominated talk or lecture.

TLK

DIFFERENTIATION
This is the process by which a teacher can help students in a single class to tackle work at their individual levels of ability and to achieve individually

appropriate cognitive levels of performance. The process has always underpinned MIXED ABILITY TEACHING, but has been given increased prominence in the light of NATIONAL CURRICULUM requirements for ASSESSMENT and TESTING. Clearly, if the assumption is that all pupils in a class cover similar areas of content within NATIONAL CURRICULUM syllabi, then differentiation in learning must be achieved through such TEACHING SKILLS as QUESTIONING and TASK SETTING. These enable the teacher to 'grade' the cognitive demands made on pupils in accordance with their ability and the stages of understanding they have currently reached; and they provide mechanisms of FEEDBACK to teachers on how individual pupils are performing. The issue of differentiation is sometimes connected to the debate about streaming or GROUPING BY ABILITY; but differentiation is a problem in any student group however 'homogeneous' it is alleged to be.

TLK

DIRECT INSTRUCTION
One model of teaching, usually described as the didactic method. It usually involves a significant amount of TEACHER TALK. This was the standard method of schools 40 or 50 years ago and it contrasts with the more informal or progressive models which came to be favoured after the PLOWDEN REPORT, but which had their origins with ROUSSEAU and DEWEY. It still forms a significant tool in the teacher's armoury.

TLK

DISCIPLINE
Discipline is an aspect of SCHOOL ETHOS related to expectations of acceptable orderly behaviour. These behaviours may be prescribed as rules which all are expected to follow and conformity to these rules is buttressed by REWARDS and PUNISHMENTS.

Under the Education (No. 2) Act 1986, it is clear that GOVERNORS and headteachers hold major responsibility for discipline. Governors are required to produce a statement of general principles and may give guidance on particular instances of breaches of discipline. The headteacher is charged with making rules and imposing them within the parameters of the general principles. (The same Act abolished corporal punishment in state schools, a requirement that came into force in 1987.)

A major report, 'Discipline in Schools', sometimes known as the Elton Report, made recommendations in response to growing concern about violence and indiscipline in schools (see Section 4, 'Legislation').

The sanctions aspect of discipline often overshadows the reward aspects, and among sanctions, corporal punishment and *detention* are perhaps the most discussed. Sections 46 and 47 of the Education (No. 2) Act 1986 concerned abolition of corporal punishment in state schools in England, Wales and Scotland. Independent schools were not included in the legislation but corporal punishment may not be used in an independent school against pupils whose fees are paid by the state. Detention after school hours (as opposed to detention during school breaks) and detention of pupils for part of the lunch-time when they normally return home for lunch needs to be used cautiously. Parents should receive notice of the detention so that they are not unduly anxious about their child's whereabouts and so that, if necessary, transport arrangements can be changed. This may mean writing to parents giving them notice that their child will be detained the following day. It is widely accepted that a punishment is most effective if it follows as soon as possible after the misdemeanour attracting the punishment. When punishment needs to be delayed for a day or more, its efficacy in discouraging the offence has to be questioned. Any LEA regulations regarding DETENTION must be followed. If detention is used, parents and pupils should be made aware of this in SCHOOL BROCHURES, general information on the school and in written school rules. Its effectiveness as a deterrent should ideally be monitored.

'Assertive discipline', an approach used in some schools in the USA, is also becoming popular in Britain. It involves strict adherence to a set of rules and gradually increasing sanctions which do not vary. All teachers and pupils know the inevitable consequences of inappropriate pupil behaviours.

Further reading

DES (1989) *Discipline in Schools* 'Elton Report' (HMSO).

MF

DISCIPLINE (TEACHER ACHIEVING/MAINTAINING)

The notion of discipline in schools means different things to different users of the term. Some would tend to be heavily influenced by authoritarian ideas: discipline in this context is something 'imposed' as a form of 'external control' by a 'good disciplinarian' probably on a group of 'disruptive' students. This cluster of terms and concepts applied to the classroom is dependent on notions of controlling behaviour by the teacher, using either physical means or the techniques of social control. It is probably better to define classroom discipline in terms of order rather than control. A disciplined relationship between teacher and students, then, is not so much an imposed situation but an agreed one. The discipline becomes an orderly set of behaviours intrinsically valued by everyone for the sake of achieving some defined goal: in this case, learning information or a skill. Disruption is viewed negatively – at least by the majority – because it interferes with orderly progress towards the shared goal. This more positive view accepts the practical reality of most schools: that indiscipline is a minority problem. It explains why the ETHOS OF THE SCHOOL is so significant a factor in successful schools.

Of course, in every class there are incidents which (if unchecked) would destroy the intrinsic orderliness, i.e. the discipline of the class. Most of these are relatively trivial: for example, chatter which is irrelevant or disturbs others, eating or drinking, minor mistreatment of school property, or unsafe practices like running in a science laboratory. Teachers develop skills for dealing with situations like these. Typical skills include: negotiating ground-rules on first encounter with a class, preparing lessons thoroughly, keeping work interesting, being mobile around the classroom, giving clear instructions, being vigilant, developing good voice control. Sometimes more serious situations develop, often because the teacher has failed in some aspect of these skills initially. This escalation of a problem may need more deliberate intervention, such as removing a disruptive pupil away from others for a time. Occasionally, a situation will arise which is very serious: such as an assault on the teacher. In these cases immediate assistance must be obtained from senior colleagues, and the school's normal procedures as set out in the school's policy documents must be followed. Maintaining good classroom discipline is one aspect of CLASS MANAGEMENT. It may involve REWARDS or occasional recourse to PUNISH-MENTS. The skills of the teacher in maintaining discipline are a sub-set of TEACHING SKILLS. The ability to sustain discipline is a 'sine qua non' of all teaching; but it should be viewed as the context in which the real purpose of the classroom – the furtherance of learning – takes place rather than as an end in itself. Failure to achieve this is one of the most significant factors in STRESS in teachers.

TLK

DISCOVERY (GUIDED DISCOVERY)

The discovery method is a method of teaching and learning advocated particularly by child-centred teachers. It argues that learners who find out things for themselves (rather than being shown or told) learn better. It is claimed that discovery learning is better, encouraging pupils' interest, understanding and ability to think for themselves. Discovery is really 'guided discovery' because the teacher structures tasks and information in such a way that the child is aided to discover what the teacher wishes to convey, say a mathematical relationship.

As one of a range of methods, it can be useful as a way of teaching aspects of some areas of the curriculum.

MF

DISCUSSION

Discussion is one TEACHING METHOD commonly employed by teachers, often, but not exclusively, in the Humanities to engage pupils' interest in, and commitment to, particular subject matter. Reasons commonly given by teachers for engaging pupils in discussion are:

- to increase pupils' self-confidence;
- to teach the ability to argue clearly;
- to make children think;
- to draw out issues in contemporary events;
- to help pupils formulate opinions;
- to encourage mutual respect and tolerance among pupils;
- to prepare pupils for the adult world;
- as a stimulus to later written work.

Discussion requires particular skills of teachers. An effective discussion leader needs to:

- present the problem clearly and make clear the group's task;
- create an atmosphere in which people are not afraid to give their opinions;
- be a good listener;
- show sensitivity to the feelings of individuals in the group;
- protect minority opinions;
- promote respect between individuals in the group;
- provoke participants to support their views with reason;
- ask open questions to which there are many acceptable answers, rather than closed (one answer) questions;
- avoid making statements;
- keep the discussion relevant to the stated problem;
- allow digression where appropriate;
- encourage pooling of knowledge;
- provide information when called upon to do so;
- avoid stating his/her own opinion;
- sum up at the end.

Techniques and procedures for handling discussion probably vary slightly according to the purpose of the discussion.

Discussion was a medium particularly favoured by Lawrence STENHOUSE, who also utilized the concept of the neutral chairman.

TLK

DISPLAY

Display in classrooms is mainly associated with primary education. The purposes of display are to stimulate learning – hence the use of visual aids to illustrate spelling, telling the time; motivating children – through the exhibition of good examples of their work; and to create an attractive LEARNING ENVIRONMENT. The best examples of display work usually contain a balance of material produced by children and material produced or selected by the teacher. Display is most effective when classroom learning flows into and out of it. The key word is impact. Teachers can use every level of the classroom (doors, windows, notice-boards), with attractive backing paper or drapes used to show off work in a way that speaks of quality. To sustain impact displays need to be changed regularly; and the teacher needs to check for neat mounting of work, imaginative use of colour, opportunities for the children to interact with the displays (to touch, smell), attractive lettering and correct spelling. There is a temptation for teachers in secondary schools/FE colleges to underrate the power of display as a learning medium. Given the opportunity most students respond well to an attractive learning environment and to the display of work; teachers of older students would do well to learn from the primary sector on this topic.

TLK

DISTANCE EDUCATION
(See: OPEN EDUCATION)

DOCTOR'S DEGREE

The third and highest 'degree' of academic attainment after BACHELOR's and MASTER's. The degree of doctor is normally awarded for a thesis containing original research by the student. The universities reserve the Doctor of Philosophy degree (Ph.D.) for this purpose: some refer to it as a D.Phil. The degree is awarded in all faculties. There are also 'higher doctorates', usually D.Sc. (doctor of science) or DD (doctor of divinity), which can be obtained for outstanding published work and nationally or internationally recognized research. Many universities reserve most higher doctorates as honorary doctorates – given to notable academics for outstanding achievement and as a mark of recognition. The titles of such awards are often anachronistic e.g. D.Univ. (doctor of the university), DCL (doctor of civil law) or D.Litt. (doctor of letters). It is regrettable, perhaps, that this honorary system has been cheapened in academic terms by awards to those who have achieved in non-academic fields: such as football or pop music. There is an increasing tendency for universities to seek a 'taught' route to a doctorate, and several are now experimenting with a taught Ed.D. (doctor of education) degree, which will probably rank below the Ph.D. in the same way that a taught M.Ed. does alongside the M.Phil. by research. The trend is a commendable and market-led response to those who aspire to doctorate level work but who do not have the means to carry out original large-scale research.

TLK

D.PHIL.
(See: DOCTOR'S DEGREES)

DRAMA
While it is not one of the core or foundation subjects of the National Curriculum, drama is used to illuminate other subjects from English to history. It can be studied at GCSE and A-level. In institutions of higher education it may be part of a course in the theatre which involves academic study and the practice of drama.

Dance and drama courses are not designated in the Department for Education as attracting mandatory grants. LEA's award at their own discretion student grants for dance, drama and stage management. Scholarships, charitable endowments and bursaries are available.

Entry to drama school is by interview and audition and there is intense competition for places. Many drama schools also offer courses in stage management as well as drama.

Address

National Council for Drama Training, 5 Tavistock Place,
London WC1H 9SS
tel: 071 387 3650

MF

DRUG ABUSE
Learning about the effects of drugs and the dangers of their misuse is one way of tackling abuse. The Health Education Authority and TACADE

offer audio-visual materials and publications suitable for use with students. Address enquiries to:
Health Education Authority, Hamilton House, Mabledon Place,
London WC1H 9TX
tel: 071 631 0930
The Advisory Council on Alcohol and Drug Education (TACADE),
1 Hulme Place, The Crescent, Salford M5 4QA
tel: 061 745 8925
Action on Smoking and Health, 5–11 Mortimer Street, London W1N 7RH
tel: 071 637 9843

MF

DRUGS
(See: HEALTH EDUCATION)

DYSLEXIA
Dyslexia refers to a spectrum of reading and writing disorders in which a learner's reading, writing and spelling are at a level much below what would be expected for his or her age and presumed intelligence.

Dyslexia may involve some or all of the following:

• significant delay in reading progress compared with others of the same age;
• writing problems such as letter or word reversal;
• erratic spelling;
• confusion over left and right directions;
• clumsiness;
• difficulties with sequencing (e.g. following instructions involving a series of tasks);
• poor speech fluency;
• difficulties with numbers.

The Joint Council for GCSE can allow examination concessions of extra time for dyslexia candidates whose dyslexia is confirmed by a report from an educational psychologist.

(See also: Section 3, DYSLEXIA INSTITUTE)

The British Dyslexia Association works through affiliated local dyslexia associations and corporate member associations to offer counselling, advice

and a referral service. A publications list is available, together with further information, from:
British Dyslexia Association, 98 London Road, Reading, Berks RG1 5AU
tel: 0734 668271/2

MF

EDUCATION

Peters (1966), exploring the term education in his earlier writings (his view was modified over subsequent years), provides a useful framework, stating: 'It implies that something worthwhile is being or has been intentionally transmitted in a morally acceptable manner.'

Key words here are 'worthwhile', 'intentionally' and 'morally acceptable'. Vigorous debate has taken place and continues about what 'worthwhile' means which is influenced by historical and cultural context among other factors. At the time of the Education Act 1870, it was considered 'worthwhile' that elementary education should concentrate on basic subjects such as English and arithmetic and religion whereas today our idea of what is worthwhile is much wider, encompassing foreign languages taught from an early age for example. In Muslim cultures a close study of the Koran is considered the bedrock of education whereas in Britain at least a token recognition of a Christian past enters the notion of education.

A consensus view of worthwhile content would be that it is the knowledge, skills, attitudes and values which society endorses. Education then, enables learners to occupy competently various roles: worker, citizen, perhaps parent and spouse. It also encourages personal growth and autonomy.

Turning to the 'intentional' nature of education we can recognize that learning can be informal and unstructured; it is the incidental learning we acquire almost without realizing. Education, however, implies intentional, structured experiences aimed at facilitating learning.

The 'morally acceptable manner' aspect of education has to do with the process by which worthwhile content is transmitted. Education implies freedom to consider differing views or information and come to a reasoned conclusion. Where this element is lacking we would speak of indoctrination. This issue is not clear cut. A teacher with strong religious convictions might justify indoctrinating pupils with his or her religious beliefs because (in his or her view) to be initiated into these beliefs enhances and reveals the whole meaning and purpose of life and nothing could be more morally acceptable. The ends justify the means. However, more enlightened educators would recognize that even religious beliefs which are as dependent on faith as on reason can be shared in a way which encourages discussion and reasoned conclusions rather than acceptance based exclusively on faith. It is appropriate then to speak of religious education. A dilemma still exists because we can envisage someone committed to religious education who does not have a religious faith and it is the faith element which some believe can be conveyed as unarguable tenets to be accepted or not accepted by the grace of God. However, looking at INDOCTRINATION and education as different points on a continuum, while a grey area exists in the middle, indicates that there are useful distinctions between the two.

Training implies limitations of both content and process. If education enables learners to occupy roles as workers and citizens and other roles, an aspect of teaching and learning which focuses exclusively on an occupational role, implying a limitation of content, is usually called training. Also in terms of process, training is one approach to learning but if it were the only one used, we would tend to avoid the word education for what was happening. It implies a rather more limited approach and is often used in relation to skills, although in professional training, knowledge and attitudes and values can be part of the course. The limitation of process seems to be related to that of content in that in professional training the trainee is implicitly saying, 'I will accept the knowledge, attitudes and values of this occupation in order to become part of the group that carry out the occupation.'

Training can be considered a part of education. If at the same time as occupational training was taking place the learner sufficiently encountered wider content and participated in wider processes, then the training would be seen as a contribution to his wider education.

A similar view can be taken of processes such as instruction or rote learning. If used exclusively they would not constitute an appropriate process for education, but they can contribute to a wider conception of process including such approaches as guided discovery learning which taken together would constitute an acceptable range of processes to be called educative.

To be 'educated implies that the educated person has been changed by the experience of education in terms of behaviour towards others, ability to understand the world (or aspects of it) and in ability to do things in the world. The transformation is integrally related to the concepts of knowledge and understanding' (Barrow and Woods, 1982).

Further reading

Barrow, R. and Woods, R. (1982, second edition) *An Introduction to Philosophy of Education* (Methuen).
Peters, R. S. (1966) *Ethics and Education* (Allen and Unwin).

MF

EDUCATION COMMITTEE
In England and Wales, an education committee is formed from the members of an elected council of local government (the local education authority). The education committee also has co-opted members who may, for example, represent community organizations.

MF

EDUCATION JOURNALS
Periodicals containing academic articles about aspects of education and pedagogy. There are numerous examples, of which only a limited selection can be quoted here. Journals tend to subdivide by topic.

1. Those concerned with educational research

These contain reports of investigative work in schools and colleges of higher education (HE). Examples would be the British Educational Research Journal; the British Journal of Educational Psychology; the NFER journal called Educational Research, and the British Journal of the Sociology of Education.

2. Those concerned with curriculum issues

Examples here are the Curriculum Journal, Curriculum Inquiry and Journal of Curriculum Studies. These contain substantial investigations into curriculum innovation and effectiveness.

3. Those concerned with the initial and in-service training of teachers

Among these, the British Journal of In-Service Education is foremost in looking at research and issues for those engaged in in-service education. The Journal of Education for Teaching, the Journal of Teacher Development, and Teacher and Teacher Education are also concerned with initial and continuing teacher education.

4. Those concerned with teaching specific subject areas

Most subjects are supported in some way by a specialist journal. Among these, examples include Teaching History, Mathematics Teacher, Maths in Schools, School Science Review, English in Education, British Journal of Moral Education, Geography, and the British Journal of Religious

Education. Areas like reading, too, have specialist journals: Reading, The British Journal of Educational Technology and the British Journal of Music Education are other examples. The phases of education are also represented by journals such as Education 3–13.

5. *Those concerned with educational issues generally*

Some journals provide a mix of research material and reflective or speculative articles. The Cambridge Journal of Education and Westminster Studies in Education are good examples of this type, as is British Journal of Educational Studies. Comparative Education looks at international issues.

6. *Those published by particular professional associations*

Many journals already listed are published as organs of professional associations. Other examples include Education Today, from the College of Preceptors.

7. *Those concerned with the management and administration of education*

A growing field is the study of educational management, and important journals here include: Journal of Educational Administration, Management in Education, Educational Management and Administration and School Organization.

Journal articles are usually refereed (i.e. vetted for quality, accuracy, originality, etc.) before publication; thus journals contain the most-up-to-date thinking in their fields. All teachers should make a professional habit of keeping up with recent published material by accessing journals related to their main subject/professional interests. Copies of key journals are usually held in the libraries of INSTITUTES OF HIGHER EDUCATION.

TLK

EDUCATION OFFICER

An administrator appointed by a LOCAL EDUCATION AUTHORITY to carry out set tasks in relation to the delivery of educational services by that Authority. Education Officers may hold various grades of seniority (assistant, senior, principal); and he/she can be responsible for a variety of functions (such as special needs, or a phase of schooling), or for a geographical division of the Authority. Education Officers normally work alongside other LEA professionals, such as INSPECTORS or ADVISERS. The most senior officer is the CHIEF EDUCATION OFFICER (in shire counties often called the County Education Officer).

TLK

EDUCATION SUPPORT GRANTS (ESG)
Education Support Grants are a particular category of grant available through GEST for IN-SERVICE training of teachers.

TLK

EDUCATION WELFARE OFFICERS AND SERVICE
The Education Welfare Service offers support to families, students and schools on all aspects of child welfare, school attendance and child employment, and is provided to help pupils get the maximum benefit from their education. Education Welfare Officers' support is available to pupils and parents who need help with such difficulties as BULLYING, a child not settling into a new school or class, or home difficulties and problems that may be affecting the child's progress at school. The Education Welfare Officer is an experienced and professional member of the LEA Education Service who is skilled in dealing with complex and personal problems, and who, if not able to help directly, is able to advise upon the most appropriate organization or person to contact. Education Welfare Officers may be contacted either through your child's school, or if more appropriate, by writing to the Local Education Authority direct.

CAK

EFFECTIVE SCHOOLS
The debate about what makes schools effective continues. The government has recently attempted to define effectiveness in terms of measurable products such as low truancy rates and high levels of examination performance. But these products are often the outward signs of an underlying ETHOS which is essential but hard to define, and the issue is pursued in more detail under that heading.

TLK

EFFECTIVE TEACHER
Precisely what constitutes teacher effectiveness is open to debate, but research suggests that the following characteristics are important. The effective teacher will:

• provide a safe psychological climate for all pupils;

- be fair and consistent in dealing with lapses from good behaviour;
- not be too dominant;
- know each pupil individually by name;
- show a knowledge of the pupil's background;
- be *au fait* with and value the subject matter of lessons;
- be aware of individual learning needs;
- accept pupils' initiatives in work or activities;
- ask leading questions;
- cope with a variety of tasks in progress simultaneously;
- organize transitions from one activity to another quickly and efficiently;
- be aware of social groupings within the class;
- be a good organizer;
- know how to use feed-back from pupils;
- encourage warm classroom relationships between pupils;
- know what standards can reasonably be expected from pupils;
- be able to describe, and cope with, exceptional pupils;
- be able to analyse teaching objectives;
- provide an interesting range of commercial and teacher-made resources;
- admit his/her mistakes and learn from them.

In addition, one should note that PUPILS' VIEWS OF TEACHER EFFECTIVENESS are likely to emphasize a different, if complementary, set of characteristics. Even the most effective teacher may occasionally teach an INEFFECTIVE LESSON.

TLK

EGALITARIANISM

In an egalitarian education system, all learners would be treated equally. This does not mean that all would be treated identically for this in itself would give rise to inequalities, the blind child being expected to read normal print, to put it at an absurd extreme. Equal treatment, then, to make any sense must mean treating people the same except where there are differences between them which justify treating them differently in certain respects.

In this respect equal treatment is the same as impartial treatment. (Barrow and Woods, 1982). This does not help us decide the grounds on which impartial and partial treatment are justified, but it indicates that arguing for different kinds of education for different learners, such as Grammar Schools for some and say Technology Schools for others, does not have to be inegalitarian.

(See also: ELITISM)

Further reading

Barrow, R. and Woods, R. (1982, second edition) *An Introduction to Philosophy of Education* (Methuen).

MF

ELECTED GOVERNORS

The Education (No. 2) Act 1986 provides the framework for governor elections and the rules apply to both PARENT GOVERNORS and TEACHER GOVERNORS with one or two minor variations. The LEA in maintained schools and the governing body in voluntary-aided schools is responsible for making all the arrangements for the elections.

For PARENT GOVERNOR elections, all parents are to be informed of the vacancy/vacancies and forthcoming election by post (this may include 'pupil post'), and nominations invited. If there is to be an election, candidates may be asked to provide a short personal statement to be circulated to parents. The ensuing ballot is a secret ballot. The count is conducted by the nominated responsible officer, and all parents informed of the result.

It should be noted that, in addition to the actual parents of a child, 'parent' can include any person who is not the actual parent of the child but has parental responsibility for him or her or who has care of the child. Thus legal guardians and foster parents would count as parents for the purpose of election as a parent governor. In cases where the status of the adult is in some dispute, the LEA will be called upon to determine exactly who is a parent for the purpose of parent governor elections.

Much of the paragraph relating to the conduct of elections mentioned above is relevant when conducting ballots for TEACHER GOVERNORS, but it should be noted that local representatives of the professional associations should be consulted on the proposed arrangements for the election.

CAK

ELITISM

Educationalists such as Bantock (1965) take a view of art including music, literature, dance and fine arts, which is more to do with appreciating it than creating it. Such educationalists are sometimes known as cultural elitists. Education, in Bantock's view, should involve the appreciation of excellence, which implies controls and limitations on the freedom of children to produce creative work. If a child's work is not expected to meet standards derived from models of excellence, then the child will not come to appreciate excellence. He is therefore not being educated. Such models of excellence are drawn from what could be called 'high' culture, which is seen as superior to 'popular' culture. Society should, in this view, nourish the production of high culture and its appreciation. It may not be possible for all members of society to acquire the sensitivity, knowledge, and intelligence thought to be a prerequisite to an appreciation of higher culture. Therefore, education, to the extent to which it implies initiating learners into higher culture, may be relevant only to a minority. Such is the elitist view. It does not say that only a minority are entitled to be initiated into higher culture but that in an imperfect world it may be possible for only a few to be initiated.

(See also: EGALITARIANISM)

Further reading

Bantock, G. H. (1965) *Education and Values* (Faber).

MF

EMOTIONAL BEHAVIOURAL DIFFICULTIES (EBD)

Children with emotional and behavioural difficulties used to be known as 'maladjusted' and much of the pioneering work with such children in the early part of the twentieth century took place in residential special schools or communities such as Red Hill in Kent and the Mulberry Bush in Oxfordshire.

The 1959 publication 'The Handicapped Pupil and Special School Regulations' described maladjusted pupils as ones: 'who show evidence of emotional instability or psychological disturbance and require special educational treatment in order to effect their personal, social or educational readjustments'.

The expression EBD refers to emotional and behavioural and relationship difficulties which are:

1. developmentally inappropriate;
2. of sufficient duration and severity to cause:
    (a) the child persistent suffering or disability and/or
    (b) the family or community distress or disturbance.

Such pupils may be taught in mainstream schools, perhaps in separate classes or in a unit on the school campus. They may also be taught in special units or schools.

Address

Association of Workers for Children with EBD, Red Hill School, East Sutton, Maidstone, Kent ME17 3DQ
tel: 0622 843104

Publications

Clarke, M. (1990) The Disruptive Child: a handbook for care and control, Northcote House.

MF

ENGLISH (IN THE NATIONAL CURRICULUM)

If you are not familiar with National Curriculum terminology, before reading this subject entry, you may find it helpful to first read the entries on:

Attainment Targets
National Curriculum
Programmes of Study
Standard Assessment Tasks

See also the entry NATIONAL CURRICULUM, in which English is used as the working example.

The attainment targets (AT) and the levels of statements of attainment (SoA) relating to them are shown below.

AT1	Speaking and listening (levels 1–10)	The development of pupils' understanding of the spoken word and the capacity to express themselves effectively in a variety of speaking and listening activities, matching style and response to audience and purpose.
AT2	Reading (levels 1–10)	The development of the ability to read, understand and respond to all types of writing, as well as the development of information-retrieval strategies for the purpose of study.
AT3	Writing (levels 1–10)	A growing ability to construct and convey meaning in written language, matching style to audience and purpose.
AT4	Spelling (levels 1–4)	
AT5	Handwriting (levels 1–4)	
AT4–5	Presentation (levels 5–7)	

It is possible to identify a number of strands in the English ATs and SoA, though these are not systematically developed over all ten levels. For example, there is a strand relating to knowledge about language which starts at Level 5 in all ATs. Other strands are specific to each AT, e.g. group discussion (AT1), drafting (AT3), information-retrieval skills (AT2). The key stages relate to levels of attainment in the following way:

KS1	–	Levels 1–3
KS2	–	Levels 2–5
KS3	–	Levels 3–8
KS4	–	Levels 3–10

Turning to programmes of study (PoS), these are related to key stages. Each Programme of Study (PoS) contains general provisions for the PoS as a whole and detailed provisions for the key stage or stages which it covers. For most ATs these detailed provisions include material specifying what pupils working towards a particular level should experience.

These Programmes of Study are defined in English.

1. Speaking and listening:
   (a) for Key Stage 1;
   (b) for Key Stages 2 to 4.
   These cover the range of situations, audiences and activities designed to develop pupils' competence, precision and confidence in speaking and listening.
2. Reading:
   (a) for Key Stage 1;
   (b) for Key Stage 2;
   (c) for Key Stages 3 and 4.
   These cover the range of reading material and the knowledge, skills and understanding to be developed.
3. Writing, Spelling and Handwriting:
   (a) for Key Stage 1;
   (b) for Key Stage 2;
   (c) for Key Stages 3 and 4.
   These cover the range of contexts, purposes and audiences for writing; the conventions of writing and the knowledge about written language to be developed.

Further reading

DES/WO (1990) *National Curriculum* (HMSO).
O'Connor, J. (1994) 'The English Curriculum' in the series Farrell, M. (Ed.), *Education for Teaching* (HMSO).

MF

ENGLISH AS A FOREIGN LANGUAGE (EFL)

English is taught to overseas students as a foreign language mainly in private language schools based in London or the south-east of England. The focus may be specific; English for business or travel for example.

Address

Association of Recognized English Language Schools, 2 Pontypool Place, Valentine Place, London SE1 8QF
tel: 071 242 3136
Publishes 'Learn English in Britain', which gives information on courses in English as a foreign language. Free.

MF

ENGLISH AS A SECOND LANGUAGE (ESL)

If a school can demonstrate that it values the languages other than English which its pupils are able to speak this may motivate pupils whose native language is not English and enhance their general school performance.

Extra support may be needed for a pupil for whom English is a second language. If this is given in a mainstream classroom rather than in withdrawal groups, it can benefit the pupil by allowing him or her to share the activities pursued by classmates.

Address

National Association for Teaching English and Other Community Languages, National Centre, Hall Green College, Floodgate Street, Digbeth, Birmingham B5 5SU
tel: 021 778 2311, ext. 290

MF

ENVIRONMENTAL EDUCATION

Environmental education includes education concerning the protection of the environment and the wise use of natural resources. It is a cross curricular theme of the National Curriculum taught through local environmental projects, case studies and other activities. In primary schools, environmental education often arises from children's responses to (and their interaction with) the natural world. This is used by the teacher to help pupils comprehend their surroundings.

In Scotland, environmental education is part of the 5 to 14 Development

Programme. In primary schools it is one of five areas while in secondary schools 'social and environmental' studies is one of eight modes.

Addresses

Council for Environmental Education, Faculty of Education and Community Studies, University of Reading, London Road, Reading RG1 5AQ
tel: 0734 875234, ext. 218
Environmental Education Advisers Association, Richard Mosely (Membership Secretary), Education Department, Cornwall County Council, County Hall, Truro TR1 3BA.

MF

EQUAL OPPORTUNITIES

Equality of opportunity means different things to different people. Some people use it as a broad umbrella term relating to groups identified according to gender, race, nationality, religion, social class, special need, sexual orientation or some other characteristic. In a more restricted sense, the term concerns equal opportunities for girls and women.

Also, equality of opportunity can mean the following:

1. equality of access; ensuring that people have the same available opportunities;
2. equivalent experience; enabling each person to fulfil their potential;
3. overcoming limitation; such limitations being on experience and learning because of earlier experiences of stereotyping;
4. equality of outcome; ensuring that different groups (e.g. girls) reach equal levels of achievement compared with other groups (e.g. boys).

Our focus here is on equal opportunities and gender. Under the Sex Discrimination Act 1975 it is unlawful for educational institutions, including schools, to discriminate because of sex. The legislation applies to:

1. the terms and conditions of admitting students;
2. refusal to admit a student (single sex schools being exempt);
3. refusing access to any courses or facilities provided by the school;
4. excluding or unfavourably treating students.

Discrimination, a related concept, is defined in law as less favourable treatment. Direct discrimination arises when a girl receives less favourable treatment than a comparable boy has received and the treatment is based on sex. Indirect discrimination occurs when a condition or requirement is applied to boys and girls equally but a significantly small proportion of girls compared with boys can comply (and vice versa).

Useful addresses

Equal Opportunities Commission, Overseas House, Quay Street, Manchester M3 3HN
tel: 061 833 9244

Further reading

Weiner, G. and Hackney, A. (1994) *Valuing the Individual* in the series Farrell, M. (Ed.) *Education for Teaching* (HMSO).

MF

ETHOS OF THE SCHOOL

Also known as climate, tone or atmosphere. Considerable research has been carried out to explore how far this affects students' development and also to assess this rather elusive quality more closely. There can be little doubt that students in some schools perform better than in others, and that this would be true even if it were possible to control precisely for the standards of academic work in the school. Some schools are happier places than others. So how do these 'climatic' effects come about? Some early research concentrated on material factors such as buildings and resources. Other research suggested the answer lay in the out-of-school backgrounds, i.e. the homes and communities from which the students came. More recently the research explored aspects of interpersonal relationships: the quality of relations between the students and staff, between student and student, and among the staff themselves. This line of thinking also identified the crucial role of the head or principal in climate-setting.

One of the largest studies of ethos across schools was Michael Rutter's research (1979) in the book *Fifteen Thousand Hours*. Rutter studied a wide variety of variables and concluded that, when all these are compensated for, a further quality (climate or ethos of the school) existed which marked out some schools from others. In these 'better' schools academic attainment was markedly higher, e.g. the average examination score for low ability children in the successful school was as good as that for the high ability students in the least successful school. Rutter's research highlighted a number of factors indicative of a successful school ethos:

- high academic standards were expected of the students, and matched by the PROFESSIONALISM of the staff e.g. in marking homework;

- good levels of TEACHING SKILLS were widespread;
- effective DISCIPLINE was based on positive behaviour such as praise;
- the students were given responsibility and opportunities for leadership;
- there was an effective COUNSELLING and tutoring system in place.

These findings were mirrored by HMI in a report called *Ten Good Schools: a secondary school enquiry* (1977). HMI added some other factors:

- good schools set their objectives and plan towards them;
- academic work is effective in DIFFERENTIATION;
- good schools have effective HOME-SCHOOL links and links with the community;
- headteachers in good schools have well developed LEADERSHIP skills.

These studies have concentrated on the secondary sector, but there can be little doubt that the same principles apply across the age-phases. Fundamental to the issue is the quality of MANAGEMENT in the school, but achieving a good climate is a subtle blend of factors that requires the co-operation of all staff and, ultimately, of all students.

TLK

EXCLUSION

Exclusion may be a rare event for a school, but power is invested in the head to exclude a pupil if he or she is causing particular concern by unreasonable behaviour. Exclusion is generally used as a last resort, and the decision to exclude is usually only taken after lengthy discussions. Once exclusion has been agreed, the head must inform the parents (if the pupil is under 18) that their child has been excluded, and explain why; he/she must also tell the parents that they have the right (or the student if he/she is over 18) to take up the matter with the governing body and the local education authority. The Education Act 1993, Section 261, places restrictions on the power of headteachers to exclude pupils by preventing indefinite exclusions and restricts the number of fixed-term exclusions to not more than fifteen school days in any one term. EDUCATION WELFARE OFFICERS are able to advise in cases of exclusion; their address may be obtained from the local education authority or the headteacher.

CAK

EXPERIENCE (EDUCATION THROUGH EXPERIENCE)

Everything can be considered as experience, including a pupil's experience of a formal 'chalk and talk' lesson. However, what is implied in the expression 'education through experience' is that the experience involves active participation. At a generally accepted level, educating through experience involves a teacher:

(a)   relating teaching to a learner's experience;
(b)   providing appropriate and worthwhile experiences to assist learning (e.g. making a field visit before teaching a related geographical point);
(c)   encouraging learning to develop directly from a learner's experience.

In this way, it is anticipated that the learner will see relevance to the learning and will therefore learn more effectively.

At a more contentious level, educating through experience is a view in which a learner's experiences are taken as the criterion against which to determine what should be taught. Problems arise if we consider children from educationally impoverished backgrounds whose bedrock of experience which one could draw on to achieve educational objectives is limited. Few teachers would want to accept the limitations and not want to extend them. Should a child whose parents read rarely and who read a limited range of material not be encouraged to read often and widely? Also, if aspects of a child's experience are bad and antisocial it is difficult to see how a teacher could use these as a criterion for what should be taught.

MF

EXPERIENTIAL LEARNING

A view of education that holds that more effective learning is achieved if children can experience what is being taught (see also ACTIVE LEARNING) rather than simply be passive listeners. Experiential learning, to quote a simple example, would attempt to put across the concept of, and empathy with, blindness by putting a blind-folded student in a strange environment – as opposed to describing the symptoms of blindness. There can be little doubt of the value of experiential learning, though there have been some politically-motivated attempts to label it as 'trendy' and to play down its value in favour of academic knowledge and data acquisition. Experiential learning is most often used with students of primary age, but is probably most effective with all age-groups. Royal Air Force and airline pilots, for example, are trained in this way using flight simulators.

TLK

EXPLAINING

Explaining is a key TEACHING SKILL at every level of education. Explaining means giving understanding to another person. It involves an explainer (the teacher), explainees (students/pupils) and something to be explained (an aspect of the CURRICULUM). Research indicates that teachers may talk for up to 66 per cent of all classroom time; much of this talk will involve explaining. Explanations are sometimes divided into different kinds. Interpretive explanations answer What? questions in the minds of students (e.g. What is oil?). Descriptive explanations answer How? questions (e.g. How is oil produced?). Reason-giving explanations are directed at Why? questions (e.g. Why is oil an important fuel?). To explain effectively teachers need to be aware of these kinds of function served by explanations. When preparing an explanation it is helpful for teachers to analyse the topic to be explained into its main components, to establish the links between the components, to identify any rules or principles to be illustrated, to use an appropriate kind of explanation (see above) and to remember to adapt the proposed explanation to the audience. This last point means that the language of the explanation must be monitored, and the needs of the most and least able taken into account. Effective explainers define new ideas and technical terms; they use precise language free of ambiguity, they use voice control effectively to give appropriate emphasis and utilize silence to allow for thinking time.

Good explanations are characterized by an effective use of 'linguistic moves', i.e. phrases like 'first . . .', 'next . . .', 'an important point is . . .', 'take special note of this . . .'. Often learners benefit most from an explanation when there are plenty of good examples given, both positive and negative (It works like this . . . but not like this . . .). Many explanations benefit from illustration using AUDIO-VISUAL approaches, so that the verbal/intellectual approach is supported by the concrete/tactile. Above all, an explanation must be given in a clear and logical sequence; and the teacher will pause from time to time to ask QUESTIONS and receive FEEDBACK, so as to check on the learning which is taking place. The commonest failings of an explanation are that the explainer fails to understand the topic him/herself, that one of the key components is omitted, that the explanation is rushed, that the language is inaccessible, or that the explainer forgets to check the pupil's understanding. Talking is not, of itself, explanation.

TLK

FASHION AND TEXTILES
(See: TECHNOLOGY)

FEEDBACK
The means of using students' non-verbal, oral or written responses to teaching as a means to assess its effectiveness. For example, a teacher uses

right or wrong answers to track how well children understand the material being studied.

TLK

FEEDER SCHOOLS

The primary schools the bulk of whose pupils form the intake for a local COMPREHENSIVE school; similarly, in some areas, the infant schools supplying pupils to a local junior/middle school.

TLK

FIRST CERTIFICATE/DIPLOMA

Vocationally-oriented qualifications awarded by the BUSINESS AND TECHNOLOGY EDUCATION COUNCIL which are broadly equivalent to four or more GCSES

(See also, Section 3, 'Directory of Organizations', under Business and Technology Education Council)

MF

FIRST SCHOOLS

(See: PRIMARY SCHOOLS)

FIRST GOVERNORS

'First' governors sit on the governing body of a GRANT MAINTAINED (GM) SCHOOL, which, prior to GM status, was a former county school, i.e. not a 'VOLUNTARY' school. As with co-opted governors of an LEA controlled school, it is expected that some members will be from the local business community who are ready to show a long-term commitment to the school. Unlike parent and teacher governors, who serve a term of four years, 'first' governors will serve for between five and seven years, the actual term length to be decided by the GOVERNING BODY.

CAK

HUMANIST EDUCATION

(See: PLATO)

FLEXIBLE LEARNING

A once popular system in schools in which students were allowed to pace and time their own work provided they completed a set quantity over a school day/week. The pressure of syllabus and ASSESSMENT asserted by National Curriculum has militated against its use. It is still employed in some further education and adult learning situations, and has the advantage of recognizing the maturity and self-determination of students.

TLK

FOOD TECHNOLOGY
(See: DESIGN AND TECHNOLOGY)

FORMATIVE
The term 'formative' is currently most widely used when referring to formative assessment, a form of assessment required by the National Curriculum. Such assessment helps 'form' teaching and learning. It provides information which helps the teacher decide how a pupil's learning ought to progress. It gives the pupil information about his or her progress and provides targets for learning. It also indicates when diagnostic tests may need to be administered to a pupil.

MF

FORMATIVE ASSESSMENT
(See: ASSESSMENT IN THE NATIONAL CURRICULUM)

FOUNDATION GOVERNORS
'Foundation' governors sit on the governing body of a GRANT MAINTAINED SCHOOL, which, prior to GM status, was a former church or other voluntary school. Foundation governors are expected to provide continuity for the governing body of the school, and as a result, their period of office exceeds that of PARENT and TEACHER GOVERNORS. The actual term of office is decided by the governing body, but it is expected to be between five and seven years.

CAK

FOUNDATION SUBJECTS
(See: NATIONAL CURRICULUM)

FRAMEWORK FOR INSPECTION
The Framework for Inspection is the document which forms the basis for ensuring the quality and reliability of inspections of schools. REGISTERED INSPECTORS are required to comply with the Framework and conduct the Inspections in accordance with its general principles together with any special conditions that may attach to the school being inspected. The Framework sets out the conditions for Registered Inspectors in two

sections, viz.: Section 1, which describes the principles on which inspections are based and the criteria against which their quality is assessed, and Section 2, which sets out the specific inspection requirements.

CAK

FROEBEL, FRIEDRICH (1782–1852)
A German educator who regarded education as a way of encouraging a child to develop 'naturally', Froebel founded the kindergarten system.

MF

FUNDING AGENCY FOR SCHOOLS (FAS)
The Funding Agency for Schools established by the 1993 Education Act was set up to administer and promote the Grant Maintained sector. Launched in April 1994 the Funding Agency for Schools works in tandem with the Local Authority once 10 per cent of pupils are in opted out schools; when this figure reaches 75 per cent, the Agency will assume total control. A new method of funding Grant Maintained schools has been devised, the COMMON FUNDING FORMULA (CFF).

Further details of the work of FAS and funding may be obtained from: The Funding Agency for Schools, 25, Skeldergate, York YO1 2XL tel: 0904 661661

CAK

FURTHER EDUCATION (FE)
Further education is an area of education dealing with FURTHER EDUCATION COURSES leading to qualifications other than degrees, diplomas or professional qualifications. Under the FURTHER AND HIGHER EDUCATION ACT (see Section 4, 'Legislation') the FURTHER EDUCATION FUNDING COUNCIL (FEFC) (see Section 3, 'Directory of Organizations') is given statutory duties regarding FE. While much takes place in COLLEGES OF FURTHER EDUCATION, the FEFC may also allocate funds for FE provided by institutions in the HIGHER EDUCATION sector.

MF

FURTHER EDUCATION COLLEGES
Colleges accepting students at 16+ years of age, typically to study vocational courses such as BTEC. These colleges cater substantially for those students who do not wish to remain in the 'sixth forms' of schools or in SIXTH-FORM COLLEGES. However, increasingly FE colleges compete for 16–18-year-old students, and often offer a menu of GCSE/GCE subjects as well as the vocational work. Many larger FE colleges also provide some

higher education opportunities such as HNDs; and again the tendency is to recruit older i.e. adult students, and to expand HE work in competition with universities and other providers. In the present entrepreneurial climate some colleges have taken over aspects of ADULT EDUCATIONprovision, too. FE colleges, while separately funded in part, were, until April 1993, under LEA control. But the 1992 ADULT EDUCATION ACT removed funding control to the FURTHER EDUCATION FUNDING COUNCIL and colleges became 'incorporated', i.e. independent of LEA control. The work of FE colleges is significantly influenced and funded through the local TRAINING AND ENTERPRISE COUNCILS.

TLK

FURTHER EDUCATION: COURSES
The Further and Higher Education Act 1992 defines the nature of FE courses as follows:

(a) a course which prepares students to obtain a vocational qualification which is, or falls within a class, for the time being approved for the purposes of this sub-paragraph by the Secretary of State;
(b) a course which prepares students to qualify for –
   (i)   the General Certificate of Secondary Education, or
   (ii) the General Certificate of Education at Advanced Level or Advanced Supplementary Level (including Special Papers);
(c) a course for the time being approved for the purposes of this sub-paragraph by the Secretary of State which prepares students for entry to a course of higher education;
(d) a course which prepares students for entry to another course falling within paragraphs (a) to (c) above;
(e) a course for basic literacy in English;
(f) a course to improve the knowledge of English of those for whom English is not the language spoken at home;
(g) a course to teach the basic principles of mathematics;
(h) in relation to Wales, a course for proficiency or literacy in Welsh;
(j) a course to teach independent living and communication skills to persons having learning difficulties which prepares them for entry to another course falling within paragraphs (d) to (h) above.

TLK

FURTHER EDUCATION CURRICULUM: DOCUMENTATION
Each validating body will have its own requirements for documentation to be provided by colleges. But in a climate of quality assurance, the college's

own internal mechanisms will probably require all course tutors to document curriculum for Academic Boards. The following checklist indicates some key issues in documenting the FE curriculum:

- the purpose and rationale for the course;
- the target group(s) at whom the course is aimed;
- the overall aims and intentions of the course;
- the entry requirements;
- the need for the course and how this has been established;
- the liaison processes, e.g. with employers;
- the consultation processes, e.g. in the college's committees;
- the place of the course within the college/department 'portfolio';
- the validation process: stages and time-scales;
- the staffing resource implications of the course and how they are to be met;
- the financial implications of the course (equipment, material);
- the physical resources required (accommodation);
- the management of the course;
- the time allocations relating to staff, students and components of the course, including timetables;
- the professional preparation and continuing development of tutors;
- the course content: the syllabus, its component parts and their integration;
- the common skills and core elements for the course;
- the resultant student learning: competences, skills, knowledge and understanding;
- the practical aspects of learning, e.g. simulated work environments;
- the work-placement requirements of the course;
- the teaching and learning methods to be promoted in the curriculum;
- the assessment methods to be used for each component, practical and theoretical;
- the support, tutorial, profiling and reporting procedures of the course, including the commitment to equal opportunities;
- the success criteria or performance indicators for the course;
- the processes for monitoring, reviewing and evaluating the course.

TLK

FURTHER EDUCATION – INCORPORATION

On 1 April 1993 Further Education and Sixth-Form colleges were freed from their ties with local education authorities, and assumed a status not dissimilar to the grant maintained status of schools. Incorporation is the term used to describe the process. Each institution has a Governing Body which is free to manage itself financially, with its money now coming from, in the case of English colleges, the FURTHER EDUCATION FUNDING COUNCIL (FEFC). As part of the transition from LEA control to independent status, the FEFC has made provision for the first year's budgets (1993–4) to be at levels which might have been expected under LEA control.

CAK

GENDER
(See: EQUAL OPPORTUNITIES)

GENERAL CERTIFICATE OF SECONDARY EDUCATION (GCSE)
The GCSE replaced the previous General Certificate of Education O level and the Certificate of Secondary Education (CSE) with a single system of examinations at 16+. The Scottish equivalent is the Scottish Certificate of Education (SCE) Standard Grade.

GCSEs may be taken in a wide range of subjects and while there may be some continuous assessment and assignment work, the final examination is important. GCSE syllabuses are based on national criteria. Some GCSE courses use differentiated assessment whereby pupils of different abilities are given work suited to their ability; a pupil with higher ability in the subject can work for the highest grades while a pupil with lower ability in the subject can follow work leading to lower grades. The grades are 'criterion referenced' rather than 'norm referenced'. Essentially this means that the pupil passes if they achieve objective criteria irrespective of how many other pupils pass or fail in any particular year.

Address

Joint Council for GCSE, 8th floor, Netherton House, 23–29 Marsh Street, Bristol BS1 4BP
tel: 0272 214379

MF

GENERAL NATIONAL VOCATIONAL QUALIFICATIONS (GNVQs)
GNVQs are the qualification introduced by the Government and NCVQ for students at 16+. They are designed to equip young people with the

knowledge, skills and attitudes valued by industry, and are nationally recognized and accepted as an alternative route into Higher Education. They complement the existing A level and AS level examinations and provide for young people the opportunity to study at varying levels. Level III GNVQ is broadly equivalent to two A level passes, with Level II equivalent to 4 GCSE at grade C or better. Each programme of study is full time and takes up two-thirds of a two-year course and two-thirds of a one-year course respectively. GNVQ courses can be combined with other courses of study.

CAK

GEOGRAPHY (IN THE NATIONAL CURRICULUM)
If you are not familiar with National Curriculum terminology, before reading this subject entry, you may find it helpful to first read the entries on:

Attainment Targets
National Curriculum
Programmes of Study
Standard Assessment Tasks

There are five attainment targets (ATs) in geography with AT3, AT4 and AT5 being referred to as 'Themes'. Within each AT, the statements of attainment (SoA) are grouped into 'strands' of linked content as shown below.

Skills	AT1	Geographical skills	The use of maps and fieldwork techniques.
Places	AT2	Knowledge and understanding of places	The distinctive features, similarities and differences between places in local, regional, national and international contexts; the relationships between themes and issues in particular locations.
Themes	AT3	Physical geography	Weather and climate; rivers, river basins, seas and oceans; landforms; animals, plants and soils.
	AT4	Human geography	Population, settlements, communications and movements; economic activities.
	AT5	Environmental geography	The use and misuse of natural resources; the quality and vulnerability of different environments; the possibilities for protecting and managing environments.

The key stages relate to the levels of attainment as follows:

KS1 –   Levels 1–3
KS2 –   Levels 2–5
KS3 –   Levels 3–7
KS4 –   Levels 4–10

There is a Programme of Study (PoS) which corresponds to each key stage. Each PoS is divided into five sections which correspond to the five ATs.

Geographical Skills – AT1

An enquiry approach and fieldwork should be undertaken where appropriate, along with opportunities to use information technology.

Places and themes – ATs 2–5

Each key stage PoS is further divided into:

- a PoS for all pupils in the key stage;
- a PoS for pupils working towards the highest levels of attainment in the key stage.

AT2 offers pupils opportunities to study important specified places. It also provides logical contexts in which to develop aspects of the thematic studies required for ATs 3, 4 and 5. The order sets out a minimum requirement for knowledge about the British Isles, Europe and the world in the form of a series of maps. Geographical skills (AT1) should be integrated into all geography work and not taught in isolation.

At Key Stage 4 (KS4) pupils may follow a short course in geography, which consists of a selection from the content of the full course. Content is specified by a reduced number of Statements of Attainment in ATs, 1, 2 and 5 and a choice of strands from ATs 3 and 4.

The initial intention was that, by 1994, ATs and PoS would apply to all key stages. The first statutory assessment for each key stage was planned to take place in the Summer of the years: 1993 (KS1), 1995 (KS2), 1994 (KS3) and 1996 (KS4).

However, revised rulings on these matters has meant that Attainment Targets and Programmes of Study now apply to KS 1 to 3 and no statutory requirement will be made for KS4. Assessment at KS 1 and 2 will be non-mandatory and the KS3 requirement is under review. At KS4, geography will continue to be taught and assessed by GCSE courses and grades.

MF

GIFTED

In this Handbook the word ABLE is used. Giftedness tends to be a more restricted term, applying only to the most highly talented of the able group of students.

TLK

GOVERNING BODY

The governing body, with at least two-thirds of its members present, must decide upon the structure and membership for each of its sub-committees, and the procedure for electing the chairperson. Working parties may be established to draft items such as the SCHOOL MANAGEMENT PLAN or the ANNUAL REPORT TO PARENTS; these must be presented to the full governing body for comment and approval.

CAK

GOVERNORS

Governors powers and duties are set out in the ARTICLES OF GOVERNMENT which, together with the INSTRUMENT OF GOVERNMENT, each governor should receive upon appointment.

The powers conferred on governors are to be exercised by the governing body as a whole, not by individual governors or SUB-COMMITTEES unless the power has been delegated to them by the whole body.

Governors' duties include:

- admission of pupils;
- annual reports and meetings;
- appointments of staff;
- charging for school activities;
- collective worship and religious education;
- discipline;
- equal opportunities' policy;
- financial management of the school's delegated budget;
- grievances and dismissals;
- health and safety;
- overseeing conduct;
- overseeing the curriculum;
- publishing a statement about the ethos and values of the school in the school brochure;
- school premises.

The full GOVERNING BODY must meet at least once a term, but in today's climate and with the increased responsibility of the governing body, many meet more frequently. The number of governors appointed to a school depends on its size, and the Education (No. 2) Act 1986 revised the composition of county and voluntary-controlled school governing bodies. It laid down the number of governors for schools of different sizes and who should appoint them. For voluntary-aided and special agreement schools the exact size and composition of the governing body is set out in the instrument of government. In LEA controlled schools appointed governors include those appointed by the County Council, district council or other local government body, and may reflect the political composition of the ruling party. The remaining members include those elected as TEACHER AND PARENT GOVERNORS. The APPOINTED and ELECTED GOVERNORS are required to invite people from commerce and industry to join the governing body, and these members are CO-OPTED GOVERNORS. Head teachers may choose to be a governor, in which case he or she is treated as an 'ex officio' member; a headteacher who chooses *not* to be a governor has a right to attend and speak at all governors' meetings, including committees.

Although members of the governing body do not have individual powers or rights, they do have the responsibility to get to know the school, the staff and the pupils. Governors should, therefore, visit the school on a regular basis and arrangements for this should be made with the headteacher. The visits should be a learning and information gathering process for the governor, whilst at the same time allowing the staff and pupils to make informal contact.

The governing body of each school must publish an ANNUAL REPORT TO PARENTS, and is also responsible for publishing the SCHOOL BROCHURE. Many local authorities support the work of school governors by establishing a GOVERNOR SUPPORT UNIT, from whom further information about the work of governors may usually be obtained.

In Grant Maintained schools governors are responsible for every aspect of the school, including its budget and all its resources, each governing body having received a clear statement of its legal powers and responsibilities as set out in the school's INSTRUMENT and ARTICLES OF GOVERNMENT. As well as taking those decisions that relate to finance and resource, governors in Grant Maintained schools will take on responsibility for the school premises, acquire and dispose of land and enter into contracts. The governing body of a Grant Maintained school will comprise:

- five parent governors, elected by the parents;
- either one or two teachers, elected by the teachers;
- the headteacher, and

- a number of 'FIRST' or 'FOUNDATION' governors greater than the total of the other governors.

CAK

GOVERNOR SUPPORT UNIT

Governor Support Units have been established by local education authorities to provide a programme of support and training for governors of LEA and maintained schools. The purpose of the programme is to enable governing bodies to fulfil their responsibilities confidently and effectively.

Help is given in the form of day training for both newly elected and established governors, and for clerks to governing bodies. Many Support Units run a 'help-line' with trained staff able to offer instant advice; in some, well run library facilities have been established and regular information is provided in the form of a journal. Advice is also given to parents and members of the public who wish to know more about becoming a school governor. The address of the Governor Support Unit may be obtained from the LEA.

Governors from the Grant Maintained Sector can seek and obtain advice from:

The Director, Grant Maintained Schools Centre, 36 Great Smith Street, London SW1P 2BU

tel: 071 233 4666   fax: 071 233 2795

CAK

GRANT MAINTAINED SCHOOLS (GM SCHOOLS) – ALSO KNOWN AS SELF-GOVERNING SCHOOLS

Grant Maintained schools are those which are no longer maintained by the LOCAL EDUCATION AUTHORITY but receive their funding direct from the DEPARTMENT FOR EDUCATION. GM Schools receive funding at approximately the same level that they would have received had they remained within the control of the LEA; however, they do receive other funds to meet their extra responsibilities, e.g. TRANSITIONAL GRANT, ANNUAL MAINTENANCE GRANT (AMG), SPECIAL PURPOSE GRANT and CAPITAL GRANT. Grant Maintained schools keep the same policy for admitting pupils as they had under LEA control; thus, if their status were that of an 11–16 comprehensive school under the LEA, as a GM school it would continue to admit pupils of the full ability range. Any application for a significant change to the school's status must follow the prescribed guidelines, the application must be submitted to the Secretary of State, who considers each proposal on its merits. All LEA maintained primary, middle and secondary schools can consider the option of becoming grant maintained; at the time of writing, nursery schools and special schools are ineligible to apply.

Responsibility for every aspect of GM school life is vested in the GOVERNORS. The GOVERNING BODY must include parents, teachers (including the headteacher) and others from the local community. At schools which were formerly 'voluntary' schools, FOUNDATION GOVERNORS provide the community representation, whilst FIRST GOVERNORS are those chosen by the other governors to serve on the boards of former county schools. The membership of grant-maintained governing bodies comprises:

- five parent governors, elected by the parents of pupils at the school;
- at least one, but not more than two teacher governors, elected by the teachers at the school;
- the headteacher; and
- first or foundation governors, the number of which must be greater than the total of the other governors. This last category must include at least two who are registered parents at the school.

Terms of office for governors at Grant Maintained schools vary; parent and teacher governors serve for four years, while first or foundation governors serve for between five and seven years, the actual length being determined by the governing body.

The duties and responsibilities of Grant Maintained schools are similar to those for local authority and LEA maintained schools. GM schools are required to:

- provide a broad and balanced education for all their pupils, and for pupils of 5–16 this means following the NATIONAL CURRICULUM, including its arrangements for assessment and testing;
- provide education free of charge, with the exception of charging for those extras as defined within the 1988 Act;
- provide daily worship for the whole school, and religious education as defined in the 1988 Act;
- be subject to the inspection of Her Majesty's Inspectors of schools;
- look after the needs of pupils with special educational needs;
- fulfil other established duties, e.g. the publication of admission procedures, the following of employment regulations; setting up procedures for considering curriculum complaints, etc.

At the present time, LEAs retain certain responsibilities for all pupils in their area, regardless of whether the pupils attend grant or county maintained schools. These responsibilities include:

- the identification, assessment, and where appropriate, the statementing of pupils with special educational needs;
- the enforcement of attendance at school;
- the provision of home to school transport in accordance with the government's requirements or the authority's published criteria, where the latter is more generous than the statutory requirement.

The INSTRUMENT and ARTICLES OF GOVERNMENT apply to Grant Maintained as well as local authority schools. In the case of GM schools, these documents are set up by the Secretary of State after consultation with the governors.

CAK

GRANTS FOR EDUCATION SUPPORT AND TRAINING (GEST)

Grants for Education Support and Training: a system by which the government gives money to LEAs (and hence schools) on an annual basis to support IN-SERVICE EDUCATION OF TEACHERS and similar initiatives. GEST is distributed by bid following an annual Circular advising of the sub-divisions of money available. LEAs have to provide 40 per cent of cost, the government 60 per cent usually up to a pre-determined ceiling. By controlling the categories of money available, and through audit, the Government can, and does, effectively control the development of in-service training and the resultant activity in schools.

TLK

GROUP TASKS

A classroom TASK set by a teacher to be completed by several students collectively rather than by each pupil individually. Group tasks require team-work and co-operation, so that the individual student's work feeds a specific contribution to a group goal. Learning takes place in the AFFECTIVE DOMAIN as well as the cognitive.

TLK

GROUP WORK

Group work involves a number of pupils (typically from 2 to 8 in number) working on a task which is shared by them, and to which they all have to contribute to ensure success. Group work is NOT organizing seats so that pupils can sit with their friends while the teaching remains in the WHOLE CLASS mode.

Possibly the best answer to the question of when to use group work is when the task which the teacher wishes the pupil to complete is likely to be carried out *more appropriately* by the use of small groups than through the other main TEACHING MODES, i.e. WHOLE CLASS TEACHING or INDIVIDUALIZED LEARNING. In practice, what this means is that the teacher will have to make judgements about the relationship between the skills or information which pupils need to acquire and the most appropriate teaching methods for communicating them. In practice, judgement will be coloured by factors such as the teacher's preferred teaching style, the pupils' preferred learning style (which may vary from class to class), the facilities available (i.e. the classroom, its furniture and equipment) and the resources (the nature, quantity and availability of books or audio-visual software).

Group work is particularly useful for:

- pursuing PROJECTS
- DISCOVERY LEARNING
- problem solving.

Some examples of its appropriate use:

- in a social studies lesson pupils were looking at problems of population explosion. They were asked to work in groups, each group being assigned a separate topic. During the lesson observed, several groups were provided with materials appropriate to their topic for study. The teacher was thus free to 'teach' a particular statistical skill for calculating population trends to one group, whose tasks demanded this knowledge.
- the organization of a science lesson relating to digestion was on the 'roundabout' principle. Six experiments were laid out around the room. Pupils were divided into six groups. Each group completed an experiment and then passed in a clockwise direction to the next. All pupils carried out the experiments but a minimum of apparatus was needed. Any dead time between completing one experiment and starting another was absorbed in writing up the results and conclusion from the completed work.
- an RE teacher was studying the very long story of Joseph with first year secondary pupils. He wanted pupils to be especially aware of the personalities in the story and the dilemmas in which they found themselves. He divided the story into scenes from a play. Each scene was written by a group of pupils, who had to analyse the situation encapsulated in it and try to put over the issues in modern English. The whole play was subsequently slotted together and performed.

- Miss Jones wanted her class to solve a problem. She set out the problem on the blackboard and the class talked over some of the difficulties which might be encountered. Having cleared the ground in this way, Miss Jones split the pupils into groups of four and asked each to present a solution within half an hour. The pupils worked together on these solutions and later in the lesson each group of four suggested its solution. These were compared and discussed by all the pupils.

Some advantages of group work are that:

- it helps pupils to learn to work co-operatively;
- it allows pupils to learn from each other and removes the stigma of failure from slow pupils;
- it gives teachers the opportunity to circulate and correct individual pupils' work;
- it teaches youngsters to be INDEPENDENT pupils;
- it gives pupils a chance to work at their own pace.

Teaching skills required for group work include the following:

- preparation and planning;
- organizing and maintaining discipline;
- vigilance;
- pitching CLASSROOM TASKS at the correct level;
- control of movements and changes of activity;
- concern for safety.

TLK

GROUPING BY ABILITY
(See: STREAMING)

HEADTEACHER
The headteacher is responsible to the Board of Governors for the management, organization and discipline of a school. The modern headteacher, dealing with such developments as LOCAL MANAGEMENT OF SCHOOLS, needs to have business knowledge and skills particularly in marketing and finance as well as general management skills and educational expertise. Less tangibly, but equally importantly, the headteacher plays a key role in setting the tone and developing the ethos of the school.
    With so many changes such as the National Curriculum and the effects

of education legislation, the administrative load on headteachers and the pressures to keep up with developments have been very high in the late 1980s and early 1990s.

In many primary schools and small schools, including special schools, headteachers may teach for all or part of the school day.

Addresses

National Association of Headteachers, 1 Heath Square, Boltro Road, Haywards Heath, East Sussex RH16 1BL
tel: 0444 458 133   fax: 0444 416 326
Secondary Heads Association, 130 Regent Road, Leicester LE1 7PG
tel: 0533 471797
Headteachers' Association of Scotland, Jordanhill College of Education, Southbrae Drive, Glasgow G13 1PP
tel: 041 950 3298   fax: 041 950 3268
Association of Headteachers in Scotland: address and telephone/fax details as for the Headteachers' Association of Scotland.

MF

HEAD OF DEPARTMENT

In secondary schools and colleges of further/higher education staff tend to be grouped into subject-based organizations called departments, managed by a head of department, who will be paid on an enhanced scale for the responsibility. The duties of the head of department are usually grouped around aspects of managerial control:

- the management of the curriculum in the subject area, including oversight of each course for which the department is responsible;
- the management of the teaching staff (e.g. timetables, professional development, welfare and pastoral care);
- the management of any non-teaching staff such as laboratory technicians or other administrative and support workers;
- the management of the department's spending of financial allocations;
- the management of plant, equipment and consumables belonging to the department.

Often the head of department is a member of a management group made up of other heads of department and more senior personnel. In this ROLE he/she will have a wider share in policy-making. The degree of autonomy enjoyed by a head of department will depend on the MANAGEMENT STYLE of institutional head. In colleges, and to a lesser extent in schools, related departments may be grouped together into larger units called faculties, with a faculty head managing the work of several heads of department.

TLK

HEALTH EDUCATION

Health education permeates subjects of the National Curriculum including science and design and technology as a cross curricular theme and may also be delivered through specific courses in schools.

Among the issues particularly important in health education are the following:

- sex education (including AIDS);
- drug use and abuse (including alcohol, tobacco and solvents);
- road safety and home safety;
- the value of the family life in society;
- exercise and good health;
- hygiene;
- psychological factors in good health;
- environmental factors in good health;
- nutrition.

Address

Health Education Authority, Hamilton House, Mabledon Place, London WC1H 9TX
tel: 071 630 0930

MF

HER MAJESTY'S INSPECTORS (HMI)

Her Majesty's Inspectors (HMI) are the official arm of OFSTED. They:

- devise inspection criteria;
- regulate and monitor the new system;
- train and assess inspectors;
- assure the quality of the system.

They also carry out inspections, and interpret the findings of the independent inspectors throughout England. This means they are able to:

- evaluate standards and quality of education;
- identify national trends;

- evaluate the effects of education policies;
- advise the Secretary of State, the Department for Education and others on educational provision.

Further information about HMI may be obtained from:
Elizabeth House, York Road, London SE1 7PH
tel: 071 925 6541   fax: 071 925 6784

CAK

HIDDEN CURRICULUM

The hidden curriculum concerns aspects of school life which are not fully encompassed by the stated curriculum. It includes attitudes and conduct concerning such topics as social class, gender, ethnicity, dress, appropriate behaviour and teacher conduct and expectations. Where official policy contradicts the underlying values of the school whether through ignorance or hypocrisy then the effects are divisive.

MF

HIGHER EDUCATION (HE)

The standard of higher education is beyond that of A LEVELS, the higher grade of the Scottish Certificate of Education, NATIONAL CERTIFICATE, NATIONAL DIPLOMA, International BACCALAUREATE, and Advanced GENERAL NATIONAL VOCATIONAL QUALIFICATIONS. Higher education leads to first or higher degrees, diplomas and professional qualifications. The venues for such courses are UNIVERSITIES and COLLEGES AND INSTITUTES OF HIGHER EDUCATION. Courses may be full or part time.

Applications to universities and colleges of higher education for full time and sandwich courses are made to the Universities and Colleges Admissions Service (UCAS), which also provides information and materials including application forms and handbooks which give guidance on admissions.

Address

UCAS, PO Box 28, Cheltenham GL50 3SA
tel: 0242 227 788 (for applicant enquiries)
0242 222 444 (general office)   fax: 0242 221 622

Further reading

Higher Education in the United Kingdom: A Handbook for Students and Advisors (Longman) [annually].

MF

HIGHER NATIONAL CERTIFICATE/DIPLOMA

Vocationally-oriented qualifications awarded by the BUSINESS AND TECHNO-LOGY EDUCATION COUNCIL (BTEC) which approach pass degree standard.

(See Section 3, 'Directory of Organizations', under Business and Technology Education Council.)

MF

HISTORY (AND THE NATIONAL CURRICULUM)

If you are not familiar with National Curriculum terminology, before reading this subject entry, you may find it helpful to first read the entries on:

Attainment Targets
National Curriculum
Programmes of Study
Standard Assessment Tasks

The attainment targets (ATs) for history are as follows:

AT1	Knowledge and understanding of history	The development of the ability to describe and explain historical change and cause, and analyse different features of historical situations.
AT2	Interpretations of history	The development of the ability to understand interpretations of history.
AT3	The use of historical sources	The development of pupils' ability to acquire evidence from historical sources and form judgements about their reliability and value.

'Strands' apply to AT1, which has more Statements of Attainment than AT2 or AT3, reflecting the importance of 'knowledge and understanding of history'. Three strands are traceable upwards through the levels. Strand 1 goes through levels 1 to 7; strand 2 can be traced through levels 1 to 9 and strand 3 goes through levels 2 to 9. All three strands combine into one strand of attainment at level 10. The three strands are shown below:

1. Change and continuity: understanding that history is concerned with change, knowing about and distinguishing between different kinds of change;
2. Causes and consequences: knowing about and understanding the causes and consequences of historical events and developments;
3. Knowing about and understanding: the key features of past situations and the distinctive characteristics of past societies.

The programmes of study for history comprise two elements:

(a) general requirements which apply to all Programmes of Study (PoS);
(b) PoS for each key stage.

The general requirements contain important statements about the opportunities which should be provided in each 'study unit' (see below) for the development of each AT. Pupils should also be enabled to explore links between history and other subjects; develop their capability in information technology and develop the knowledge, understanding and skills related to cross-curricular themes. Provision should be made for pupils with special educational needs. The Programmes of Study should enable pupils to develop knowledge and understanding of British, European and world history.

The PoS for each key stage consist of four sections:

• key elements, such as concepts to be taught and types of historical sources to be included;
• opportunities pupils need to meet the ATs;
• the methods by which pupils can find out about the past and communicate the results of their investigations;
• study units to be taught.

Concerning 'study units', there is one at KS1 which must be taught throughout the key stage.

At KS 2–4 the PoS are made up of:

• core study units;
• supplementary study units which complement or extend the core.

At KS2 pupils should be taught nine study units. At KS3 pupils should be taught all five core and three supplementary study units. At KS4 pupils will be able to follow one or two models. Model 2 contains a core study unit and is designed to be taught as a short course on its own or in combination with another subject. Model two is an extended course and is designed to fulfil the requirements for a GCSE qualification in history.

Planning and teaching National Curriculum history involves thinking about the ATs and PoS simultaneously. Pupils can only meet the ATs by acquiring the knowledge of the historical content prescribed in the PoS. As they progress up the levels, pupils should be able to demonstrate a wider and deeper knowledge of the content in the PoS.

The relationship between the key stages and levels of attainment are as follows:

KS1 – Levels 1–3
KS2 – Levels 2–5
KS3 – Levels 3–7
KS4 – Levels 4–10

Attainment Targets and Programmes of Study apply to KS1 to 3 and no statutory requirement will be made for KS4. At KS4, history will continue to be taught and assessed by GCSE courses and grades.

HISTORY OF EDUCATION

The history of education gains its importance for the same reason that history itself is important: that it provides a distinct perspective on its subject matter. Educational history remains important because history is not about amassing a set of incontrovertible facts about the past, even if that were possible. It is as much concerned with the continuing reinterpretation of the past through the concerns of the present. As present concerns change from generation to generation, so the need to reappraise history continues. For example, any historical examination of the education of girls written today with our concern for equality of opportunity would be very different from such an examination written in the early 1900s when to a much greater extent the prospect for a woman was to be a wife and homemaker.

For such reasons, the interpretation of historical trends (or whether events constitute a trend at all) will vary from time to time. The relative insight given to particular data and evidence will also vary.

Bearing this in mind, the history of education can show us the waxing and waning of various influences; National Government, charities, the Church, parents, local government, and so on. This can help explain the state of affairs in the present.

Even a brief chronological outline of government reports and education acts (see Section four, 'Legislation') can provide the beginning of data which can show the varying concerns of education over time. A more detailed study will indicate who was being educated, by whom, how and for what purpose. The influence of political, economic and other social forces are other important factors.

The history of education then is an essential facet of the study of education combining a capacity to explain and to explore.

Further reading

Lawson, J. and Silver, H. (1973) *A Social History of Education in England* (Methuen).

MF

HOME EDUCATION
(See: ALTERNATIVE EDUCATION)

HOME–SCHOOL RELATIONS
Relationships between home and school ideally ensure that parents can take part in school life, that teachers gain a fuller understanding of a pupil's home life and that the parent–teacher partnership helps the child's education.

For parents, activities which foster partnership include supporting school work by encouraging home learning including formal homework, helping where appropriate in the school, supporting parent–teacher association activities and, more formally, being involved as a parent school governor.

Schools need to develop and maintain good two way lines of communication with parents through such means as meetings, newsletters, open evenings and home–school message books.

See also Section 3, THE NATIONAL CONFEDERATION OF PARENT-TEACHER ASSOCIATION (NCPTA)

MF

HOMEWORK
Work set by teachers to be carried out by pupils in out-of-school time is normally called homework, occasionally preparation or prep. Such work augments pupil learning, effectively extending the working day for pupils. For this reason it is best used sparingly (pupils already spend up to six and a half hours a day in school – close on a normal 'working day' for many employees). Schools should include a homework policy as part of their SCHOOL MANAGEMENT PLAN: and teachers, parents and students should adhere to it. Homework régimes of two and a half to three hours nightly are found – and are likely to lead to overload and be counterproductive. Similarly, the use of homework as PUNISHMENT imbues a positive educational activity with negative overtones. Effective homework may often be in the form of a reinforcement task; or it may be the application of knowledge acquired in the classroom; or it may require pupils to carry out tasks which cannot be undertaken in class, such as an environmental study.

At KS4 and in the sixth form, pressure (by teachers and often by parents) for homework builds. Moderation is probably a wise counsel: students need lives beyond and outside school-related tasks in order to refresh themselves for study. Some schools stay open beyond the 'normal' school day for an hour or two to allow pupils a supervised and quiet facility in which to complete homework before going home, and such systems seem popular with pupils. PROFESSIONALISM demands that work set by teachers should also be subject to prompt MARKING and FEEDBACK to have real value.

TLK

HOSPITAL SCHOOLS SERVICE

Each year thousands of children are hospitalized and for many of these young people the education process continues, whether their stay in hospital is for a short time – say a week – or for a more prolonged period. The Hospital Schools Service is staffed by qualified, experienced teachers, and working within the framework of the National Curriculum is a priority. Where appropriate, students are prepared for, and sit, external examinations. Research in both the educational and medical fields has shown that the recovery process of a child in hospital is, in the majority of cases, helped by attendance at school.

CAK

HUMANIST EDUCATION
(See: PLATO)

HUMANITIES

An imprecise term, humanities can mean various things. Geography and history combined, sometimes with the addition of literature or language or both are its most common manifestation. Aspects of religious studies may also be included.

Integrating subjects in this way can be appropriate for the study of a different culture.

MF

HYPERACTIVITY

Hyperactivity is a term which is often inappropriately used towards a child who is simply lively and gregarious. It is more fittingly used where children are excessively noisy (screaming, shouting); are disruptive and aggressive;

have poor concentration, co-ordination and speech; sleep poorly or insufficiently; and are excessively restless.

Address

Hyperactive Children's Support Group, 71 Whyke Lane, Chichester, Sussex PO19 2LD

MF

INDEPENDENT LEARNER

A phrase used to describe a pupil or student who, because he or she is equipped with proper STUDY SKILLS and is operating within an appropriate INTELLECTUAL CLIMATE, can work without close teacher supervision for a reasonable period of time. Independent learners need to be able to pace themselves effectively and – up to a point – assess their own progress for limited periods. The phrase contrasts with DEPENDENT LEARNER.

TLK

INDEPENDENT SCHOOLS

An independent school is one which receives no direct income from either local or central government, and is funded wholly or largely by fees paid by parents. Independent schools do not have to follow the NATIONAL CURRICULUMand can employ teachers who lack QUALIFIED TEACHER STATUS.

There are more than 2,500 day and boarding independent schools in the United Kingdom, and these cover the age ranges from 2 to 19. The schools themselves are widely different the one from the other – there are selective and non-selective schools; boarding or day; single-sexed or mixed; rural or urban; large and small. About 80 per cent of independent school pupils are day pupils, though the school day may be longer than that experienced by a student in a state school. Usually independent schools set an entrance examination to satisfy themselves that the child they admit can cope with the demands of the school work. Most schools, however, admit children of a wide ability range and take a great pride in getting the best possible results for all children, whatever their abilities. Nearly all independent schools prepare pupils for public examinations and for entrance to higher education.

Many independent schools are endowed as charitable trusts while others are run as businesses and have to make a profit. A small number of independent schools meet religious needs and include schools for Muslims (see ISLAMIC EDUCATION), Quakers (see QUAKER EDUCATION) and other groups.

CAK

INDIVIDUAL LEARNING

A common classroom scenario in which pupils are carrying out a task privately, e.g. writing an essay, drawing, doing mathematical examples, etc. Often the same task is set to all pupils in a context of WHOLE CLASS TEACHING. This is not to be confused with INDIVIDUALIZED LEARNING.

TLK

INDIVIDUALIZED LEARNING

Often a teacher will set the whole class off on a task while he or she circulates and monitors learning. These contacts with single pupils may be INDIVIDUAL LEARNING, but they are not individualized learning. Strictly, individualized learning is where each pupil's needs are assessed and then he or she is provided with a set of distinctive tasks to perform different from those set to other pupils in the class.

The advantages of individualized learning include the following:

- it allows tasks to be set which are appropriate to the pupil;
- it allows pupils to proceed at their own pace;
- it may allow some pursuit by pupils of personal interests;
- it provides a useful mode for pupils who like to work independently some of the time;
- it can give individual FEEDBACK to teachers about specific pupils, their strengths and weaknesses.

Individualized learning should be used:

- as part of a varied teaching strategy;
- to help diagnose problems or level of ability;
- to give pupils a chance to be creative or distinctive;
- to try out individual pupils' level of understanding.

Some examples of its appropriate use include the following:

The class is studying village life as a theme. One pupil shows enthusiasm to tackle this from a literary point of view. The teacher equips him with a tape recorder and tape to listen to Dylan Thomas's *Under Milk Wood*. Later, the pupil uses the style to write his own village story.

Mary has been away sick for a few days. While the class does some reinforcement work the teacher uses the opportunity to go over missed work with her.

At GCSE level, students have to tackle projects. Each project requires a personal choice of title, methodology and style of reporting within the basic examination requirements.

Teaching skills required for individualized learning are:

- the ability to set meaningful classroom TASKS;
- knowledge of individual pupils and their progress;
- RECORD-KEEPING about pupils' progress;
- understanding of pupils' personal interests.

Compared with other TEACHING MODES individualized learning is exceptionally demanding on the energy of the teacher and on preparation.

TLK

INDOCTRINATION

Indoctrination involves intentionally imparting beliefs which it cannot be demonstrated are true or false, as if they were true. Political, religious and moral beliefs tend to be of this unprovable kind, e.g. 'God is omnipotent and omniscient.' In indoctrination, the aim is to make the beliefs unshakeable by ways which include non-rational forms of persuasion, such as appeals to authority (e.g. We know Jesus is the son of God because the Bible says so).

Teachers of politics, religion and morality work in areas where indoctrination can overtake education, as do teachers dealing with interpretations of history or the arts. Particular care is necessary in the teaching of these subjects if the teacher is to educate not indoctrinate. The non-rational aspect of the methods used in indoctrination makes it antipathetic to education, which uses morally acceptable means of teaching, that is means which can be justified according to reason.

However, for those who begin from a position where the doctrines they hold seem irrefutable and fundamentally true, it could be seen as morally acceptable (indeed morally essential) to induct others into those doctrines. Therefore some doctrinal teachers who would seem to others, outside the doctrine, to be indoctrinators, could see themselves as educators.

MF

INDUCTION
(See: NEWLY QUALIFIED TEACHER)

INDUSTRIAL TRAINING
(See: VOCATIONAL EDUCATION)

INEFFECTIVE LESSONS
Even in the best ordered classrooms, where CLASS CONTROL is normally good and there is an EFFECTIVE TEACHER, it is possible for some lessons to go astray. Some factors causing ineffectiveness are listed here, with advice on possible remedial action:

Insufficient lesson material. It is better to have too much than too little material. The teacher can always edit as he/she goes along, but one can't create new material in mid-lesson. Also, one needs some 'spare' material suited to the extremes of ability in the class, who may find the planned work unsuitable.

Failure to bring all the necessary equipment or know how to use it. Many student teachers, and even experienced ones, carry heavy bags of resources around from lesson to lesson. These are the ones who have learned that the best lessons can disintegrate if, at the vital moment, one doesn't have the worksheet/pair of scissors/pipette, etc. you thought you had! If the teacher has a base room, he/she will carry less because access to equipment will be more efficient. If using apparatus or audio-visual aids, the teacher must know how to use them.

The activities planned are boring. Lessons need to begin with impact, but they need to be sustained with interest. Sometimes boredom results from poor lesson planning: the teacher has some good idea, but fails to build on them. Sometimes it results from poor choice of content, of work which is too hard, too easy or repetitive. It may result, too, from some of the factors which follow.

Lack of variety in lessons. Over a series of lessons the teacher may fail to build in a variety of activities. Lessons then become predictable, and pupils will start to become bored. But material can be tackled in a variety of ways: role play, didactic methods, discussion, audio-visual presentation, drama, quizzes, games and so on.

Poor voice control. Many otherwise competent teachers fall down on voice control. They fail to use simple techniques like varying intonation, varying pace of delivery, pausing, emphasis and volume to make their voices interesting. One way to learn expertise here is to listen to professional broadcasters, especially those who tell stories for children. Some good examples are Johnny Morris, Thora Hird, Willie Rushton and Martin Jarvis. Their styles are quite different, but they all have superb voice control.

Sustaining one teaching mode too long. A common error is to plan a lesson around just one TEACHING MODE. Most lessons are successful if activities are broken up by periods when there is a change of work, even if it is only for a few minutes. For example, a lesson where pupils are working on individualized tasks, can be sustained by a minute's whole class work on an issue of common interest to the pupils. Or a whole class lesson, perhaps a discussion, can be profitably interrupted for a short session while pupils look up new information or form small 'buzz' groups.

Poor explanations. One of the worst things that can happen is that pupils fail to understand the lesson. See: EXPLAINING SKILLS.

Poor instructions. A related fault is that pupils set off to carry out tasks but they fail to understand clearly what to do. Instructions are simply a kind of explanation, so that the same advice applies here as above. The best instructions are clear, step-by-step, sequenced correctly, with key points emphasized, and revised and repeated as necessary.

Failure to control the transition from one activity to another. In other words, in changing from whole class to group work, or group work to individualized learning, the teacher may have to move pupils around the room, rearrange the furniture, provide resources and so on. These processes need to be preplanned, controlled and supervised – with perhaps only a few pupils moving at a time.

Insufficient vigilance. When pupils are actually working the teacher may be too desk-bound. Pupils may form queues around the desk and block vision. Or the teacher may simply be unobservant. The teacher should never allow more than one pupil at the desk at a time; be mobile; learn to see out of the edges of the eyes; use the eyes like strobes to sweep the room constantly; learn to use ALL the senses (it is possible to *smell* a packed lunch being eaten on the back row!).

Interruption may occur. Pupils are quite good at trying to put inexperienced teachers off. Usually it's not malicious, just a game. Teachers learn not to be deflected. As one gains experience, one learns which apparent 'red herrings' it is possible to pursue productively.

TLK

INFORMATION TECHNOLOGY

Information technology (IT) concerns information handled by modern technology, particularly the COMPUTER. The application of IT to learning in subjects and in cross curricular activities is an important and expanding area of education.

Generic software including word processors, databases and spreadsheets can be used to support, enhance and extend learning in a wide range of curriculum areas developing language skills and data manipulation skills. Text can be developed to include words, pictures and sounds. Data may be collected and investigated using databases and spreadsheets or logged directly into the computer using datalogging equipment comprising sensors and computer interface.

Subject-specific software can be used to develop understanding in particular curriculum areas. Integrated learning systems may be used to deliver and support learning.

A wide range of hardware and software is currently in use in schools and colleges. This includes portable computers, CD ROM, scanners and peripherals to enable children with special educational needs to access the curriculum.

See also COMPUTER-ASSISTED LEARNING and PROGRAMMED LEARNING.

Address

National Council for Education Technology, Milburn Hill Road, Science Park, Coventry CV4 7JJ
tel: 0203 416 994   fax: 0203 411 418
A registered charity funded by the Department for Education, NCET works to help teachers, lecturers, trainers and learners to make the best use of technology.

MF

INITIAL TEACHER TRAINING (ITT)

Initial Teacher Training is the process by which teachers obtain QUALIFIED TEACHER STATUS (QTS). Teachers in the schools sector must qualify by taking either a first (BACHELOR'S) degree in a subject area of the National Curriculum – plus a one-year POSTGRADUATE CERTIFICATE IN EDUCATION; or a four-year B.Ed. course in an INSTITUTE OF HIGHER EDUCATION. The processes of initial teacher training have come under recent government scrutiny and a number of proposals are currently put forward by government. These include routes into teaching through LICENSED AND ARTICLED TEACHER schemes. Some of these schemes are retrogressive in terms of ensuring graduate status for the profession. Among the government's proposals are three-year, and even two-year B.Ed. schemes for older students with some Higher Education. A more effective proposal is to make the PGCE qualification more accessible to existing graduates by encouraging part-time and distance-learning courses alongside full-time ones. A few part-time courses do exist at present; and pioneering work on distance-learning for the PGCE has been undertaken by Brunel University on a small scale, and nationally by the OPEN UNIVERSITY and by the Distance

Education for Teaching Project. Changing training methods and funding arrangements for Initial Teacher Training have put more emphasis on school-based training, where experienced teachers act as MENTOR to the student. The government is encouraging schools and consortia to bid to establish PGCE courses of their own; a radical departure viewed sceptically by the profession. The move to school-based training has also highlighted the centrality of teaching COMPETENCES to the new style training. The least palatable of the government's ideas has been characterized as the 'Mums' Army' proposal: a new one-year course for mature students qualified for higher education, and with accreditable experience of working with children, who wish to specialize in teaching nursery and infant pupils up to the end of KS1. This appeared to put back the professional clock by decades to the time when there were significant divisions in the profession – such as between primary and secondary teachers, and between the pay of male and female teachers. The proposal has been shelved at present because of professional resistance, but constant vigilance is necessary to guard against the devaluation implied here. The control of initial teacher training, including its funding, is to be taken away from the COUNCIL FOR THE ACCREDITATION OF TEACHER EDUCATION (CATE) and given to a new body, the TEACHER TRAINING AGENCY. In the further education sector it is possible for lecturers to be appointed on the basis of professional and academic qualifications without teacher training. Such staff are sometimes given access to training on-the-job through the CITY AND GUILDS COURSE (such as CG7301) or the Certificate in Education (FE).

TLK

IN-SERVICE EDUCATION

In-service education is the process whereby teachers continuously update their skills while continuing their employment: the process is also known as PROFESSIONAL DEVELOPMENT. While it is true that teachers have, for decades, given up time voluntarily in order to update – by attending Saturday courses, evening events such as those organized by TEACHER'S CENTRES, or longer courses or conferences, e.g. in vacations – it is only since 1988 that every teacher within every school in the state sector has been required to attend training compulsorily as part of his/her contractual workload. The then Secretary of State for Education, Kenneth Baker, introduced five days a year as training days – sometimes known as 'Baker Days'. Schools are free to choose the dates of these or to negotiate them with their LOCAL EDUCATION AUTHORITIES. Topics covered should relate to the school's overall MANAGEMENT OR DEVELOPMENT PLAN, and schools may be held accountable, through INSPECTION, for the effective use of these days. From time to time the government may issue guidance for the use of some of the training time; and in any case money to support these and other in-service training is delivered by the government. For schools with GRANT MAINTAINED status the training money is delivered direct to school funds by the Government. Schools in LEA control receive money through the LEA as intermediary. This money is in the form of a grant for specific purposes, which require an LEA contribution before it can be accessed.

The grant has been known by a variety of titles in its short history – Grant Related In-Service Training (GRIST), Teacher Related In-Service Training (TRIST), and as the Local Education Authority Training Grant Scheme (LEATGS); but is currently called Grant for Education Support and Training (GEST). Part of the grant is delivered as an Education Support Grant (ESG), which is usually a sum to provide not training as such but a form of support such as books for the NATIONAL CURRICULUM or the services of an ADVISORY TEACHER. Until the GEST system was introduced, with tighter rules about the devolution of money direct into schools, LEAs tended to take a strong lead in managing the grant and providing training programmes for teachers, usually using the work of education ADVISERS. However, the GEST rules have helped diminish the LEAs' roles in training, and it seems likely that, in future, schools will either become increasingly self-reliant or will have to become skilled at buying in services either from the old LEAs (now reorganized on a commercial basis as business units), or from new-style educational consultants. HIGHER EDUCATION institutions traditionally offered a wide range of courses to their local teachers, often with accreditation as an incentive. More and more teachers are being forced to pay their own fees if they wish to access this advanced training. GOVERNING BODIES have a duty to keep an eye on the quality of in-service training available to teachers in their schools, which is often done through the medium of a report from the headteacher.

TLK

INSPECTIONS

From 1993 all maintained schools will be inspected once every four years by teams of inspectors appointed by the OFFICE FOR STANDARDS IN EDUCATION (OFSTED). Inspectors are required to make reports on:

- the quality of education;
- the educational standards;
- whether finances are managed effectively;
- the spiritual, moral, social and cultural development of pupils.

Private and local authority inspection teams bid to OFSTED and Her

Majesty's Chief Inspector for the opportunity to inspect those schools selected for inspection. An inspection is measured in 'inspector days' and will depend on the size and nature of the school. At present the range falls between four inspection days for those schools with around 100 pupils on roll and 57 for the largest secondaries. A reduced schedule of inspector days will also apply where the head of small schools is also a full-time class teacher. Where inspectors believe a school is not providing an acceptable standard of education, then that school is declared 'at risk'. 'At risk' schools are advised on ways to improve the standards of the school; if the school then fails to improve it may be taken out of the hands of the authority or governors and put in the care of a new kind of 'educational association', appointed by the Secretary of State. The Inspectors' reports must be produced within five weeks of the inspection ending.

GOVERNORS have duties both before and after the Inspection; before the Inspection they must provide the documents and information required by OFSTED and arrange for a meeting between parents and the REGISTERED INSPECTOR so that parents' views may be heard and considered. After the Inspection the governors must:

- send a summary of the Report to parents;
- make the Report available for public inspection;
- draw up an action plan within 40 working days and send copies to OFSTED, the LEA if a county school, the Secretary of State if grant maintained, parents, all employees at the school, and in the case of secondary schools, to the local TEC;
- include progress on that action plan in every subsequent ANNUAL REPORT TO PARENTS.

CAK

INSPECTION TEAM MEMBERS

REGISTERED INSPECTORS need to be able to call on other inspectors to form the team to conduct the inspection of each school. Inspection team members will support the registered inspector by inspecting different facets of the school's work and contributing to the overall judgement of a school and to the report. They may have expertise in particular aspects or subjects or in finance or management. It is the responsibility of the registered inspector to form the team for each inspection so that he or she is confident that all the relevant parts of the FRAMEWORK FOR INSPECTION can be covered.

Each inspection team must also include at least one lay member. By 'a lay member' is meant someone without personal experience in the management of any school or the provision of education in any school (otherwise than as

a governor or in any other voluntary capacity) and whose prime function on the team is not that of providing financial or business expertise. The purpose of the lay member is to provide a sensible, objective view of a school through the eyes of someone outside education. It is up to the registered inspector to decide what specific tasks to assign to the LAY INSPECTOR(S), but it is intended that lay inspectors should be fully involved in as many aspects of the inspection as possible, including the observation of pupils at work.

Before an inspector (including a lay inspector) may act as a member of a team, he or she must have satisfactorily (in the opinion of HMCI) completed a course of training. In the first instance the training will be provided by HMI, and will comprise a five-day course in the use of the Framework for Inspection.

Once an inspector – lay or otherwise – has successfully completed training, his or her name and area of expertise (including lay) will be placed on a list held by HMCI. This list will be available for consultation by registered inspectors who wish to build up inspection teams. A register of registered inspectors will be held by HMCI, and inspectors who wish to make themselves known to registered inspectors may ask HMCI for the names of those operating in their area.

TLK

INSPECTORS
Until the 1992 Education Act each LOCAL EDUCATION AUTHORITY was required to sustain a group of inspectors to monitor standards in education at the local level. The work of these inspectors was parallel to, but distinct from, the quality control exercised by HER MAJESTY'S INSPECTORS (HMIs). The LEA inspectors were also referred to as ADVISERS, and it is under this entry that the pre-1992 roles are described. From 1993 the government reformed inspection arrangements for schools, creating three new roles: REGISTERED INSPECTORS, INPSECTION TEAM MEMBERS and LAY INSPECTORS.

TLK

INSTRUMENT OF GOVERNMENT
The Instrument of Government is, to all intent, the constitution of the governing body, and is made by order of the LEA for those schools within the LEA system, i.e. county controlled schools. In a maintained school, the head and governing body must be consulted before a new instrument is produced; in voluntary schools the governing body and the LEA must agree the provisions. Under the Education (No. 2) Act 1986, an Instrument of government requires review after four years. Governing bodies can suggest

Changes to their Instrument of Government, and the LEA must consider the proposals.

The Instrument of Government for Grant Maintained schools is drawn up by the Secretary of State after consultation with the governors.

CAK

INSURANCE

While schools and its employees within the control of the LEA are usually covered by the LEA under a global third-party liability insurance policy against claims of negligence, governors of LEA schools are advised to enquire of their authority exactly what cover is provided. Many councils, for example, do not hold personal accident insurance cover for employees, voluntary helpers, governors or pupils. Some insurance companies specialize in this cover and will arrange cover via the Parent/Teacher Association or similar body if enough parents at any one school express interest. Governors of Grant Maintained schools have to make all their own insurance arrangements and are expected to conform to the same standards as authority schools. It is their responsibility to obtain adequate insurance cover for both persons and plant, and advice on this may be obtained from the Grant Maintained Schools Centre.

CAK

INTEGRATED SCIENCE
(See: COMBINED/BALANCED SCIENCE)

INTEGRATION–SEGREGATION
Integration refers to the principle of educating pupils having special educational needs and other children together. It is an aspect of a broader aim of 'normalization' which advocates people with special needs having equal opportunities to everyone else and being integrated into community life.

The report 'Special Educational Needs' chaired by Mary Warnock (1978) identified three forms of integration with regard to education:

1. Locational integration, in which a special unit or class was provided in an ordinary school.
2. Social integration in which the disabled pupil participates in broadly social activities in school such as assemblies and break times.
3. Functional integration in which the disabled pupil takes part in the academic curriculum.

These three forms are listed in ascending order of completeness of integration.

The 'Warnock Report' led to the Education Act 1981, which promotes the continued integration of children with special educational needs into ordinary schools. The Act gives an important role to parents in arguing the case for integration.

The alternative to integration is the segregation of pupils in special schools, for which the Warnock Report envisaged a continuing role. Where pupils with special needs are patently not thriving in mainstream schools and where their presence has a sufficiently deleterious effect on the education of other pupils, the special school remains an alternative. Also, initial segregation into a special school, where there is often a concentration of specialist expertise and resources which cannot be matched elsewhere can lead to integration into the community in later life which might otherwise have been less effective.

Further reading

Cole, T. (1989) *Apart or a Part?* (Open University Press).

MF

INTELLECTUAL CLIMATE
Pupils learn most effectively when there is motivation to learn, and one way of feeding motivation is to create a suitable intellectual climate in the classroom. This climate will materialize when, for example, the teacher signals that learning is valued, perhaps through the use of praise, but also by example – when the teacher shows a personal enthusiasm and interest in learning. To organize learning regularly as a problem-solving activity stimulates an intellectual approach; and the effective use of QUESTIONING SKILLS by teachers and the stimulation of CURIOSITY in pupils are contributing factors. More generally, the teacher will encourage pupils in broad interests (hobbies, world news), will debate controversial issues, will promote openness of opinion, and will promote cultural activity (e.g. through extra-curricular activity) and conversation. Intellectual climate is most likely to be effective when the SCHOOL ETHOS is right and attention is paid to the overall LEARNING ENVIRONMENT of the institution.

TLK

INTELLIGENCE AND INTELLIGENCE TESTS
Intelligence was thought to be a general ability which was innate, fairly constant over time and measurable by tests administered to groups or

individually. The criticisms of intelligence testing have concentrated on their relative freedom from or contamination by cultural bias and the extent to which they measure learned knowledge and acquired skills rather than tap any underlying general ability.

Intelligence tests are designed so that the average person for his or her age scores 100 on the test. Scores sufficiently below 100 are taken to indicate a below average level of intelligence while scores sufficiently above 100 are taken to indicate an above average level. Equally important, in tests which use a battery of activities to assess intelligences is the score for each 'component' indicating say verbal or spatial intelligence.

Where schools use such tests in selecting pupils or when teachers draw on information provided by such tests, it is important to remember that intelligence tests should be only one of several assessments.

MF

INTERACTION ANALYSIS

Interaction analysis is a tool of classroom research for analysing the transactions which take place in classrooms. These transactions can be of many different kinds and can be sub-divided into verbal behaviour, non-verbal behaviour (see: COMMUNITY IN THE CLASSROOM and COGNITIVE activity). These sub-divisions often represent teacher ROLES and activities: organizing, consulting, marking, administering, managing, etc. Some researchers have concentrated their research efforts on analysing the interactions involved in these activities. For example, the American Ned Flanders, *Analysing Teacher Behaviour* (New York: Addison-Wesley, 1970) invented a system for categorizing all the verbal activity by the teacher and students in a classroom. Thus, using the category system, researchers could record manually, for example, what kinds of things teachers said (instructions, explanations, questions, rebukes) and what kinds of things pupils said (responses, initiating remarks, asking new questions, etc.).

The research also allowed other measures, such as the degree of dominance of the teacher in terms of classroom time for which he/she spoke. In the same way, other researchers have measured non-verbal behaviour (Michael Argyle, *The Psychology of Interpersonal Behaviour*, Harmondsworth: Penguin, 1978); while yet others have tried to explore cognition in classrooms (Trevor Kerry in E. C. Wragg, *Classroom Teaching Skills*, London: Croom Helm, 1987). Interaction analysis often uses a category system, and recordings are made by observers watching 'live' lessons, though sound or video tape and even time-lapse photography are all tools of the interaction analyst. The main purposes of this style of research are usually either to record the social life of classrooms (even to such as co-operation, bullying, sexism) and to investigate TEACHING SKILLS (QUESTIONING, EXPLAINING, CLASS MANAGEMENT, etc.).

TLK

INTERESTS

One maxim of child-centred education is 'education according to a child's interests'. Two interpretations of 'interest' arise; education may be in accordance with what interests a child, or in accordance with what is in the child's interests.

Regarding the second meaning, the description of a child's education being 'in his interests', leaves open the question how we decide what is in his interests. Problems associated with agreeing this are similar to those which arise if we talk about 'education according to *need*'. Different people have different notions of what a child needs just as they have varying opinions about what is in a child's interests.

Turning to the first meaning, that education should be in accordance with what interests a child, such interests can be established much more easily, for example, by observing and talking to the particular child. The potential source of disagreement here is whether or not it is desirable for education to be in accordance with what a particular child chooses to do out of interest.

One interpretation of education according to interest would probably secure widespread agreement. This is that the teacher should seek to interest the child, perhaps by leading into a topic which the teacher considers important (but which may not yet interest the child) by drawing on the child's present interests.

What is likely to be less widely agreed is education in which the only determining factor is what interests the child, for such interests may or may not be considered of value according to one's point of view. Also, activities may be introduced to a child which may not interest him initially but which may later fascinate him.

If limitations are accepted on allowing education to be in accordance with what interests the child, then we must discuss what factors override interests (moral issues for example). At this point the insistence on interests as being the sole consideration breaks down. So the two extreme positions of anyone wanting to support education solely according to interest are that:

1. The only criterion of value is what the individual child values;
2. Given the necessary freedom, children will select worthwhile interests.

When the position is stated in this way, most people would argue for an educational definition of the term interests which rejects the two definitions above.

Further reading

Barrow, R. and Woods, R. (1988, third edition) *An Introduction to Philosophy of Education* (Routledge).

MF

INTERNATIONAL BACCALAUREATE
(See: BACCALAUREATE)

INTERNATIONAL EDUCATION
Education which is international in content and ethos is encouraged in several ways. The Commonwealth Secretariat Education Division works with member countries to organize innovations with an international character.

European education is fostered by schemes and particular schools. Some INTERNATIONAL SCHOOLS provide specifically for an international education while others are schools whose medium of teaching is English but which are based abroad. At the United World College of the Atlantic, students from 60 countries study on scholarships. The qualification associated with such international schools and colleges is the BACCALAUREATE.

Addresses

Commonwealth Secretariat Education Division, Marlborough House, Pall Mall, London SW1Y 5HY
tel: 071 839 3411
United World College of the Atlantic, St. Donat Castle, Llantwit Major, South Glamorgan CF6 9NW
tel: 04465 792530

MF

INTERNATIONAL SCHOOLS
International Schools may be international in their character and ethos or may be schools abroad which teach in English. The qualification associated with such schools is the BACCALAUREATE.

Addresses

European Council of International Schools, 21B Lavant Street, Petersfield, Hants GU32 3EL
tel: 0730 68244
ECIS provides a 'Directory of International Schools' which lists schools abroad which teach in English.
International Schools Association, C.I.C. Case 20, 1211 Geneva 20, Switzerland
tel: 41 22 733 6717
Member schools are international in character and ethos. The Association created the International Baccalaureate.

MF

INTERVIEWS (FOR POSTS)

The preconditions for effective interviewing of candidates for appointment to posts in schools and colleges are especially important in the expanding climate of industrial and equal opportunities legislation. For these reasons, as well as to sustain professionalism, all principals, heads and governors should make themselves aware of accepted ground rules for procedure. These are often set out in college, school or LEA policy statements; the guidance given here is basic only. First, proper public advertising of posts is essential, with accurate information about grades, salaries, etc. All enquirers should receive full information about the institution; and very detailed descriptions of the post. These last should include a job description, a list of the essential qualifications of applicants, a list of the desirable characteristics of applicants, and accurate data about grade, salary and application procedures (including the closing date for applications and the projected interview date). On the interview day candidates should be welcomed and helped to relax: such things as effective car-parking arrangements, facilities for the disabled, well signposted toilets, comfortable chairs and the provision of refreshment helps. A sight of the institution and the working area is desirable. During the interview the layout of the room needs to be appropriate, and the furniture comfortable. Each candidate should be given equal time access to the panel and be asked the same kinds of questions (which the panel will have prepared in advance). There should be a chance for applicants to ask questions of the panel.

Heads and principals should ensure that governors understand the necessity not to ask questions which reflect gender, racial or other biases. The skilled interviewer will formulate open questions, giving the candidate time to respond. He/she will cultivate a good listening ability, and will use verbal and non-verbal cues to encourage the candidate to talk. Between them, panel members should take (and keep, in case of later challenge) notes on the interviews: but it is distracting for the candidate if the interviewer tries to write while listening to the candidate's responses. When candidates have been interviewed they may be asked to await a decision, or the decision may be communicated later by post or telephone. They should be thanked for attendance before departure. Decisions should be made by the panel after full discussion each in strict accord with the job description and the published criteria of the post. Delays in informing the candidates should be minimized and candidates should have been forewarned of the likely mode of information. Candidates should be advised how to claim expenses due for attendance. After the decision is reached the chair of the interview panel should arrange for all application forms, notes and related paperwork to be stored safely and in confidence. Where a candidate is not appointed but the interview is seen to be rigorous, fair, professional yet relaxed, the candidate will maintain goodwill towards the institution and retain positive attitudes about it.

TLK

INTERVIEWS (FOR RESEARCH)

Interviews can be used as a form of evidence in educational research. A typical example might be to interview a hundred heads of department to ask what job operations they perform in this role. From an analysis (on tape or in written record) of their replies a profile of the Head of Department's job could be compiled. Such interviews need to be carefully prepared within the requirements of the research, and standardized across researchers.

TLK

INTONATION

One teaching skill required by every teacher is the ability to use his/her voice effectively. Given that teachers may talk for up to two-thirds of the school day, it is important that they learn voice-control: the ability to put light and shade, emphasis and variety into the voice. This skill is difficult to demonstrate on paper, but even a very small word can be invested with a wide variety of meaning when said in a particular way, as the following table aims to show:

The single word 'No' can alter its meaning according to the way in which it is said.

	Expression	Message
No.	matter-of-factly	I didn't do, or don't know, the thing you have enquired about.
No.	defiantly, petulantly	I won't do what you have just asked me.
No?	interrogatively, with mild surprise	Surely that didn't *really* happen to old so-and-so?
No.	expectantly	I don't know, but I'm waiting for you to tell me.
No!!!	incredulously (with exhalation of breath)	That idiot of a slip-fielder has dropped *another* catch.
No.	insecurely	Yes – but I'm lying.
No.	submissively	Honest answer to: 'You won't do it again, will you?'
No . . .	drawn out, irritable	I'd like to but I haven't the courage/haven't made up my mind.
No . . .	deliberately emphatic	That's the second time I've told you to take your hand off my knee, and I meant it the first time.
No.	horrified (with inhalation of breath)	Help!

TLK

ISLAMIC EDUCATION

There are some two million Muslims living in Britain and around half a million Muslim children of compulsory school age. Among the educational concerns of the Muslim community are:

- that Muslims recognize and exercise parental rights and responsibilities regarding the education of their children and that they are involved as, for example, school governors or as members of the local Standing Advisory Council on Religious Education;
- that collective worship and school assemblies have sufficient flexibility to allow Muslim children to worship according to their faith and that there is provision for Muslim prayers;
- that religious education in schools reflects the faith of Muslim children in the school.
- that sex education is taught in such a way that it does not conflict with Islamic principles and beliefs.

- that physical education takes into account such Islamic requirements as prohibitions on indecent clothing and free mixing between sexes;
- that, in art, Muslim pupils are not expected to pursue activities which contravene Islamic belief, namely activities involving human images or iconography;
- that musical activities are not forced upon a pupil as, strictly speaking, the use of musical instruments is forbidden in Islam;
- that Muslim children should be allowed to follow the Islamic dress code and that, where a school expects uniform to be worn, flexibility is allowed;
- that Muslim children are allowed holidays to celebrate the two major annual festivals of Id ul Fitr and Id ul Adha;
- that school meals do not violate Islamic codes of eating.

An important development is the establishment of independent Muslim primary and secondary schools in Britain of which there are about thirty. There are many hundreds of supplementary schools, called madrasahs. However, none of the schools has been awarded voluntary-aided status under the Education Act 1944.

Addresses

The Islamic Academy, 23 Metcalfe Road, Cambridge CB4 2DB
tel: 0223 350 973   fax: 0223 350 976

(See also: Section 3, Directory of Organizations)

Muslim Educational Trust, 130 Stroud Green, London N4 3RZ
tel: 071 272 8502   fax: 071 281 3457
Publications obtainable from and published by the Muslim Educational Trust: *Islam: A brief guide*; Sarwar, G. (1994 revised edition) *British Muslims and Schools*; Sarwar, G. (1992 with a 1994 updated insert) *Sex Education: The Muslim Perspective*.

MF

JEWISH EDUCATION
In independent or state-aided Jewish schools, subjects such as Hebrew and Jewish history are studied. Part-time Jewish religious schools offer Jewish religious education outside normal school hours for pupils who do not attend Jewish schools.

The Board of Deputies of British Jews provide religious education facilities for Jewish boarders in public schools, inspect provincial classes and give advice to promote Jewish religious education. Further information may be obtained from:
Board of Deputies of British Jews, Education Department, Woburn House, Upper Woburn Place, London WC1H OAP
tel: 071 387 3081

Publications

The *Jewish Year Book* (Jewish Chronicle Publications) lists Jewish schools and Jewish organizations.

MF

KEY STAGES (KS)
Key stages (KS) are those periods in the education of each pupil to which elements of the National Curriculum apply. There are four Key Stages, normally related to the age of the majority of pupils in a teaching group as follows:

KS1   beginning of compulsory education to 7 years old
KS2   7 to 11
KS3   11 to 14
KS4   14 to the end of compulsory education.

MF

KNOWLEDGE (AND THE SCHOOL CURRICULUM)
In order to determine an appropriate school curriculum, it is necessary to make its content explicit. Hirst (1975) gives a framework for doing this. He sought to develop a concept of education that could be defined and justified according to the nature and significance of knowledge. Such an approach would give a foundation which could resist political or social pressures and the wishes of pupils.

In the context of discussing a liberal general education appropriate for all school pupils, Hirst regarded knowledge as separable into a number of forms. (Physical sciences is one form, for example.) These forms are ways of understanding cultural experience. Each form has interrelated aspects. Also each form involves four criteria:

1.   its own distinctive concepts;
2.   a distinct logical structure;

3. expressions which are testable against experience (in accordance with criteria which are distinctive to the form);
4. techniques and skills for examining experience.

If we take the physical sciences as an example, we see that they have:

1. their own concepts (e.g. friction);
2. a distinct logical structure; (e.g. a theory of gravity);
3. expressions testable against experience (e.g. metals expand when heated);
4. techniques and skills for examining experience (e.g. the experimental method);

Applying these criteria, Hirst specified seven forms of knowledge:

1. mathematics;
2. physical sciences;
3. human sciences;
4. history;
5. religion;
6. literature and the fine arts;
7. philosophy.

Hirst also proposed 'fields of knowledge' which are based on several forms and which structure around particular phenomena. Geography is an example.

The school curriculum should be designed to introduce pupils into each of several forms of knowledge. It should cover as far as is practicable the whole range of these forms. Project approaches, drawing on various forms, can be used. However, the fundamentally important factors in the curriculum are the underlying forms. Also, each form needs to be studied as a coherent discipline if it is to be properly understood.

Returning to Hirst's four criteria for determining a form of knowledge listed above, the third criterion (testability against experience) has been criticized. The reason is that it is difficult to see how a test against experience could be used in such forms as mathematics or religion. Hirst's justification for pursuing the forms has also been challenged. He argued that the process of being initiated into the forms is the equivalent of developing a rational mind. Therefore, to question his approach is to question the point of developing a rational mind. But, Hirst continues, to pose the question at all is to assume a rational approach thereby supporting his position.

It is the first step in Hirst's reasoning that is questionable. For in his framework there is no principle of selection to determine the value of other ways of developing a rational mind (e.g. computing) that are not forms of knowledge.

A principal of selection is needed which focuses on the purposes of developing a rational mind and the pursuit of one activity over another. This introduces a broadly utilitarian justification for aspects of education (Barrow and Woods, 1988) and these justifications will vary from place to place and from time to time. This weakens Hirst's position, as he intended that his framework would be stable. However, Hirst did encourage rational argument about what should and should not be included in the curriculum, which is extremely important.

Further reading

Barrow, R. and Wood S. R. (1988) *An Introduction to Philosophy of Education* (2nd edition) (Methuen).
Hirst, P. H. (1975) *Knowledge and the Curriculum* (Routledge & Kegan Paul).

MF

LAY INSPECTOR
An INSPECTION TEAM MEMBER without personal experience in teaching or in the management of any school (otherwise than as a governor or in any other voluntary capacity) and whose prime function on the team is not that of providing financial or business expertise. The purpose of the lay member is to provide a sensible, objective view of a school through the eyes of someone outside education.

TLK

LEADERSHIP
Leadership is not to be confused with management (see: POSITIVE MANAGEMENT), but education managers need also to be leaders. Initially one could do worse than adopt Stogdill's definition:

> Leadership is not a matter of passive status, or of the mere possession of some combination of traits. It appears rather to be a working relationship among members of a group, in which the leader acquires status through active participation and demonstration of his capacity for carrying co-operative tasks through to completion.

This definition has several merits. First it avoids a dependence on restrictions of personalized characteristics or personality traits. Second, it therefore implies that leadership may be learned or acquired, or even passed within a group. Third, it emphasizes identification of the leader with the group, not his or her separation from it. Fourth, it is suggested that leadership is organizational and functional and thus related in some way, it is hypothesized, to the process of management. This leads us into an examination of broad management objectives for schools in a changing climate. In trying to examine the task of senior education managers as leaders in a time of change, and in trying to assess their potential for success, it is first necessary to attempt to identify some of the most significant objectives which they will need to achieve. The various Acts and White Papers, as well as the more informal pronouncements of politicians, suggest that the following objectives will be critical in the immediate future even where they are not already achieved:

- the generation of high-quality strategic management plans;
- increased public profile of the school/college in the community;
- improved marketing of the school/college to prospective students and their parents;
- effective resource management (human, material, financial);
- income generation;
- appraisal of other (senior) staff performance;
- quality assurance (academic and non-academic);
- curriculum delivery within national curriculum guidelines;
- institutional self-monitoring and review;
- sustenance of institutional morale;
- professional development of staff;
- introduction of innovation to ensure a 'competitive edge'.

The SCHOOL MANAGEMENT TASK FORCE put it as follows:

Recent work on the characteristics of EFFECTIVE SCHOOLS places greater emphasis on leadership, teamwork and sound management structures. School improvement requires a constant professional effort. The job is never done, but in times of rapid change there are new expectations and new accountabilities which sharpen the need for effective support and training for senior staff . . .
Moreover, our conversations with industry, commerce and other parts of the public sector have provided a parallel perspective in managing change, in which management development is seen as a crucial process in helping organisations achieve their purposes. (*Developing School Management: The Way Forward*, p. 2)

Leadership is, then, that part of the management function which provides progress towards new goals in a time of change. This progress can take place only where the leader, through collaborative teamwork and on the basis of smooth organization ('sound management structures'), achieves such progress.

Core leadership responsibilities are sometimes listed as:

- to motivate and develop the individual;
- to build and maintain the team;
- to achieve the task.

Further reading

Stogdill R. (1948) Personal factors associated with leadership; a survey of the literature. *Journal of Psychology*, vol. 25, pp. 35–71.

TLK

LEARNING DIFFICULTIES
(See: SPECIAL EDUCATIONAL NEEDS)

LEARNING ENVIRONMENT
Good schools/colleges create an environment which encourages learning. There are several aspects to the creation of a learning environment. SCHOOL ETHOS forms the context. The physical environment is important, and is partly in the control of the individual teacher, who will usually be assigned to a classroom to use as a base. Characteristics of a good base room include the following. General tidiness is important: it helps if the teacher tidies up his/her own possessions each day before leaving. A weekly rota of students responsible for general tidiness promotes ownership. DISPLAY is important, including the display of student work. Any equipment (including sets of books) should have a home and everyone should be encouraged to use it. Safety should always be a consideration: e.g. teachers should avoid trailing wires, report broken furniture and have it removed. It is helpful to have a notice board with notices neatly mounted and with a 'Today' section for urgent attention. In all display of work or notices, proprietary products should be used which do not damage surfaces when removed (blu-tack on walls rather than sellotape, etc.).

In selecting furniture the teacher should try to keep a say in the purchase, and review options in the light of qualities such as colour, design and stackability. Even in workshop areas everything can be kept clean and 'professional' in appearance. Keeping a room aired is healthy and helps to aid freshness and alertness in students. Homely touches such as pot plants may help in some instances. If space allows, a small reference library and study corner gives good signals. It is helpful to have a termly clear-out of accumulated clutter. As well as the physical aspects of creating a learning environment it is important to inculcate an appropriate INTELLECTUAL CLIMATE which encourages learning; and as part of this to help students to acquire STUDY SKILLS with a view to becoming INDEPENDENT LEARNERS.

TLK

LEARNING THEORY

A learning theory is the means whereby educationists attempt to account for how learning takes place, and why it is successful or unsuccessful. Learning theories are usually rooted in psychology, or to a degree in social psychology and/or philosophy. The theory itself attempts to provide a systematic and integrated outlook on how and why particular learning takes place. Thus, consciously or unconsciously, all teachers adopt a learning theory in their classroom behaviour; and consistency between the theory and the practice are essential. Basically there are three main strands of theory, although with each strand there are significant variations propounded by individual theorists.

Strand 1 consists of 'mental discipline' theories: according to these, learning consists of the student's mind being trained or disciplined – much as an athlete might improve physical performance by practice and by extension of the muscles of the body. Mental discipline theorists differ in the starting points: some believe the mind is basically bad and has to be disciplined; some believe that learning is the unfolding of the naturally good mind; others take a more neutral view of the mind, and see learning as a kind of mental 'athletic training' of the kind described above. Exponents of mental discipline theories include ROUSSEAU, Froebel, John Holt and A. H. Maslow.

By contrast, strand 2 consists of the 'behaviourist' theorists. For them learning is about changes in observable behaviour brought about by stimuli which produce responses (i.e. learned behaviour) in the student. These behaviourists are also sometimes known as stimulus-response conditioning theorists. At the simplest level stimulus-response conditioning is illustrated by a dog that learns to go to a feeding bowl whenever a bell sounds or its name is called – eventually it salivates at its name whether or not there is food in the bowl. More complicated versions of this theory have been espoused by B. F. Skinner, R. M. Gagne and A. Bandura. They believe that successive, systematic changes to the learners' environment increases the probability of desired responses. Thus learning, for behaviourists, tends to result from reaction to stimuli in the social or learning environments which produce habits or behavioural tendencies.

The third strand, by contrast, are the Gestalt field theorists such as J. S. Bruner. These theorists emphasize the learners gaining a changing of insights, outlooks or thought patterns. For them, learning is a COGNITIVE process or reorganizing the ways in which the learner makes sense of situations or problems. In practice, the three approaches are not mutually exclusive. Teachers and practitioners may use insights from all of them in a quite eclectic manner.

TLK

LESSON
A unit within a school/college day. In colleges/secondary schools lessons are often of quite short duration (45–60 mins) and may be subject-specific. In primary education the boundaries between individual lessons are not always so strictly observed, since the same teacher is likely to remain with the class and work may be of a more integrational nature.

TLK

LESSON PLANNING/STRUCTURE
Lesson planning is, or should be, a bread-and-butter process for all teachers and a factor in their overall PROFESSIONALISM. Lessons can be planned in a variety of ways, but all lesson plans will need to address the following key questions:

1. What are the intentions of the lesson? i.e. at the end of it what will the students have by way of:
    (a) new knowledge
    (b) new understanding
    (c) new skills?
2. What content needs to be covered to fulfil these intentions?
3. What TEACHING METHODS are best suited to achieving the intentions?
4. Which teaching mode will match the students' learning needs (i.e. WHOLE CLASS, GROUP WORK or INDIVIDUALIZED LEARNING)?
5. What class management strategies will affect the learning? e.g. does the room layout need to be altered?
6. What resources and audio/visual aids need to be prepared in advance/be available?
7. How will variety of activity be used to sustain student interest for the duration of the session?
8. How will student learning be gauged?
9. How will learning outcomes be recorded by the teacher/student?
10. How will the lesson be evaluated to inform the teacher's future work?

TLK

LESSON STRUCTURE
(See: LESSON PLANNING)

LICENSED TEACHERS
The TASC (Teaching as a Career) Organization produced the following description of the Licensed Teacher scheme in an information leaflet dated 1989:

The licensed teacher regulations came into force on 1st September 1989 creating a new route into the teaching profession. Aimed at mature entrants with suitable qualifications and experience, and also at overseas trained teachers, this route offers the chance to train as a teacher 'on the job' through IN-SERVICE TRAINING. QUALIFIED TEACHER STATUS will be granted after successful completion of this training, generally, but not exclusively, after two years. Candidates need to be at least 26 years old (unless he/she is an overseas trained teacher); have successfully completed the equivalent of two years full-time higher education in the UK or elsewhere; and have attained Grade C in GCSE in mathematics and English or the equivalent. A candidate cannot apply him/herself for the licence. It will be for the LOCAL EDUCATION AUTHORITY (or school governing body in a GRANT MAINTAINED or non-maintained school) to apply for a licence on the candidate's behalf. LEAs will determine the amount and nature of training for any particular candidate. In the case of a person who has undertaken teacher training overseas, for example, little additional training might be required. On the other hand, a UK graduate with industrial but no teaching experience, will need more extensive training. The licensed period may be between one and three years, depending upon previous experience and the candidate's performance as a licensed teacher.

People without previous teaching experience will normally take two years to reach QUALIFIED TEACHER STATUS. If satisfied with a candidate's performance during the course of the licence period it will be for the local education authority or school governing body which applied for the licence to apply for QTS on the candidate's behalf. Successful completion of the licence period will lead to QTS but no academic qualification is awarded. There is no restriction on subject or age-group taught, but the licensed teacher would normally be required to remain in the same post for the duration of the licence. Licensed teachers can be paid either on the qualified teachers' pay scale or the unqualified teachers' pay scale as the LEA or governors consider appropriate.

TLK

LISTENING
The complementary activity to SPEAKING. Students spend a long time listening to the teacher – research suggests about two-thirds of all LESSON time. Listening is an active, not a passive, process and requires very specific skills in children. They not only have to hear what is said, but sift it for sense and understanding. Often they have to order the material, and to

absorb its content so that they can write notes. Students should also be encouraged to listen to their peers when they contribute, so as to learn from one another. The skills of listening are STUDY SKILLS which need to be learned in the first instance. Effective listening results in understanding, and can be increased by the teacher's EXPLAINING skills. Teachers, too, have to listen to students not only to gain FEEDBACK, but to signal that they do in fact value student contributions. Listening in this AFFECTIVE context is a skill in being an effective TUTOR or counsellor.

TLK

LITERACY/ADULT LITERACY
Literacy comprises the basic skills of READING, writing and SPELLING and as an aspect of ENGLISH to one of the core subjects of the NATIONAL CURRICULUM.

Regarding adult literacy, local education authorities (LEAs), under Regulations introduced in 1989, must plan and monitor basic numeracy and literacy in their local area. Also, LEAs have to include provision for adults with special needs, the disadvantaged and the unemployed.

Addresses

Adult Literacy and Basic Skills Unit (England and Wales), Commonwealth House, 1–19 New Oxford Street, London WC1A 1NU tel: 071 405 4017   fax: 071 404 5038 Scottish Adult Basic Education Unit, Atholl House, 2 Canning Street, Edinburgh EH3 8EG tel: 031 229 2433

MF

LOCAL EDUCATION AUTHORITY
In England and Wales, a local education authority (LEA) is an elected council of local government which forms an education committee from its members. The education committee also has co-opted members. The committee is served by a permanent CHIEF EDUCATION OFFICER or director of education, who has a permanent staff to administer local education.

In Scotland, the responsibility for education rests with regional councils and island councils which are referred to as 'education authorities'. In Northern Ireland, education is the responsibility of the Education and Library Boards.

The influence of LEAs has greatly diminished in the 1980s and in the early 1990s and continues to do so. The reasons for this include the following developments:

- the growth of GRANT MAINTAINED SCHOOLS, which have chosen to leave LEA control;
- the development of local management of schools (LMS) which has devolved many LEA functions to schools;
- the removal of further education from LEA control.

Addresses

Association of County Councils (ACC), Eaton House, 66A Eaton Square, Westminster, London SW1W 9BH
tel: 071 235 1200   fax: 071 235 8458
Association of Directors of Education in Scotland,
W. Semple CBE (general secretary), Director of Education,
Lothian Regional Council, 40 Torphichen Street, Edinburgh EH3 8JJ
tel: 031 479 2101
Association of Local Authorities of Northern Ireland
R. McMay (secretary), 123 York Street, Belfast BT15 1AB
tel: 0232 249286   fax: 0232 326642
Association of Metropolitan Authorities, 35 Great Smith Street,
Westminster, London SW1P 3BJ
tel: 071 222 8100   fax: 071 222 0878
Council of Local Education Authorities (address as for Association
of County Councils):
Society of Education Officers, 20 Bedford Way, London WC1H OAL
tel: 071 612 6388/6389   fax: 071 323 0029

MF

LOCAL MANAGEMENT OF SCHOOLS (LMS)

From 1 April 1990 some LEA maintained secondary schools were given control over their own budgets. The remaining secondary schools and primary schools were given the same facility during the following years to total delegation by the LEA by April 1994. Delegation of school budgets has given schools considerable freedom to decide how to spend that part of the budget that is not already bespoke, e.g. staff salaries, etc.; it also allows for any end-of-year underspend to remain with the school, whilst any budget deficit must be carried over to the following financial year.

Each LEA is required to have a scheme, approved by the SECRETARY OF STATE, which sets out the formula for working out budgets for both primary and secondary schools; a copy of this scheme must be given to each of its schools. The scheme must set out details of those items of spending which do not go into the delegated budgets but for which money is held back and administered centrally. Governing bodies are expected to live within their budget, to allocate sufficient funds to allow the NATIONAL CURRICULUM to be taught, to ensure that funding is sufficient for the needs of those children with special educational requirements and to provide regular and accurate records of income and expenditure.

CAK

LOOK AND SAY
(See: READING)

MANAGEMENT: OF SCHOOLS AND COLLEGES
The process whereby an effective organization of the institution is achieved, leading in turn to overall effectiveness.
(See: EFFECTIVE SCHOOLS, POSITIVE MANAGEMENT, SCHOOL MANAGEMENT TASK FORCE.)

TLK

MANAGEMENT STYLE
Management theorists distinguish various patterns of management which predispose the management towards a particular style, e.g. on the continuum:

authoritarian ◄————————————————————► democratic
(See also: POSITIVE MANAGEMENT)

TLK

MARKING
Marking students' work serves several important ends: to provide FEEDBACK to students on their progress; to allow teachers to monitor that progress; and to provide an assessment of that progress through a mark or grade. Not every TASK set by a teacher will be formally marked; some may contribute to CONTINUOUS ASSESSMENT, or may be FORMATIVE. But, generally, teachers should not set work which goes unmarked: students find this unsatisfactory. This is overridingly true of HOMEWORK tasks. It is part of a teacher's professionalism, not only to mark work, but to do so promptly. Many teachers organize written and other markable tasks so that students receive

feedback and/or grades within a week of completion. The kind of marking which teachers do is also important. Some tasks (such as multiple examples in maths) may lend themselves to little more than a series of ticks. But most other written work is better marked when the teachers adds a comment summarizing the overall strengths and weaknesses of the work (i.e. explaining the mark), and points up specific issues within the student's text. This is often best done not by putting red ink all over the work but by using a separate 'comment sheet'. Such a sheet could be a separate blank piece of paper; but more effectiveness is achieved when teachers prepare a pro forma which has sections relating to marking criteria. These would include, typically, how closely the work relates to the problem set, its coherence, its factual accuracy, the use of evidence, the ability to sustain an argument and so on.

Naturally the assessment criteria need to be given to students when the work is set so that they are not working blind. Many beginning teachers find the sheer quantity of marking a problem, and quickly learn that – to stay on top of it – they need to temper tasks set students to those which are genuinely valuable, that they must get their time-management well-organized to cope, and that marking is a significant demand on their out-of-school time. Marking is, in effect, a dialogue between the student and the teacher; as such, it is one of the subtle factors which go to make up classroom relationships.

TLK

MASTER'S DEGREES

Traditionally, universities have awarded 'degrees' at three levels of attainment: bachelor (lowest), master and doctor. These are ancient terms and are still retained. In the earliest university structure it was necessary to study arts before proceeding to other subject areas: the minimum level to be achieved being the MA. Thus, at Oxford and Cambridge, the graduate (BA) had to give evidence of sustained study for a fixed period after graduation and could then, on payment of a fee, be awarded the degree, or status, of master, with appropriate academic dress. This still is the system at Oxford and Cambridge, but not elsewhere: in other universities the MA is an earned degree after a formal course of study.

The MA graduate, having 'gained his spurs' in Arts' was then allowed to read for a first (i.e. a bachelor's) degree in another subject, such as divinity – which is why some bachelor's degrees in ancient universities rank as higher degrees (e.g. BD, B.Litt.). As time went on, universities began to see the need to provide master's level courses in subjects other than arts and a vast range of such degrees has been constructed. Among teachers the most commonly held are M.Ed. (master of education), M.Sc. (master of science) and, increasingly for managers the MBA, (master of business administration). In general, these are awarded after successfully completing 'taught courses' of study. However, some M.Ed. degrees are given for research. Higher degrees resulting from research generally rank above those which are course-related. The commonest research master's degree is the M.Phil. This was designed as a half-way house between the taught master's and a doctorate. This is how it is used in most universities: like the Ph.D. it can be awarded in any discipline including education. There are, however, exceptions to the 'logical' picture described: University of East Anglia, for example, uses the M.Ed. as a research degree and University of Cambridge awards an M.Phil. for taught courses.

TLK

MASTER OF EDUCATION (M.ED.)
(See: MASTER'S DEGREES)

MASTER OF PHILOSOPHY (M.PHIL.)
(See: MASTER'S DEGREES)

MASTER OF SCIENCE (M.SC.)
(See: MASTER'S DEGREES)

MATHEMATICS (IN THE NATIONAL CURRICULUM)
If you are not familiar with National Curriculum terminology, before reading this subject entry, you may find it helpful to first read the entries on:

Attainment Targets
National Curriculum
Programmes of Study
Standard Assessment Tasks

Attainment targets (ATs) for mathematics and their related statements of attainment (SoA) can be set out as strands that describe how important mathematical ideas develop through the NC levels. These ATs and strands are shown below:

AT1	Using and applying mathematics	(i) Applications (ii) Mathematical communication (iii) Reasoning, logic and proof
AT2	Number	(i) Knowledge and use of numbers (ii) Estimation and approximation (iii) Measures
AT3	Algebra	(i) Patterns and relationships (ii) Formulae, equations and inequalities (iii) Graphical representation
AT4	Shape and space	(i) Shape (ii) Location (iii) Movement (iv) Measures
AT5	Handling data	(i) Collecting and processing (ii) Representing and interpreting (iii) Probability

The key stages relate to levels of attainment in the following way:

KS1 – Levels 1–3
KS2 – Levels 2–6
KS3 – Levels 3–8
KS4 – Levels 4–10

There is a Programme of Study (PoS) for each AT. Each PoS consists of elements which correspond to each of the 10 levels of attainment.

The layout of the revised Order (DES, 1991) shows PoS, SoA and examples alongside each other. The elements of the PoS are necessary in determining the scope of each SoA and should be used to plan work for pupils in order for them to achieve the assessment objectives.

The PoS for AT1 needs to be considered in conjunction with the PoS for ATs 2–5:

- work related to ATs 2–5 provides the basis of mathematical knowledge and skills necessary for pupils to use and apply in the range of ways indicated in AT1;
- work related to AT1 provides the strategies through which pupils can extend the skills and understanding dealt with in ATs 2–5.

Further reading

DES/WO (1991) *Mathematics in the National Curriculum* (HMSO).
Reynolds, P. (1994) 'The Mathematics Curriculum' in the series Farrell,
M. (Ed.), *Education for Teaching* (HMSO).

MF

MENTOR

An experienced practitioner who gives professional support and guidance to
a more junior colleague (the mentee) through the process of MENTORING.
Such a person – as well as having good and varied practical experience on
which to draw – would ideally possess certain key qualities:

* an analytical approach to teaching;
* wise judgement born of experience;
* a positive view of teaching as a skilled, complex but learnable process;
* a questioning approach;
* a personality characterized by warmth, humour, patience and enthusiasm;
* a flexible approach to problem-solving.

Mentors tend to carry out specific roles in INITIAL TEACHER TRAINING, and
in other contexts. These are: management and learning opportunities,
support, guidance and training, and ASSESSMENT. Mentors need to
understand something of the nature of ADULT LEARNING. In particular,
mentors must help students to clarify the goals of their learning, to be open
and honest with them about their development, and be able to negotiate
routes to learning.

Further reading

Watkins, C. and Whalley, C. (1993) *Mentoring: Resources for School Based
Development* (Longman).

TLK

MENTORING

This process has become particularly associated with INITIAL TEACHER
TRAINING, but can refer to any situation in which a less experienced
practitioner is supported and guided by a more senior one. At its least
effective, mentoring may be associated with an APPRENTICESHIP model of
learning – i.e. that the novice acquires skills by sitting with, observing and

emulating the expert. More recently mentoring has been used in tandem with a COMPETENCY MODEL in which the mentor guides and supports the mentee towards specific competences through FEEDBACK and training. A third model, the *reflective*, implies that the mentor will encourage the mentee to develop his/her own abilities, to look analytically at teaching and learning situations and to adopt a self-imposed and experimental approach to more effective working. This last model is close to that adopted in better APPRAISAL systems.

The three models form a kind of loose hierarchy, since in practice most teacher trainees are likely to model themselves on exemplars of good practice, only later being more systematically coached towards articulating and attaining the competences that underlie such practice, and then adopting a more fine-grained and self-analytical approach. The mentoring process is one which is relatively new for the area of learning for teaching, though the broad concept has been in existence for thousands of years. In recent times it became fashionable to adopt this practice in management training in business and commercial contexts, from which it has filtered into education. To be a MENTOR requires specific skills, and increasingly training courses in mentoring are becoming available.

TLK

MICROTEACHING

Microteaching is a form of skills' learning which evolved in the aftermath of the development of closed circuit television systems. The CCTV studio or portable video camera allows a learner-teacher, for example, to teach a session to a group. Then the teacher (as well as the tutor and students) can watch a replay of the session, analysing its strengths and weaknesses or looking for specific performance skills. Facilities such as action-replay and stop-frame can be used to study events in detail. The method allows for close scrutiny of practical skills. It accords well with the philosophy of the REFLECTIVE PRACTITIONER. The technique lends itself to other kinds of learning, e.g. management skills such as conducting INTERVIEWS.

TLK

MIDDLE SCHOOLS
(See: PRIMARY SCHOOLS)

MISSION STATEMENT
A mission statement is a succinct summary of the fundamental purpose of an institution – a school or college. Ideally such a statement would be constructed out of dialogue between the principal and staff, and amended

and/or approved by governors. Adopted by all parties, and communicated to students, parents and relevant others, it would be the central rationale by which the institution evaluated its success and progress, and would be taken into account in the quality assurance process. The construction of an effective mission statement is a skilled process, and the following table attempts to identify characteristics of strong and weak statements.

Good factors	*Weak factors*
Brief, business like	Overly long, obscure
Expressed in clear English	Rhetorical, jargonistic
Well laid out	Poorly presented
Related to reality	Too ambitious
Negotiated with all staff	Compiled by senior management
Achievable	Wedded to philosophy, not practice
Identifying clear targets	Platitudinous
Identifying intermediate stages in success	Lacking indications of progress
Putting clients at the centre	Putting the institution at the centre
Relating the institution to its context	Ignoring the contextual issues

TLK

MIXED ABILITY ORGANIZATION

Mixed ability is one method of organizing pupils into classes, as opposed to STREAMING, SETTING or BANDING. Mixed ability organization means that pupils of a given age are grouped on entry to a school or year-group without reference to ability. A mixed ability class will contain pupils across a wide, possibly the whole, range of ability in the school.

Mixed ability grouping is widely used in the primary sector, and has been for several decades – since the abolition of a universal 11 plus examination in 1965. Typically, in an average sized first or infant school, all the pupils admitted at any one time would form a single class and no attempt would be made to stream the pupils by ability. The mixed ability grouping might be retained throughout the period of primary school life.

In secondary schools, mixed ability as a form of organization did not occur commonly until the advent of the comprehensive system in the second half of the 1960s. In the 1970s it became common-place for comprehensive schools to use mixed ability groups for the first, second and even third years that pupils were in the school. Because comprehensive schools were often sizeable and received pupils from many FEEDER SCHOOLS they had to ensure a mix of ability within an entry of several hundred pupils. This was done in a number of ways:

- by random assignment of pupils to classes;
- by alphabetic division of pupils into groups, i.e. by initial letter of surname;
- by some form of friendship or catchment area grouping;
- by testing pupils for ability and spreading pupils of known abilities across all classes evenly.

The mixed ability form of organization was supported by a particular philosophy of education. This held that every child should be able to proceed at his or her own pace and to tackle work, within an overall class framework, designed for his or her ability. Pupils should have these rights within a context which minimized labelling brought about by testing or by social factors such as class, racial origin or gender. In part, mixed ability arose as a response to, and rebellion by the teaching profession from, the low ability early-leaving classes formerly created in secondary modern schools. These classes, which were often described as 'sinks' or 'ghettos', magnified the disciplinary problems in schools by concentrating the least able and most disaffected in 'blackboard jungles'. The raising of the school-leaving age (ROSLA) to 16 in 1964 meant that such pupils would remain in school for a further twelve months and forced an urgent re-thinking of appropriate CURRICULUM and of TEACHING METHOD, as well as organization.

To be faced with a class of pupils of very mixed ability required teachers to learn new skills since mixed ability organization must not be confused with MIXED ABILITY TEACHING.

Current government policy discourages mixed ability organization in favour of a reversion to more traditional streaming. Such a policy seems destined to reintroduce the problems which mixed ability was designed to solve.

TLK

MIXED ABILITY TEACHING

MIXED ABILITY ORGANIZATION is a means by which pupils are divided into groups without reference to academic ability. Underlying this form of organization are specific educational philosophies. But to teach mixed ability classes demands specific skills from teachers. They are probably not different skills, but more general teaching skills refined to a higher level and honed to the mixed ability context. In particular, WHOLE CLASS TEACHING – a regular resort of those teaching homogenous groups – becomes less appropriate except for starting off projects or lessons, and for drawing work to a conclusion. Use of GROUP WORK and of INDIVIDUALIZED LEARNING is more appropriate to mixed ability classes, since part of the underlying rationale is to allow individual pupils to proceed appropriately and at their own pace. Mixed ability lessons require teachers to be well organized because they have to deal with a wide range of activities simultaneously. When learning is in groups or individualized the teacher needs to provide a wide range of AUDIO-VISUAL RESOURCES, including self-produced resources such as worksheets. Variety in lessons is a crucial factor in holding the attention of pupils, some of whom may have reduced attention span because they have SPECIAL LEARNING NEEDS or because they are GIFTEDor of high ability.

Good mixed ability lessons require high degrees of expertise from teachers in EXPLAINING and giving clear instructions. QUESTIONING skills are important, too, not only so that teachers can receive FEEDBACK on how children are learning, but in order to promote an appropriate attitude towards PROJECT-WORK, DISCOVERY LEARNING and problem-solving. Teachers have to be skilled in TASK-SETTING, so that pupils are well occupied on tasks which have a significant degree of COGNITIVE DEMAND. Individual RECORD-KEEPING on pupil progress is vital as an aid to identifying the next task to set each pupil. Some teachers argue that mixed ability approaches are more appropriate to some curriculum areas (HUMANITIES; ENGLISH) than others (MATHEMATICS; MODERN LANGUAGES) because the latter tend to be 'linear' in nature, i.e. to require mastery of point a before progression to point b, of point b before progression to point c, etc. Research into mixed ability teaching compared with other kinds of teaching has tended to indicate that the form of organisation has less effect on pupil performance than the QUALITY of the individual teacher regardless of the organizational context. Proponents of mixed ability teaching point to improved attitudes to learning from pupils educated in this way.

TLK

MODERN FOREIGN LANGUAGES (IN THE NATIONAL CURRICULUM)

If you are not familiar with National Curriculum terminology, before reading this subject entry, you may find it helpful to first read the entries on:

Attainment Targets
National Curriculum
Programmes of Study
Standard Assessment Tasks

There are nineteen modern foreign languages which count as National Curriculum languages. These are the eight official languages of the European Community (EC) (Danish, Dutch, French, German, Modern

Greek, Italian, Portuguese and Spanish) and eleven other languages of commercial and cultural importance (Arabic, Bengali, Chinese [Cantonese or Mandarin], Gujarati, Modern Hebrew, Hindi, Japanese, Panjabi, Russian, Turkish and Urdu). Schools must offer one of the official EC languages as a foundation subject, but can offer any other language from the nineteen on the list as an option.

Attainment targets (ATs) for modern foreign languages are as follows:

AT1	Listening	The development of pupils' ability to understand and respond to spoken language.
AT2	Speaking	The development of pupils' ability to communicate in speech.
AT3	Reading	The development of pupils' ability to read, understand and respond to written language.
AT4	Writing	The development of pupils' ability to communicate in writing.

Most pupils should make rapid progress through the early levels. These offer lower attaining pupils or those with special educational needs worthwhile, realizable goals. Progression becomes steeper in the middle to upper levels, which challenge all pupils. The highest levels are suitable for very able and bilingual pupils.

The Programmes of Study (PoS) at KS3 and KS4 consist of two parts, prefaced by general requirements which apply to both key stages.

General requirements contain: important statements about the use of the target language for real purposes, in which language skills are combined; opportunities for developing information technology capability; and provision for pupils with special educational needs.

Part I – Learning and using the target language: the skills which should be developed, and opportunities which should be provided, through activities in the target language:

1. Communicating in the target language.
2. Understanding and responding.
3. Developing language learning skills and awareness of language.
4. Developing cultural awareness.
5. Developing the ability to work with others.
6. Developing the ability to learn independently.

Part II – Areas of experience (AoE): the content and contexts for learning and using a modern foreign language set out as seven AoE which should be explored through the target language in each key stage.

Area A: Everyday Activities
Area B: Personal and Social Life
Area C: The World Around Us
Area D: The World of Education, Training and Work
Area E: The World of Communications
Area F: The International World
Area G: The World of Imagination and Creativity

Further reading

DES/WO (1992) *Modern Foreign Languages in the National Curriculum* (HMSO).

MF

MONTESSORI, MARIA (1870–1952)

Montessori was a doctor of medicine as well as a pioneering educator. In 1899 she founded a school for 'feeble-minded' children and adapted her methods to young children who did not experience disabilities. Essentially hers was a psychological method in which the process of education was not completely dominated by curricular needs. Credence was also given to a child's interests and stage of intellectual development. MONTESSORI SCHOOLS have developed world-wide.

MF

MONTESSORI SCHOOLS

Usually, Montessori schools are independent nursery schools using teaching approaches and methods developed by Maria MONTESSORI. Children are encouraged to learn from their natural surroundings. All the senses are encouraged through activities such as music and dance.

Address

London Montessori Centre, 18 Balderton Street, London W1Y 1TG
tel: 071 495 6365

MF

MORAL EDUCATION

Moral education (as opposed to religious education or social education) is about the ability of pupils to make mature and balanced judgements on matters of behaviour in the light of an articulated value system of right and wrong. Much of what happens in classrooms is designed to have overtones of moral learning – from the use of Aesop's fables with primary pupils through to discussions of contemporary news events with sixth-form/ further education students.

How can one evaluate the degree of moral learning which has taken place? Taba developed an interesting series of criteria for use in social studies lessons which seem extremely pertinent for the moral component in Religious Education teaching. Using fictional and non-fictional stories as source material, a method common to Religious Education, the social studies curriculum developers asked oral or written questions designed to measure:

- pupils' sensitivity to the feelings and attitudes of others;
- pupils' understanding of, and the ability to predict the consequences of, behaviour;
- how far pupils can identify with the feelings and attitudes of people in different circumstances from themselves;
- pupils' ability to explain other people's behaviour and to appreciate the place of past experiences in determining it;
- pupils' insight and ability to 'read between the lines';
- how far pupils can be objective in discussing their own behaviour;
- the extent to which pupils bring emotional response into the field of intellectual and rational control.

This system commends itself in so far as it is relatively objective and not value-laden in terms of setting up expectations of what pupils ought to write or say in their answers or in suggesting 'model' attitudes which they ought to adopt.

Further reading

Taba, H. (1967) Nine Collected Works, in A. Simon and E. Boyer, *Mirrors for Behaviour*, vol. 5 (Philadelphia: Research for Better Schools Inc., 1967).

TLK

M.ED.
(See: MASTER'S DEGREES)

M.PHIL.
(See: MASTER'S DEGREES)

M.SC.
(See: MASTER'S DEGREES)

MULTICULTURAL EDUCATION

While a Eurocentric approach to education would focus on European achievements and culture, multicultural education recognizes the pluralistic nature of modern British society. Cultural and racial variety is respected and celebrated in multicultural education. Understanding and tolerance of people of different cultures and ethnic backgrounds is encouraged.

Multicultural education should be a philosophy, a policy and a practice that permeates the whole school curriculum and school life. It is likely to be less effective if seen as a discrete area of study.

Address

Access to Information on Multicultural Education Resources,
Faculty of Education and Community Studies, University of Reading,
Bulmershe Court, Earley, Reading RG6 1HY
tel: 0734 875 123, ext. 4871   fax: 0734 318 650

MF

MUSIC (IN THE NATIONAL CURRICULUM)

If you are not familiar with National Curriculum terminology, before reading this subject entry, you may find it helpful to first read the entries on:

Attainment Targets
National Curriculum
Programmes of Study
Standard Assessment Tasks

There are two attainment targets (ATs) for music, as follows:

AT1	Performing and composing	The development of the ability to perform and compose music with understanding.
AT2	Listening and appraising	The development of the ability to listen to and appraise music, including knowledge of musical history, our diverse musical heritage, and a variety of other musical traditions.

Regarding 'strands', each end of key stage statement relates to a strand of progression.

AT1 has five strands: the first three are linked to performing; the remaining two are linked to composing:

- playing and singing (by ear, from signs and notations);
- controlling sounds made by the voice and a range of musical instruments;
- performing with others;
- composing, arranging and improvising;
- refining, recording and communicating musical ideas.

AT2 has three strands:

- listening and identifying musical elements and structures;
- the history of music: its composers and traditions;
- appraising music: appreciation of live and recorded music.

In KS1 the second and third strands are combined in AT1, and the first and second strands are combined in AT2, making a total of six end of key stages statements.

There is not a statutory 10-level framework for music. For KS 1–3, end of key stage statements define the knowledge, skills and understanding which pupils of different abilities and maturities are expected to achieve by the end of each key stage. Programmes of study at KS4 are non-statutory.

Turning to the Programme of Study (PoS), it comprises two parts:

1. General requirements for all key stages;
2. Specific requirements for each key stages.

General requirements define:

(a) the opportunities which should be given to pupils throughout all the key stage.
(b) the range of repertoire for listening and performing.

The PoS have been set out in relation to each AT. But this does not necessarily mean that teaching activities or learning opportunities should be designed to address them separately. Each PoS statement relates to an end of key stages statement and is illustrated by non-statutory examples.

The ATs and PoS for KS4 first apply in August 1995 but are non-statutory. In England, most schools are expected to offer music to pupils wishing to continue to study the subject after the age of 14.

Further reading

DES/WO (1992) *Music in the National Curriculum* (HMSO).

MF

NATIONAL CERTIFICATE/DIPLOMA

Vocationally-oriented qualifications awarded by the BUSINESS AND TECHNO-LOGY EDUCATION COUNCIL which are broadly equivalent to A LEVELS and are accepted as a university entrance qualification for appropriate courses.

(See Section 3, 'Directory of Organisations, under Business and Technology Education Council)

MF

NATIONAL CURRICULUM

The National Curriculum (NC) is an attempt to bring consistency to the curricula of maintained schools. One of the provisions of the Education Reform Act 1988, the NC has been introduced progressively in England and Wales since the Autumn term of 1989.

It does not apply to schools in the independent sector nor to every school in the maintained sector; exceptions being made for hospital schools, nursery classes, nursery schools and city technology colleges. Otherwise every pupil in a maintained school is entitled to a curriculum which, in the words of the Act:

> promotes the spiritual, moral, cultural, mental and physical development of pupils at school and of society;
> prepares such pupils for the opportunities, responsibilities and experiences of adult life.

Government established two bodies: the National Curriculum Council and the School Examinations and Assessment Council, each with members appointed by the Secretary of State. These were replaced by the School Curriculum and Assessment Authority (SCAA) under the Education Act 1993.

The NC has 10 foundation subjects (11 in Wales) which are sub-divided into 3 core subjects and 7 other foundation subjects. English, mathematics and science constitute the core subjects with the addition of Welsh in Welsh speaking schools in Wales. These subjects embrace essential concepts, knowledge and skills. The remaining foundation subjects are technology, history, geography, music, art, physical education and in secondary schools, a modern foreign language. (Welsh is the second language in Wales.)

The 'basic curriculum' comprises the foundation subjects plus religious education, while the 'whole curriculum' includes other elements at appropriate stages. These elements are:

• careers education and guidance;

- health education;
- other aspects of personal and social education;
- across the curriculum coverage of gender and multicultural issues.

There is no prescribed time allocated to particular subjects, the Act only requires that the core and other foundation subjects are taught for a 'reasonable time'.

Attainment targets (ATs) define the main aspects of each subject. In English for example, there are the following ATs:

AT1	Speaking and listening;
AT2	Reading;
AT3	Writing;
AT4	Spelling;
AT5	Handwriting;
AT4/5	Presentation. (This is related to spelling and handwriting.)

Let us look at AT2 'Reading' as an example of an AT. The AT is concerned with:

'The development of the ability to read, understand and respond to all types of writing, as well as the development of information-retrieval strategies for the purposes of study'. (DES, 1990)

Each AT is exemplified in a list of statements of attainment (SoA) and these are grouped into several levels which describe pupils' achievement. In most, there are ten levels for each AT, level 10 being the highest. Level 1 for reading comprises four statements of attainment. The first of these is that pupils should: 'recognize that print is used to carry meaning, in books and in other forms in the everyday world'.

At level 10 in the AT 'Reading' there are five SoA. The first of these is that pupils should: 'read a range of fiction, poetry, literary non-fiction and drama, including pre-twentieth century literature'. Pupils are assessed against these SoA.

So far we have been concerned with AT's and SoA which are to do with assessment. Another feature of the NC is programmes of study (PoS) for each subject. In English there are three PoS:

1. Speaking and listening;
2. Reading;
3. Writing, spelling and handwriting.

PoS give the range of knowledge, skills and understanding that pupils should be taught.

Another important feature of the NC are key stages, of which there are four. Assessment of pupils must take place at the end of each key stage. The table below shows each key stage and the age range associated with it. (The new labels given to each school year, e.g. Y1 for 6-year-olds, are also included.)

Key Stage	New Description	Abbreviation	Age of majority of pupils at the end of the academic year
	Reception	R	5
1	Year 1	Y1	6
	Year 2	Y2	7
2	Year 3	Y3	8
	Year 4	Y4	9
	Year 5	Y5	10
	Year 6	Y6	11
3	Year 7	Y7	12
	Year 8	Y8	13
	Year 9	Y9	14
4	Year 10	Y10	15
	Year 11	Y11	16
–	Year 12	Y12	17
	Year 13	Y13	18

PoS are usually related to key stages, each PoS containing general provisions for the whole area of the subject covered and detailed provisions for each key stage.

For most ATs the 'detailed provisions' include material specifying what pupils who are working towards a particular level should experience. Key stages are associated with levels of attainment. In English, for example, the association is as follows:

KS1 – Levels 1–3
KS2 – Levels 2–5
KS3 – Levels 3–8
KS4 – Levels 3–10

This is the general structure for subjects in the NC. There are some minor variations for each subject.

MF

NATIONAL DIPLOMA
(See: NATIONAL CERTIFICATE)

NATIONAL VOCATIONAL QUALIFICATIONS (NVQs)

NVQs are qualifications designed to recognize a candidate's performance in the workplace and outside. They are competence based, using national standards and future needs to provide benchmarks against which candidates can be measured in workplace assessments. Individuals are assessed on key work-skills to gain a qualification which is nationally recognized by employers and which offers evidence that the individual can do a job to a nationally set standard.

NVQs are part of the Government's national strategy to improve the quality and delivery of training in the workplace. Established with the target of accrediting 12 million candidates by 1996, NVQs are accredited by the NATIONAL COUNCIL FOR VOCATIONAL QUALIFICATIONS (NCVQ). The NCVQ's principal role is to provide quality assurance on NVQs, not to act as an awarding body.

NVQs are designed to:

- be based on national standards;
- take account of future needs of technology, markets and employment patterns;
- be free from any barriers which restrict a candidate's access;
- be available to all and free from discrimination based on sex, race, creed or age;
- rely on work based assessment.

NVQs are awarded at five different levels, with each level made up of a series of units of competence. Within each unit are a series of elements making up the most precise specification of competence. Each of these elements is individually assessed and certified. General National Vocational Qualifications (GNVQs) are the qualification introduced by the Government and NCVQ for students at 16+.

Where there has been hesitancy on the part of British industry to commit itself to NVQs, this is probably related to perceptions about their cost and complexity, inadequate content and low assessment standards.

NVQ levels are comparable as follows:

NVQ	level 1	Below GCSE level
	level 2	GCSE
	level 3	A-level
	level 4	Higher Education
	level 5	Higher Education

CAK

NEEDS

Needs are often considered in relation to CHILD-CENTRED EDUCATION where such notions of educating a child according to his needs are expressed. It is useful to distinguish needs from wants in that 'needs' imply a particular objective whereas 'wants' may not. A child needs a pencil if he is to draw. If he wants a pencil, he may or may not wish to draw.

Need implies values so it is not always possible to agree that particular needs should be satisfied. An alcoholic may 'need' a drink for example but not everyone would agree that the need should be satisfied or that the craving for alcohol is a need at all. Deciding children's needs is by no means an objective process. Also, to assess needs it is necessary to establish what is required for a particular end. If you 'know' that you need medicine, then you assume that it is valuable to be healthy. You have to know (or believe) that the medicine will be beneficial to your health. Also, you have to recognize that you are sick.

Judging needs is complicated enough for adults. Young children are unlikely to be able to appropriately judge their needs for themselves, particularly their long-term needs. Adults differ about what they take to be children's needs. Adults views on this depend on their perspective of child psychology, their sociological knowledge, their view of what are desirable objectives and their knowledge of means to ends.

Therefore, it clarifies nothing to say that a child should be educated according to his needs. Both progressive and traditionalist educators could equally justify their approach by an appeal to a child's need.

MF

NEWLY QUALIFIED TEACHERS

Newly qualified teachers (NQTs, formerly known as probationary teachers) are men and women who have undergone a course of study to degree level and have trained professionally but who are in their first year of service within a school. It is the responsibility of schools to provide suitable support – usually in the form of a 'co-tutor', i.e. an experienced teacher or HEAD OF DEPARTMENT who can help the NQT with skills' acquisition. Another senior member of staff is likely to act as an assessor. Some LOCAL EDUCATION AUTHORITIESprovide induction programmes using the GEST training grant as a resource. The most common teaching problems which NQTs encounter are as follows:

- class management problems, i.e. problems of organising pupils and equipment;

- discipline problems – how to cope with difficult individuals or disruptive classes;
- striking the right balance (firm/friendly) in relationships with pupils;
- record-keeping techniques are often lacking and NQTs find it hard to track the progress of large numbers of pupils;
- preparation of lessons may be skimped because of pressure of work;
- interpreting a syllabus into a series of classroom lessons may be beyond some NQTs;
- awareness of children's previous learning may be lacking;
- in terms of quality of work, NQTs may not make adequate demand on pupils;
- mixed ability groups especially may require teachers to be flexible in handling teaching situations and use varied teaching styles. Many NQTs find this difficult;
- some NQTs may be excellent at teaching their own subjects, but feel insecure handling poor readers, slow learners or subsidiary subjects;

Above all:

- during college days students always have someone to fall back on, a tutor or a class teacher, as NQTs they are often alone for the first time.

TLK

NUMERACY
(See: MATHEMATICS)

NURSERY CLASSES
A nursery class is a description of a Unit attached to an LEA Infant school where specialist provision and staffing cater for Rising 5s usually on a part-time basis.

TLK

NURSERY EDUCATION
Under the Education Act 1980 section 24 (in Scotland section 25) education is not compulsory for children under five. LEAs have discretion as to whether or not they will provide nursery education in NURSEY SCHOOLS or in nursery classes attached to primary schools. The government plans to increase nursery provision as and when funds permit.

MF

NURSERY NURSE
A qualified assistant employed in a NURSERY SCHOOL, NURSERY UNIT OR CLASS, or in a similar provision for young children. Nursery nurse is possibly a misnomer: the holders of this status are not nurses in any medical sense. They have, however, undergone a period of training in the care and nurture of children aged 0–7 years. This training will typically consist of a FURTHER EDUCATION course validated by the NNEB. Alternatively, some specialist colleges, such as the Norland College in London provide recognized training. The BTEC also has a certificate course aimed at this profession. The NNEB provides a route to more advanced training – the post qualifying diploma. Unfortunately LEAs and other providers of nursery education are not obliged to use trained staff in their nurseries except where local policies dictate this. Some nursery nurses belong to professional groups such as the PROFESSIONAL ASSOCIATION OF NURSERY NURSES (PANN).

TLK

NURSERY SCHOOL
A school set up by a LOCAL EDUCATION AUTHORITY to cater for children of under five years of age. Local authorities are not required to establish such schools, nor alternatives such as NURSERY CLASSES. Where they do exist they may be staffed by qualified staff such as NURSERY NURSES, but this is again discretionary. Research tends to show that nursery education has beneficial effects not only on the child's immediate progress but on long-term educational achievement. Despite such research, and the social need for provision in a society where more and more women join the labour-market, not all LEAs are assiduous in making nursery provision.

TLK

NUTRITION AND INTELLIGENCE
Negatively it could be argued as a matter of common sense that undernourished children are likely to be more sickly than well-fed children, to miss more time in school, to concentrate less, to be less energetic and alert and so to perform less well. This kind of thinking underpinned the provision of the 1944 EDUCATION ACT which allowed for LOCAL EDUCATION AUTHORITIES to provide SCHOOL MEALS, fee school milk, and to make special dietary provision for specific groups such as delicate children. More recently controversy about nutrition in education has centred on the effect of nutrition – or at least specific kinds of foods – and the relationship with intelligence. The question here is fundamentally: can a particular diet build greater intelligence?

A number of alternative claims in this country and abroad were made in the 1980s. Since then some careful research has been established to test these claims. The results are intriguing, showing some marked patterns, but are not wholly conclusive: partly because samples have all been small and partly because experiments varied widely and so could not be directly compared. Nevertheless, the trend in the findings is that when an experimental group of children is given a daily tablet containing a range of micro-nutrients for a period of 3–6 months these children subsequently show measurable, sometimes significant, improvement in intellectual scores. By contrast, children given a similar tablet, which is only a placebo, do not improve on their test scores and may slip back marginally. However, the tests seem to show that non-verbal scores of the children given micro-nutrients improve while scores on verbal tests do not. One unsolved problem relates to the widely-held view that most British children already receive adequate levels of vitamins and minerals in their 'normal' diet. If this were true, then the research quoted might be used to suggest that micro-nutrient tablets could be used to top-up intelligence in a way that athletes use steroids to produce muscle. But a preferable, and un-researched, view is that in practice the diets of many children are actually deficient, and that the tablets used in the experiments simply compensated for the deficiency, allowing the children to reach their personal potential.

TLK

OFFICE FOR STANDARDS IN EDUCATION (OFSTED)

The Office for Standards in Education (OFSTED) was set up in September 1992 by the Education (Schools) Act 1992. Its professional staff are HER MAJESTY'S INSPECTORS (HMI). It is a non-ministerial government department headed by Her Majesty's Chief Inspector (HMCI) who has a duty to inform the Secretary of State for Education about:

- the quality of the education provided by schools in England;
- the educational standards achieved in them;
- whether they manage their resources effectively;
- the spiritual, moral, social and cultural development of their pupils.

Improvement through inspection

The purpose of OFSTED is to improve standards of achievement and quality of education through regular independent inspection, public reporting and informed advice. To do this it has set up a new, competitive system for the regular inspection of schools by independent REGISTERED

INSPECTORS and their teams, operating under contract to OFSTED. Inspections are conducted according to a new Framework of Inspection, devised by OFSTED, drawing on the vast experience of Her Majesty's Inspectors.

Individual inspections are monitored by HMI and the system is monitored against specific performance indicators and targets. A quality assurance and development unit evaluates the system.

What's 'new' about the new inspection system?

- all schools to be inspected regularly on a four-yearly cycle;
- inspections to be conducted by independent inspectors;
- inspection contracts to be won by competitive tendering;
- each team to have one lay member;
- inspections to be carried out to a published national framework;
- parents to be invited to a pre-inspection meeting and receive a summary of the final report;
- quality control for the whole system to lie in the hands of an independent government department.

The corporate aims and objectives of OFSTED are:

- to establish, manage and regulate an efficient, effective and high quality system for the regular inspection of schools;
- to meet the requirements of the Secretary of State for Education and others for advice and inspection;
- to report on the health of the components of the education system within OFSTED's remit (OFSTED provides advice to the Secretary of State on standards and quality of education in schools and teacher training institutions; and on the provision of further and higher education within institutions maintained or assisted by local education authorities), and on particular issues and aspects within the system;
- to raise awareness of, and to promote the involvement of, educational standards and quality, and to play a role in the national debate on these matters;
- to establish and manage OFSTED as an efficient and effective organization which encourages the maximum contribution and commitment of all staff.

OFSTED may be contacted at:
Elizabeth House, York Road, London SE1 7PH
tel: 071 925 6800　　fax: 071 925 6546 (press office)
(Information supplied by OFSTED)

CAK

OPEN EDUCATION

In open education or open learning the student works through specially designed booklets and other materials which structure learning with little or no face-to-face contact with a teacher. Video, audiotapes and radio and television programmes may assist the learning.

Open education allows flexibility because students can work at their own pace and when and where they wish. Its limitation is that it may not offer the enriching and motivating face-to-face contact with a teacher and other students that conventional education provides. However, some open learning courses offer limited face-to-face contact.

The British Association for Open Learning provides up-to-date details of resources and courses. Further information may be obtained from: British Association for Open Learning, Standard House, 15 High Street, Baldock, Herts SG7 6AZ tel: 0462 89600.

MF

OPEN LEARNING

Open learning involves a student using materials which can be studied at home or elsewhere and which do not necessitate regular attendance at a school or university. Text, computer software, television and radio programmes, video tapes and audiotapes may be used. This may be supplemented by occasional face-to-face and telephone contact with a tutor. Among the advantages of open learning are that it allows learners to study when and where they choose and at a pace which suits them. It is cost effective and can make optimum use of a teacher's time. The disadvantages of the approach are that it may not give the social and group support to learning nor the valuable face to face tuition that is sometimes necessary. However, a limited amount of peer support and face-to-face tuition can supplement open learning courses as can opportunities to acquire practice skills such as the use of machinery not deliverable by open learning alone.

Among the recent educational applications of open learning to teacher education is the development of materials and course structures for secondary in-service and initial teacher education under a DFE-funded project leading to the publication of materials by HMSO under the series title 'Education for Teaching'.

The British Association for Open Learning provides information on resources and courses. Further details may be obtained from: British Association for Open Learning, Standard House, 15 High Street, Baldock, Herts SG7 6AZ tel: 0462 896000

Further reading

Farrell, M. (Ed.) (1994) 'Education for Teaching', a series of open learning books covering the essentials of teaching in the secondary school: Core Studies (8 books), Science (8 books), English (9 books) and Mathematics (8 books).

MF

OPEN-PLAN SCHOOLS

Open plan describes a style of school building favoured in the 1970s for primary schools, and more rarely for (part of) secondary schools. It involved doing away with traditional classroom partition walls and closed doors, and opening up the floorspace. This had the knock-on effect that pupils were taught in more flexible groups and that the available space could be used more creatively, e.g. to provide for large group work, reading corners etc. Some teachers reacted strongly against this learning context; the main arguments being:

- classes don't have a fixed identity;
- the noise level in the school is too high;
- it wastes a lot of time in movement and organization;
- children can more easily cover up when they are not working;
- teachers lack the convenience and security of a 'home-base';
- maintaining discipline is more difficult;
- lesson preparation is more difficult;
- it is a retrograde step, back to the 'village school' concept;
- staff are not adequately trained to use effectively the teaching methods demanded by open-plan buildings.

On the other hand, exponents of the open-plan school drew attention to a number of strengths:

- staff can be used more flexibly;
- it encourages team-teaching;
- space is not divided territorially;
- it makes better use of scarce equipment and resources;
- individual staff become facilitators;
- teachers' specialist skills can reach a wider audience of pupils;
- there is more effective use of total floor space for education as opposed to administration or circulation;
- it is cheaper to build;
- it makes pupils more independent.

In practice the biggest single drawback was, inevitably, noise created not from indiscipline but from large numbers of people in a confined area. The open-plan school waned in popularity quite rapidly though examples still exist.

TLK

OPEN UNIVERSITY

Britain's Open University is one of the best known of the world's 'distance teaching' Universities. Founded in 1969 it prepares students for under-graduate degrees, postgraduate qualifications to master's and doctoral level and a range of other vocational and professional qualifications. The University also produces packs of resources including text, video and audio cassette on a variety of topics. In 1992 nearly 200,000 people studied for a degree and other courses. From the first the Open University has worked in partnership with the BBC, which has a specialist centre and specialist staff on the University's campus, Walton Hall, in Milton Keynes, a new city development fifty miles to the north of London. Academic staff across nine faculties and centres prepare the materials and courses, all of which are presented or implemented through thirteen regions. Each region has a network of study centres providing students with tutorial and counselling support. Over the last few years Open University courses and qualifications have been made available in other parts of Europe, particularly in European Community countries. Courses have also been franchised more widely in Australia, Hong Kong and Singapore, for example, and to some countries (Hungary, for example) through translation. The University has built up a significant expertise in multi-media course development, part-time study and the needs of mature entrants or re-entrants to higher level study. Staff from the Open University have, therefore, contributed to the establishment and development of most of the 'Open University' equivalent organizations established in many countries over the last two decades.

Education courses have played a prominent role in each phase of the University's evolution. In the early 1970s thousands of teachers, particularly in the primary sector, upgraded their qualification to graduate level through Open University courses. The programme design is modular in structure. Six credits, each involving 440 hours of study time, are required for a first degree. Students 'build' degrees through a combination of full credit and half credit (220 hours) courses. These courses are also given a points value under the Credit Accumulation and Transfer Scheme (CATS) with respect to transfer to a course run by another institution. Exemptions are given to those holding previous qualifications. All of the education courses can be studied in their own right and thousands of teachers who already have graduate status take one or two credits for personal 'in-service purposes'. The University has been particularly strong in developing management, psychology and special needs courses. By the 1980s with the teaching profession achieving graduate entry status a new structure of accreditation for on-going professional development was necessary. Three new qualifications were, therefore, put in place at Certificate, Advanced Diploma and Master's level. The last of these has proved particularly successful. Over 30 per cent of all students studying for master's degrees in education in Britain (around 3,000 in 1991) do so through the Open University. There is a strong possibility that through the 1990s and into the first year of the next century that study at master's level will become the expectation of the majority of teachers and, in this, the role of part-time distance education is likely to be significant. Other universities, for example, are now adopting similar methodologies using distance teaching texts, evening or weekend tutorials, residential schools and a credit based programme. It is in this context of twenty years' development that the University is launching one of Europe's largest programmes for the initial training and education of teachers.

Over many years the Open University has received requests from students to provide a routeway to qualified teacher status, either through concurrent education and training of the type associated with the B.Ed. programme taken by many intending teachers, particularly primary teachers, or through the POSTGRADUATE CERTIFICATE IN EDUCATION (PGCE) that accredits the one–year courses provided for those who have already achieved graduate status. In the late 1980s a first initiative in this area was taken in developing course materials to support professional development work on part-time courses run by other departments of education in institutions of higher education. Between two and three hundred students a year have gained QUALIFIED TEACHER STATUS (QTS) in this way.

In 1990, however, the decision was made to investigate seriously how many students amongst the existing undergraduate population would be interested in obtaining a teaching qualification solely through Open University part-time study. A survey carried out in one densely-populated region, the West Midlands, showed that half of all students had thoughts of teaching as a career and that 19 per cent were very interested. The interest divided equally between those thinking of primary or secondary subject teaching.

The government showed interest in the scheme and the first recruits to the Open University's PGCE course came on stream in February 1994.

TLK

OPTING OUT

The decision to opt a school out of local authority control rests with parents. Any LEA primary or secondary school can hold a ballot of parents on whether to forward an application to the Secretary of State for GRANT MAINTAINED STATUS. From January 1994 governors in LEA maintained schools must 'consider' once a year whether to hold a ballot of parents on whether or not the school should seek GM status. The result of this consideration must be reported in the next governors' ANNUAL REPORT TO PARENTS. A grant is available from the DFE (up to £700 plus £1 for every child in the school) to cover expenses incurred informing the parents about Grant Maintained status during a ballot. The Secretary of State decides each case on its merits.

CAK

ORACY

In an educational context oracy means learning by talking. In practice, talking in the classroom means students not only talking to the teacher but talking to each other. Different kinds of talking, in different contexts, and to different audiences may be appropriate. Thus, the teacher who wishes to promote learning through talking must consider the purpose of that talk: to solve a problem, to persuade, narrate, explore, argue a case, evaluate or summarize. The student-talk must then be organized to fit that purpose and to suit the potential audience which might be: a peer, an adult, an individual, a small or large group, of the same, opposite or mixed gender. The talk will need structure: it may need to be planned, may be from notes or memory, or defined spontaneously; it may feature anecdotes, discussion, a report and so on. In the process students will become aware of, and use, a variety of skills and techniques: improved vocabulary, technical language, use of BODY LANGUAGE, negotiation, timing, sequencing. If the oral skills are practised in a context of dialogue, the student must also develop LISTENING SKILLS. Oracy is an important skill because it helps the student to develop in an area in which all adults need to be fluent, whether in social or business relationships and transactions. Oracy requires both COGNITIVE and AFFEC-TIVE SKILLS from pupils, and a well-developed ability by the teacher not to slip into DIDACTIC MODELS OF TEACHING. Thus oracy is usually practised in a GROUP WORK context and often with collaborative learning as part of its goal.

TLK

OUTDOOR ACTIVITIES/OUTDOOR EDUCATION

School journeys often involve outdoor education and have been the subject of recent legislation. Charging for school journeys and educational visits in schools maintained by Local Education Authorities was an issue covered in the Education Reform Act 1988. Charges cannot be made for educating pupils in normal school hours. No charge can be made for transporting pupils to or from any venue, outside the school premises, in which education is provided. If a pupil is on a residential trip, then the school may charge for the pupil's board and lodging.

Addresses

National Association for Outdoor Education, 50 Highview Avenue, Grays, Essex RM17 6RU
School Journey Association, 48 Cavendish Road, London SW12 ODG
tel: 081 675 6636
Scottish Environmental and Outdoor Education Centres Association Ltd., Scottish Centres, 57 Melville Street, Edinburgh EH3 7HL
tel: 031 226 6391

Publications

Safety in Outdoor Education, by the DES with the Scottish Education Department, the Welsh Office and the Department of Education in Northern Ireland (HMSO).

MF

OVERACHIEVEMENT
A concept which states that some pupils outperform their real, or measured, levels of ability, on particular occasions. The concept is certainly spurious. It seems altogether more plausible that (barring occasional fluke circumstances such as a lucky run of test questions or cheating) a pupil can only perform at his or her 'real' level of ability – though the pupil may often disguise this as a symptom of UNDER ACHIEVEMENT.

TLK

OVERHEAD PROJECTOR (OHP)
Use of the OHP enhances the impact of lessons. Transparencies can be made by hand using special pens or by means of a photocopier or word processor. Colour can be added. Commercial transparencies even allow the depiction of working models. To a degree the OHP replaces the blackboard and allows the teacher to face the class rather than turn away to write.

TLK

PAIRED LEARNING
(See: PEER GROUP TUTORING)

PARENTAL CHOICE
Each school has an area that it traditionally serves, and although most parents are happy for their child to attend the local school, they do have the right to choose another school. Usually the child will be accepted into the school of the parents' choice if the school is appropriate for the child's age, his/her aptitude and ability, and if there is room within the planned admission limits. In the case of an LEA school, if there are more applicants for places than there are places available, then the authority will have to decide which children to accept and which to refuse. If a request is refused parents do have the right of appeal to an independent appeals panel. If the child is accepted at a school outside the area designated for transport purposes, then the responsibility for getting the child to school, and the cost involved, rests with the parent.

CAK

PARENT GOVERNORS
Parent governors are elected by the parents of registered pupils at the school, with the number of parent governor places varying according to the number of pupils on roll at the school. At the time of election, parent governors must have a child registered as a pupil at the school. Parent governors are elected for a term of four years from the date of election, but are not required to stand down if their child leaves the school during the parent governor's term of office. A parent governor may stand for re-election at the termination of the four-year period if he or she still qualifies. If, after an election has been held, there are still vacancies for parent governors, then the other governors may appoint parents to those vacancies.

CAK

PARTICIPANT OBSERVATION
A technique used frequently in ACTION RESEARCH whereby the researcher is also a participant in the process of the research.

TLK

PART-TIME EDUCATION
Part-time courses are a popular feature of Colleges of Further and Higher Education, where they allow learners to continue working or fulfilling other

commitments while fitting in study. The courses include a variety of academic studies and work-related courses, and can lead to formal qualifications including a degree.

MF

PASTORAL CARE

Pastoral care in a school is an indication of the teacher's broad role in standing 'in loco parentis' to the pupil. The teacher is not simply a teacher as such but is also interested in the child as a person. Also good pastoral care complements effective teaching. A teacher who is aware of the child's wider needs can help that child more effectively to benefit from education.

Pastoral care aims to ensure and enhance the pupil's educational, personal and social well being. It can include:

- advising the pupil on his or her educational progress;
- career guidance;
- picking up signs of unhappiness or distress and taking any necessary action;
- personal and social education.

Most secondary schools have a structured pastoral system with form tutors, heads of year (or heads of house) and senior management concerned with pastoral issues. Some school have a counsellor, who may be full-time or who may visit several schools on a peripatetic basis.

Addresses

National Association for Pastoral Care in Education, Department of Education, University of Warwick, Coventry CV4 7AL
tel: 0203 523810

Further reading

Lewis, I. and Watkins, C. (1994) 'School Organisation and Ethos: Including PSE' in the series Farrell, M. (Ed.), *Education for Teaching* (HMSO).

MF

PASTORAL MANAGEMENT

Research into pastoral management in schools is hampered by the lack of a clear definition of what constitutes pastoral provision. The emphasis may be on vocational guidance, or life skills, or on care and support for troubled pupils. This last may skew the pastoral care system towards a pathology unit for the few rather than support for all. Douglas Hamblin, the guru of pastoral care in schools, argues for a pastoral system which provides both continuity of care for all pupils and early identification of those at risk. Some exponents see the main purpose as being to remove barriers to learning. Recent research suggests that pastoral systems may be diverted to serve the end of the school's senior managers to sustain discipline. Certainly there are tensions implicit in any pastoral care system which fails to identify and articulate purpose and policy through the SCHOOL MANAGEMENT PLAN and to communicate that in the SCHOOL BROCHURE. There is a close and organic link between the establishment of a good pastoral care system and the SCHOOL ETHOS.

TLK

PEER GROUP TUTORING

While much learning emanates from the teacher or from teacher-provided materials, the role of peers in the learning process is nevertheless important. Peers bring to the classroom a variety of abilities, skills and experiences which can be shared. In addition, many classroom TASKS lend themselves to peer assistance: for example, learning vocabulary in a foreign language. AFFECTIVE education requires peer co-operation. Often peer learning takes the form of paired learning. Even in the primary school students might listen to one another read. Experiments in classrooms have showed that paired learning does produce learning gains. The system of 'buddy pairs' is more common in American education than here. Some critics claim it is a cheap and ineffective substitute for teacher attention; but the realism with classrooms with teacher: student ratios of 1:30 probably justifies it as just one of a range of legitimate practices to enhance learning.

TLK

PERSONAL SOCIAL EDUCATION (PSE)

PSE is a cross curriculum area of the National Curriculum concerned with pupils' personal and social development through the school curriculum and a pupil's whole experience of school. PSE encompasses the school's ethos and the personal-social aspects of school life and learning.

Specific planned occasions to promote PSE include special courses on health, careers, etc., and tutor group meetings.

Further reading

Lewis, I. and Watkins, C. (1994) 'School Organisation and Ethos Including PSE' in the series Farrell, M. (Ed.), *Education for Teaching* (HMSO).

MF

PESTALOZZI, JOHAN (1746–1827)

Pestalozzi was a Swiss educationalist born in Zurich. He was influenced by Rousseau and in particular by his concept of 'natural' education and his concern with psychological development. From 1774 to 1780 Pestalozzi founded and worked in the Neuhof or new farm, a residential institution where he educated poor children according to his theories. The experiment was a financial failure. Between 1780 and 1798, he wrote social and political books and articles. Pestalozzi took charge of an orphan children's home from 1798 to 1799 and, between 1800 and 1804, he was head of a school at Burgdorf. Finally, from 1804 to 1825, he worked at Yverdon running a large secondary school where he developed his theories. His own exposition of his methods was published as 'How Gertrude Educates Her Children' in 1801.

Address

Pestalozzi Children's Village Trust, Sedlescombe, Battle,
Sussex TN33 0RR
tel: 0424 870 444　　　fax: 0424 870 655

MF

PH.D.
(See: DOCTOR'S DEGREES)

PHILOSOPHY OF EDUCATION

Philosophy is an activity or skill which can be informed by study but which tends to improve with practice.

The philosophy of education is concerned with widening and deepening our knowledge of education and with focusing the tools of philosophy on educational ideas, theories, arguments, issues and problems. It includes an examination and clarification of central concepts such as 'education', 'knowledge' and 'curriculum' so we can understand the concepts better and so we can be more aware of the implications of holding particular ideas. Philosophizing about education makes it harder to hold uncritical views. It moves us towards having a clear set of coherent concepts which can be debated and assessed.

Philosophy of education entails studying the various movements and ideologies of education and the ideas of particular philosophers who have had an impact on educational ideas. Philosophy enables us to recognize when language is being used descriptively and objectively and when it is being used evaluatively and emotively. It gives tools to assess the validity or invalidity of an argument.

MF

PHONICS
(See: READING)

PHYSICAL EDUCATION (IN THE NATIONAL CURRICULUM)
If you are not familiar with National Curriculum terminology, before reading this subject entry, you may find it helpful to first read the entries on:

Attainment Targets
National Curriculum
Programmes of Study
Standard Assessment Tasks

There is only one attainment target (AT) for physical education. It encompasses the strands of planning, performing and evaluating whilst retaining progression in aspects of health-related exercise. Progression can be traced through the strands in the end of key stage statements across the key stages (KS).

There is no 10-level framework for physical education, although at KS4 a level framework will be developed for GCSE.

The programmes of study (PoS) comprise three parts:

1. General requirements relating to PoS. These requirements should apply to all key stages and be taught through all areas of activity.
2. Programmes of study (general). These set out what must be taught to pupils during each key stage in order to meet the objectives set out in the end of key stage statements.
3. Programmes of study (activity specific). Six areas of activity are defined:
   • athletic activities;
   • dance;
   • games;
   • gymnastic activities;
   • outdoor and adventurous activities;
   • swimming.
   Requirements relating to the areas of activity vary according to key stage.

The PoS are related to the key stages in the following way. At KS1 and

2, all six areas of activity should be experienced, but at KS1 and KS2 emphasis should be on dance, games and gymnastic activities. All pupils should be able to swim at least 25 metres unaided and demonstrate an understanding of water safety by the end of KS2. If swimming is taught during KS1 pupils should start the KS2 swimming programme at the appropriate point. The provision relating to swimming came into effect from August 1994.

At KS3, pupils should pursue the PoS for a minimum of four areas of activity, with games compulsory each year (swimming having been incorporated into other areas of activity).

At KS4, at least two activities should be experienced either from the same area of activity or from two different areas.

Further reading

DES/WO (1992) *Physical Education in the National Curriculum* (HMSO).

MF

PLATO (428 BC–*c*.347 BC)

Born into an aristocratic family, Plato was strongly influenced by Socrates. About 389 BC he began teaching in Athens where his school came to be called the Academy. His educational ideas are revealed in written dialogues (e.g. *Crito*) often featuring Socrates, and in the *Republic* and *Laws*.

In the *Republic*, Plato envisages an ideal state in which citizens comprise three groups; industrial, military and ruling (philosopher) classes. As infants, both the military and the ruling class should, Plato recommended, be told moral tales. Play was not to be overlooked. Early education should comprise musical and gymnastic training (training in the manual or useful arts was not considered appropriate for the higher classes); calculation and geometry should begin in childhood, forming a preparation for dialectic (philosophy) to be studied later as higher education for those chosen to be the ruling class.

From among the groups educated in this way, the best are tested and selected as rulers and the remainder became soldiers. Rulers pursue higher education comprising arithmetic, geometry, astronomy, the theory of music, which all lead to the highest science dialectic (philosophy).

At the age of 20, men and women are to be selected to be trained in mathematics for ten years. At 30 years old a further selection is made of those who will go on to study philosophy for five years. From 35 to 50 these rulers are to go back to practical life as commanders in war or offices of state. After 50, rulers should contemplate 'the Good', pursuing philosophy and when the time is ripe working in politics.

In the *Republic*, the education of the artisan classes is not covered. In the *Laws*, Plato states that someone who is to be, say, a builder in later life should be given as a child mimic tools with which to practice.

The aim of education is to benefit the individual and serve the safety of the state, because an educated person is a good person who will act nobly and defeat enemies in war.

The humanist tradition in western education was established by Plato, who probably influenced subsequent educational thought more than anyone else before or since.

MF

PLAY

Play is an activity pursued for its own sake, which normally has no serious aim and which is done predominantly for pleasure.

Play can be a great aid to learning. It can involve social skills (taking turns, following and negotiating the rules of a game). Imagination is developed particularly in fantasy games and in role playing. Exploring materials through play can be a helpful precursor to more structured learning about qualities such as size, texture, shape and weight. Social play can particularly encourage and develop language.

In general, play helps children to explore and make sense out of their physical, social and emotional world.

MF

PLAYGROUND SAFETY

Similar principles and guidelines for safety apply to both public and school playgrounds.

Children falling onto hard play surfaces is a major hazard. The areas beneath and around play equipment from which children can fall should be impact absorbing surfacing such as tiles or a wet pour surface.

Play equipment should not be too high. For example, a slide could be built into a natural grassy slope. Swing areas should be clearly demarcated to avoid children inadvertently walking in front of a swing and being knocked over. Swing seats should be made of strong, light material rather than heavy wood. Equipment should be regularly inspected, using a safety checklist, and properly maintained.

Careful but not over zealous supervision is essential. In general, the aim should be to provide opportunities for safe but stimulating and enjoyable play.

MF

POLICE LIAISON

Under the terms of the 1988 EDUCATION ACT it is incumbent upon CHIEF EDUCATION OFFICERS to liaise with Chief Constables to ensure that positive attitudes are generated towards the police. What this means in practice is that many police forces set up schools' liaison schemes using officers to visit schools. Typically such schemes have objectives such as:

- to provide pupils with increased understanding about the role of the police service in the community;
- to establish closer relations between pupils/schools and the police;
- to undertake educative programmes, for example relating to drugs education, the dangers faced in the community (the 'never go with a stranger' programme), or physical dangers (walking over iced ponds in winter);
- to participate with teachers in lessons about social responsibility.

Some forces go so far as to produce lesson materials, linked with the NATIONAL CURRICULUM, which can be used by teachers and/or officers and which are published in textbook format. Related to this work, but often carried out separately, is ROAD SAFETY EDUCATION. Police forces are usually pleased to be approached, often through their community relations branches, by governors or headteachers with a view to closer co-operation.

TLK

POSITIVE MANAGEMENT OF SCHOOLS

Some characteristics of positive management and their negative corollaries:

In attitudes and beliefs:

positive managers	*as opposed to*
have an optimistic belief in education	retreating into pessimism
keep a sense of humour	treating everything indiscriminately seriously
regard managerial situations as opportunities	looking on management situations as a chore

In personality:

positive managers	*as opposed to*
have a determined personality	being timid
show charismatic leadership	deferring decisions
are prepared to take risks	always cautious
are creative in finding solutions	relying on conventional situations

can live with insecurity	fearing to cope with the unknown
prepare a range of solutions	relying on a limited range of strategies
have an interventionist style/take initiatives	being weighed down by the system
keep a view of the future	retreating into history

In actions and strategies:

positive managers	*as opposed to*
consult widely	handing decisions to others
set overall goals (short, medium and long-term)	lacking a sense of direction
accept incremental target attainment	expecting rapid results all the time
can live with intermediate setbacks	seeing setbacks as failure
tackle the attainable	wasting energy on the impossible
nurture colleagues through change	protecting colleagues from change
acting in competition with him/herself	acting in competition with others
manage people effectively	leaving staff to their own devices
handle resources effectively	believing everything is down to poor resourcing
manage plant effectively	allowing surroundings to reflect demoralization

TLK

POST GRADUATE CERTIFICATE IN EDUCATION (PGCE)

This is the standard route to QUALIFIED TEACHER STATUS (QTS) for graduates. It has traditionally consisted of a one-year full-time university course on the theory and practice of teaching, with periods of observation and practice in classrooms. Recently, Government has attempted to modify this route into teaching in various ways:

- by encouraging the development of part-time courses;
- by supporting Institutes of Higher Education to develop distance learning materials to support entry of existing graduates into the profession without the need for full-time attendance;
- by encouraging professional skills to be given a higher profile as teaching competences;
- by increasing the school-based element of the training, in particular the amount of time spent in school and the increased role of teachers as MENTORS;

- by encouraging (consortia of) schools to develop PGCE courses independently of the Institutes of Higher Education.

The content of PGCE courses was strictly controlled by the COUNCIL FOR THE ACCREDITATION OF TEACHER EDUCATION and more recently by the TEACHER TRAINING AGENCY. These bodies deal with funding issues. The Department for Education requires tight syllabus guidelines of PGCE providers.

TLK

POSTGRADUATE STUDY
Any formal qualification or period of study undertaken by someone who is, and is required to be, a graduate at BACHELOR'S DEGREE level before embarking on the study. Some university certificates and diplomas, as well as higher degrees, have this requirement. The commonest example among teachers is the PGCE.

TLK

PREPARATORY SCHOOLS
(See: PRIMARY SCHOOLS)

PRE-PREPARATORY SCHOOLS
(See: PRIMARY SCHOOLS)

PRIMARY SCHOOLS
In England, Wales and Northern Ireland, the years of statutory primary education are 5 to 11 In Scotland, the corresponding ages are 5 to 12. Primary education takes place in one of the following types of school:

- Infant schools for pupils from 5 to 7 years;
- Junior schools for pupils from 7 to 11 years;
- Infant/Junior schools or Junior Mixed Infant (JMI) schools for pupils from 5 to 11 years;
- First Schools for pupils from 5 to 8 or 9 years.

Middle schools deemed primary take children from the age of transfer from First school until the age of 12 or 13 therefore the earlier years of middle school from 8 or 9 to 11 correspond to the years of primary schooling.

Preparatory schools, which take pupils from 8 to 13 years, are independent schools which prepare pupils to take the Common Entrance Examination in order to enter an independent secondary school.

Pre-preparatory schools, which take pupils from 5 to 8 years, are independent schools which prepare pupils for entry to a preparatory school.

MF

PRISON SERVICE EDUCATION

Prison Service Education Deparments throughout establishments in England and Wales provide a wide range of programmes and facilities which mirror educational opportunities in the general community. Opportunities are available for prisoners to improve on their basic skills or vocational skills, whilst on the academic side there is the possibility, in at least 80 establishments, for prisoners to read for a degree with the OPEN UNIVERSITY. Seven London Colleges of Further Education offer a range of full-time Access courses which students from HM Prison Holloway may attend daily on day parole release. A number of prisons have developed links with TECs, which have resulted in imaginative schemes. Prior to 1993 education in the Prison Service was undertaken by LEAs through Colleges of Further Education, but the Government White Paper 'Competing for Quality' meant that in 1993 competitive tendering for the provision of education in prisons was introduced. Further details of HM Prison Service may be obtained from:

HM Prison Service HQ, Cleland House, Page Street, London SW1P 4LN tel: 071 217 3000

CAK

PROFESSIONALISM

Teachers perform according to certain standards of skill and COMPETENCE. Professionalism requires that a teacher has an attitude of always performing to the highest standards and trying to improve (e.g. by using the techniques of REFLECTIVE PRACTITIONER). However, as well as competence, teachers adopt and exhibit values in their work (in areas such as attitudes to pupils and the skills of dealing with parents). Professionalism reflects both the teacher's high level of skill and his/her exhibition of appropriate values.

TLK

PROFESSIONAL DEVELOPMENT

The expression 'professional development' is often used interchangeably with IN-SERVICE EDUCATION, but there are differing nuances of meaning which are explored here. Professional development implies a continuous, career-long process of learning about the teacher's role – not just through attendance at courses and conferences but by the continuing personal reflection and ACTION RESEARCH which becomes an attitude or philosophy of individual PROFESSIONALISM. In this sense, professional development is not just something imposed – as training may be – but something for which the professional takes personal responsibility with a view to meeting carefully thought-out targets. Some local education authorities established PRO-FESSIONAL DEVELOPMENT CENTRES to support this process.

(See also: PROFESSIONAL DEVELOPMENT – schools' responsibilities)

TLK

PROFESSIONAL DEVELOPMENT: SCHOOLS' RESPONSIBILITIES

Headteachers and governors have responsibilities to see that staff in schools receive effective PROFESSIONAL DEVELOPMENT and IN-SERVICE EDUCATION. Much of this is delivered using the five statutory Baker Days available to all schools, but this responsibility does not end there. Schools have to administer GEST training monies. Each school also has to include professional development planning as part of its SCHOOL MANAGEMENT PLAN.

While it remains true that most schools welcome the introduction of 'Baker Days' and these have been regarded widely as a useful part of the teaching calendar, they have nevertheless helped schools to identify a number of key questions about professional development. These questions include the following:

- how can professional development be made to link both individual and institutional needs and aspirations?
- how can schools gain the most effective professional development on these days?
- how can this professional development be made cost-effective?
- how can schools be sure that 'Baker Days' are producing gains for pupils as well as staff?
- how can 'Baker Days' be recommended to parents and the community as both valuable and essential?

No one could doubt, therefore, that institutions in the future need a range of skills which include the following:

- the ability to plan professional development;
- time and opportunity to examine the professional development training market and what it has to offer;

- access to criteria for judging quality of professional development activities;
- financial skills to budget for professional development;
- adequate knowledge to link development to other legal and curriculum requirements;
- opportunities to tailor professional development to be relevant in the context of the appraisal of individual teachers and lecturers;
- skills in promoting professional development to parents, governors and the public;
- increased accountability for decisions about professional development policy;
- organizational skills in using professional development from a range of providers and tailoring it to meet the needs of the institution;
- the ability to ensure that professional development affects classroom teaching performance, leading to enhanced results by pupils and students;
- skills in providing training experiences for a teaching force which is becoming increasingly sophisticated, and who increasingly compare their experiences with those of the world of business and commerce.

TLK

PROFILE COMPONENTS
(See: ASSESSMENT IN THE NATIONAL CURRICULUM)

PROGRAMMED LEARNING
Learning which allows the use of linear and branching computer programs to aid the student. Early programmed learning was a relatively limited affair, but with developments such as CD-ROM can now be very sophisticated: whole encyclopaedias including illustrations can be called up, for example
(See also: COMPUTER ASSISTED LEARNING)

TLK

PROGRAMMES OF STUDY (PoS) IN THE NATIONAL CURRICULUM
Programmes of study comprise the subject matter, skills and processes which are taught to pupils during each Key Stage so that they are able to meet the objectives set out in the attainment targets.

For example, in English the PoS are defined as follows:

1. Speaking and listening:
   (a) for KS1
   (b) for KS2 to 4.
   These cover the range of situations, audiences and activities designed
   to develop pupils' competence, precision and confidence in speaking
   and listening.
2. Reading:
   (a) for KS1
   (b) for KS2
   (c) for KS3 and 4.
   These cover the range of reading material and the knowledge, skills
   and understanding to be developed.
3. Writing, spelling and handwriting:
   (a) for KS1
   (b) for KS2
   (c) for KS3 and 4.
   These cover the range of contexts, purposes and audiences for writing;
   the conventions of writing and the knowledge about written language to
   be developed.

As will be apparent, the PoS in English are related to Key Stages and
each PoS contains general provisions for the PoS as a whole as well as
detailed provisions for the Key Stage(s) which it covers. For most English
attainment targets the detailed provisions include material specifying what
pupils working towards a particular level should experience.

Examples of PoS can be found in the entries for the various subjects of
the National Curriculum.

MF

PROJECT WORK

Project work is a descriptor sometimes used synonymously in the primary
school with TOPIC WORK. Here, we shall deal with it as the descriptor of
work undertaken by pupils on a specific theme, usually in the secondary
school. In this sense, project work is usually a sustained piece of personal
investigation or study, on a given theme, usually resulting in a file of written
work or a report. At KEY STAGE 4 it may be part of the assessed work for a
GCSE course, alongside examination work. Teachers tend to favour the
use of project work because it captures pupils' interest, it develops
investigational skills, it requires knowledge to be applied, it asks pupils to
discipline themselves to use conventions of presentation and it teaches time
management. It has spin-offs in that pupils have to develop skills in

accessing libraries and other sources and in taking personal responsibility for their work. Pupils, too, usually report positively about project work for similar reasons, though for pupils undertaking a lot of subjects there is a danger of project overload. Recently, as part of its campaign for higher standards in education, the Government has tried to diminish the quantity and role of project work in schools. It is alleged that objective testing forces teachers to develop a more consistent curriculum and that objective testing 'proves' the better acquisition of knowledge. These apparent advantages of the test over project work are unproven – and probably unprovable. Project work more nearly mirrors the kinds of skills most adults have to undertake in daily occupational lives.

TLK

PSYCHOLOGIST

There are many ways in which a psychologist can help a child at school either by working through teachers or by working directly with the child.

Educational psychologists are normally required to have taught and then pursue further training to qualify in educational psychology. They may advise a school on educational and psychological matters such as the use of tests, and the education of children with learning and behaviour difficulties. They may also carry out assessments of pupils. Parents and others may contact an educational psychologist through the child's school, the school psychological services, the family doctor or child guidance clinic. If a child has emotional and/or behavioural difficulties, then a clinical psychologist or a child psychotherapist may help. They could offer counselling or psychotherapy for the family or for the child. Points of contact are child guidance clinics, hospital paediatric departments, private clinics or the family doctor.

MF

PSYCHOLOGY AND EDUCATION

Psychology is a social science concerned with the systematic study of human (or animal) behaviour. The behaviour may be overt (observable) or covert (mental states and processes). Methods used in psychology include both introspection and observation.

Educational psychology seeks to apply findings and principles from general, social and child psychology to education. In particular, it helps us to understand the learning process better, not just factual learning but social and moral learning too.

It studies the behaviour of children and adults comprising physical, mental, social and emotional behaviour. Through this, educational psychology seeks to establish what affects the quality and quantity of learning.

Studying individuals in various settings it develops hypotheses about the conditions of learning, which can be tested. We can assess the similarities and differences between individual learners. This helps us to provide for them more effective settings for learning. Educational psychology enables us to evaluate the strengths and weakness of teachers and learners.

Among the topics included in the remit of psychology and education are motivation, perception, learning theories, memory, intelligence, personality, creativity and special needs.

Further reading

Child, D. (1981) *Psychology and the Teacher* (third edition) (Holt, Rinehart and Winston).
Kutnick, P. (1994) 'Development and Learning' in the series Farrell, M. (Ed.), *Education for Teaching* (HMSO).

MF

PUBLIC SCHOOLS
In England and Wales, public schools are independent schools with a particular historical reason for acquiring the name. Among independent schools, certain elite boarding establishments came to be known as 'great' schools in the eighteenth century partly because they were attended by the sons of aristocratic families.

These included the following:

Winchester (founded in 1382 by bishop William of Wykeham);
Eton (founded in 1440 by Henry VI);
St Paul's (reconstituted by Dean Colet in 1508);
Shrewsbury (founded in 1552 as a King Edward VI Grammar School);
Westminster (refounded in 1560 by Elizabeth I);
Merchant Taylors' (established 1561 by the Merchant Taylors' Company);
Rugby (founded in 1567 by Lawrence Sheriff, a wealthy grocer);
Harrow (founded in 1571 by John Lyon, a yeoman of the parish);
Charterhouse (founded in 1611 as a London city charity school).

In the eighteenth century it was legitimate to call any endowed schools 'public' schools to distinguish them from the private schools. In time however, the so-called great schools came to be known as public schools and the more general use fell away.

The Clarendon Commission reported in 1864 on the nine schools listed above. The School Enquiry Commission (the Taunton Commission) reported in 1868 on endowed, proprietary, and private schools. The distinction implied in having two separate Commissions for the great schools and others which in some cases were very similar led to a certain amount of resentment among some headmasters, for example Edward Thring, the headmaster of Uppingham. The result was that the Head-masters' Conference was formed which became the voice of the public schools. A definition of a public school today is therefore a school which is a member of the Headmasters' Conference.

In Scotland a public school is a state school, that is one available to the general population of children. In the United States of America, a public school is also a state school.

MF

PUNISHMENT

Punishments are one factor in schools' efforts to maintain DISCIPLINE; though to administer a punishment means that all else has failed. Every school should have a policy on discipline, set out in its SCHOOL MANAGEMENT PLAN and published to parents. The range of sanctions approved by the school should be stated, and all teachers should adhere to this code. Ultimate sanctions, such as EXCLUSION, will rest with the headteacher. Corporal punishments should form no part of a punishment policy. These have often been regular occurrences in state schools in times past – some of them official, such as caning; some of them unofficial, such as the pro-verbial 'clip round the ear'. Neither is now acceptable, although some inde-pendent schools do maintain beating as a punishment. Teachers who do punish children must be aware that case law has set precedents that lay down that all punishments should be such as a reasonable parent might use. It should be in accordance with the school code, be moderate, and not admin-istered from wrong motives (for example, in the heat of anger or because of personal dislike). Reasonable punishments might include extra work, detention, a telling-off or being sent to a senior member of staff. In more serious cases, students may be 'put on report', or parents might be brought in to discuss the child's behaviour. Though it cannot always be avoided, punishment should be a last resort. Teachers are better advised to improve CLASS MANAGEMENT skills so as to anticipate and then forestall problems.

TLK

QUAKER EDUCATION

Quaker schools in England were founded originally for the children of Friends, but for many years now have welcomed pupils from all creeds and

faiths and from a wide variety of backgrounds and nationalities. Pupils are encouraged to co-operate with others and to compete against themselves, seeking high standards in all areas of life. Each school offers a rich variety of artistic, musical, athletic and other creative pursuits as well as setting high academic standards. Quaker schools seek to develop within their pupils a self-discipline that is sensitive to the needs and interests of others, and to make pupils aware of the values of compassion and tolerance through Quaker belief and experience. Quaker education offers co-educational facilities within a boarding atmosphere, though day places are available for children who wish to attend a Quaker school and who live in close proximity. Further information may be obtained from:
The Friends Schools Joint Council, Friends House, Euston Road, London NW1 2BJ.

CAK

QUALIFIED TEACHER STATUS
The recognition by the DEPARTMENT FOR EDUCATION that a person is trained to be a teacher in a state school. Qualified teacher status is conferred after successful completion of:

- a B.ED DEGREE;
- other equivalent degrees;
- a subject degree plus a PGCE;
- a LICENSED TEACHER course;
- a recognized teaching qualification in an overseas country.

TLK

QUESTIONING: PROBING SKILLS
In looking at QUESTIONING in the classroom we indicated that this was a global TEACHING SKILL, made up of sub-skills. One of these sub-skills is that of 'probing'.

The purpose of probing is not simply 'to keep the conversation going'. Inexperienced teachers or students often feel that they have done well if they keep the pupils talking regardless of the quality and relevance of the ideas being expressed. In Turney's view probing is questioning in order to sustain thinking. This probing serves a number of purposes:

1. *To clarify*: here the pupil has to re-phrase a response or idea. In other words, to make it more accessible, e.g. 'What do you mean by the phrase "higher class"?'

2. *To support a point of view*: the teacher can seek evidence to sustain an argument the pupil has advanced, e.g. 'What leads you to say that Shaw is prejudiced?'

3. *To seek a degree of consensus*: here the teacher involves the rest of the class to test that they agree or disagree with the speaker and to make them feel involved, e.g. 'Which of you would share Jane's opinion?'

4. *To test accuracy*: the respondent is asked to produce or suggest a proof of a statement made, e.g. 'How could you test your theory to show that it must hold true in all circumstances?'

5. *To ensure relevance*: the teacher asks the pupil to demonstrate that a statement does, in fact, bear on the topic, e.g. 'Why do you think, John, that his age is important to the way he acts?'

6. *To elicit examples*: this helps pupils to apply knowledge across a range of situations or to support a generalization by specific citing of concrete examples, e.g. 'You say colour in animals can be a means of camouflage, Ann; what examples can you think of among birds, moths or fish?'

7. *To raise a consciousness of complexity*: a pupil may stumble upon a good idea but be only partially aware of its significance. The teacher can help highlight the other facts by further questioning, e.g. 'Your religion will determine some of your moral attitudes, but what other experiences will also fashion this moral sense?'

The skill of probing helps teachers to get pupils to think more deeply and more widely, often about issues they themselves have raised. It is beneficial, too, in helping pupils to express more fully and clearly what they have in mind. Practised over a long period with a class it will improve pupils' willingness to talk, their construction of responses and their grasp of thinking skills. *They will eventually probe their own thoughts without stimulus from the teacher, and the whole level of classroom dialogue will improve in quality.*

TLK

Further reading

Turney, C. (1975) *Sydney Micro Skills Series 2* (University of Sydney).

RACIAL DISCRIMINATION

Race is usually taken to include a person's colour, nationality or ethnic origins. The Race Relations Act 1976 forbids direct or indirect discrimination. Schools and colleges in both the state and independent sectors must not discriminate:

- in the terms offered for admission to an educational establishment;
- by refusing (or deliberately not accepting) an application for admission;
- in the way a student is given access to benefits, facilities or services;
- by excluding a student.

Under DES circular 16/89, LEA schools and Grant Maintained schools have to collect ethnically related data. This concerns pupils entering primary or secondary school. Parents are asked to volunteer information on their child's ethnic origin, religion and language spoken at home.

The Commission for Racial Equality considers evidence of discrimination and provides advice. It holds a list of addresses of local Community Relations Councils and publishes a variety of information leaflets.
Details may be obtained from:
The Commission for Racial Equality (CRE), Elliot House,
10–12 Allington Street, London SW1E 5EH
tel: 071 828 7022

MF

RATIONALITY

An aim of education is to encourage rationality, so it is important to be clear about the term. Rationality centres on the process of reasoning brought to bear on knowledge, attitudes, beliefs, values, feelings and behaviour. A rational argument coherently moves from premises to conclusions in reasoned, relevant steps which follow logically from one another. If you are a rational person, you value rationality and behave accordingly. You reflect and form opinions based on reason rather than say because such opinions are held by others in positions of power. You seek relevant information, pose pertinent questions and consider alternative views before coming to an informed judgement. Encouraging and developing such capacities in learners is at the heart of education.

MF

READINESS

The term readiness has been used in connection with child-centred education pertaining to the method of educating. In child-centred education, teaching should take place when the child is 'ready'.

Two uses of 'ready' emerge. Firstly, it can mean being able to carry out a task with some success. In this uncontentious sense we talk of readiness to read. This implies that there is a physiological and psychological 'readiness' which makes learning to read possible and that logical steps preceding reading have been taken, for example, recognizing that marks on paper have a relation to making sounds.

A second more restrictive meaning is that someone:

(a)   has an ability;
(b)   is interested in demonstrating the ability;
(c)   recognizes he has the ability.

It is the second sense that seems to be meant by child centred theorists. However, it is unlikely that teachers would want to defer teaching every topic or task until a child had shown these three criteria. Decisions would need to be made at some point that although a child had not shown an interest, it was time to try to encourage interest in reading (or whatever).

MF

READING: METHODS OF TEACHING

There is no single recognized way of teaching a student to read. Methods commonly in use are as follows:

1.   *Phonic approaches* in which students learn sounds and letters, analyse and synthesize words from the beginning, i.e. work attack skills.
2.   *Look-and-say method* – in which words are taught as a 'sight vocabulary'. The method can be built into sentence recognition. Having acquired a 'vocabulary' children progress to a reader, generally adding new words.
3.   *The learner-centred or language experience approach* – in which students are exposed to books and a stimulating language environment. The student wants to record his/her experiences and the teacher writes for him/her – this is the first reader.
4.   *Individualized approaches* – in which the student, surrounded by a variety of materials, self-selects items of interest and then is helped by the teacher towards accessing them.

Generally a mixture of methods 1, 3 and 4 are seen in classrooms. Primary schools should set out their reading policies in the SCHOOL BROCHURE so that parents who want to help their children can use appropriate methods and materials.

TLK

RECORD KEEPING

Schools are required to keep a record of each child on the register which includes the following information:

- academic achievement;
- skills and abilities;
- progress made.
- attendance absence;

School records may also include:

- reports from people outside the school (e.g. a social worker);
- information on a pupil's development;
- information on home background.

Records must be updated annually or more frequently. From 1990, certain aspects of records became available to the interested parties. In the case of a registered pupil up to the age of 18 years the parents may have access to certain aspects of the record. Regarding a pupil of 16 years or older, the pupil may view the record.

Parents of pupils over 16 years old who wish to see the records should write to the school governing body. It is they who are responsible for ensuring that the records are maintained and they must comply with the request within fifteen school days. Schools must give the opportunity for any inaccuracies in the educational records to be corrected.

Among aspects of the record which may not be viewed are the following:

- ethnic data on the individual pupil;
- any reference on the pupil written either for a prospective employer or for another educational establishment to which the pupil may be intending to transfer;
- school reports on the pupil written for Juvenile Courts; information which could identify another pupil;
- any information which, if revealed, could cause serious harm to anyone;
- any information related to child abuse (actual or alleged).

Records kept by teachers of each pupil's work have always been important, for without such records, the teacher is unable to, for example:

- monitor a pupil's progress;
- compare the pupil with others of the same age group;
- diagnose difficulties so appropriate remedial action can be taken.

The NATIONAL CURRICULUM seeks to systematize such record keeping.

Records need to be selective, for it is clearly not appropriate to record information simply because it is possible to assess it. However, records should identify individual pupil achievements against all the applicable

National Curriculum ATTAINMENT TARGETS. Such records need to be frequently and systematically updated in order to form a basis for reporting attainment and progress to parents. Samples of pupils' work are used as evidence to support the teacher's records.

The OFSTED guidance is that teachers should ensure that they use records effectively to regularly review pupils' progress and set appropriate targets for the future. Good records can help teachers to evaluate how effective their teaching programmes are and can influence curricular planning and lesson preparation.

Records can be used to assist continuity and progression when a pupil moves from one teacher to another or from one school to another. Also they can help teachers to assign pupils to teaching groups formed according to certain criteria. Records should be used to decide on the entry tiers for pupils regarding national tests and General Certificate of Secondary Education examinations.

Records of achievement are commonly used in schools. Often, they are employed as a process which recognizes positive attitudes and achievements and gives the opportunity for pupils and teachers to engage in a dialogue. Because such records, in practice, often reflect affective skills (rather than cognitive skills), it is important for records and profiles to be updated to:

* cover the whole range of pupils' skills;
* set specific targets for pupils and teachers to address in both general and subject-specific contexts;
* take full account of National Curriculum requirements.

Such record can help to support an integrated process for assessment, recording and reporting. DFE circular 14/92 strongly advises schools to use the National Record of Achievement as a vehicle for this purpose.

Further reading

Office for Standards in Education (1993) Handbook for the Inspection of Schools, Part 5, Technical Papers, Paper 5, Assessment, recording and reporting (HMSO).

                                                                    MF

RECORDS OF ACHIEVEMENT
As from January 1993 new regulations came into force which required all secondary schools to give leavers a record of their achievements, using the

National Record of Achievement. It is expected that students will present their record when applying for admission to further or higher education, or when they go for work interviews.

Under these regulations changes were also made to the style of the annual report to parents about their child's progress. Included in the more detailed individual reports, comparative information on their children's contemporaries in the same school and nationally will be given. Records of accomplishments will now be passed on to the new school when a pupil/ student transfers.

CAK

RECURRENT EDUCATION
(See: ADULT EDUCATION)

REFLECTIVE PRACTITIONER
A term used to describe a teacher who reviews his/her own practice systematically, perhaps using research tools. The term often refers to participants in ACTION RESEARCH. It is a desirable outcome of PROFESSIONALISM. The reflective practitioner uses skills of analysis to experiment with TEACHING SKILLS with a view to extending personal PROFESSIONAL DEVELOPMENT. A reflective practitioner could be described as a dynamic and continually growing professional.

TLK

REFLECTIVE PRACTITIONER MODEL
Reflective teachers exhibit key characteristics which mark them out as engaging in constant self-appraisal by:

- a concern with aims and consequences;
- constant self-monitoring and evaluation;
- awareness of techniques and CLASSROOM RESEARCH;
- open-mindedness to change;
- a willingness to discuss with, and learn from, others.

Further reading

Pollard and Tann (1987) *Reflective teaching in the Primary School: a handbook for the classroom* (second edition) (Cohen Cassell: London).

TLK

REGISTERED INSPECTORS

Registered inspectors will be at the heart of the new system of school inspection set up under the Education (Schools) Act. From September 1993 in the case of secondary schools and from September 1994 in the case of primary and special schools, most full inspections of the school will be arranged by Her Majesty's Chief Inspector of Schools in England (HMCI) and will be undertaken by teams of independent inspectors led by registered inspectors.

Once the programme of inspections for each term has been decided, registered inspectors may be invited to tender for the inspection of the schools included in the programme, on the basis of specifications prepared by HMCI in consultation with the schools' governing bodies. Before tendering, registered inspectors will need to select their INSPECTION TEAMS (drawn from those who have satisfactorily completed the requisite course of training, and including at least one LAY INSPECTOR).

Once they have secured a contract, they will be responsible for the conduct of the inspection, including the deployment of the inspection team, and for providing written reports, including a summary report for parents. The Act also requires the registered inspector to hold a meeting with parents before the inspection takes place. The conduct of inspections and the format of the written reports will be the subject of registration set down by HMCI or of guidance issued by him.

To be registered as an inspector, a person will need to satisfy HMCI:

(a) that he/she is a fit and proper person to perform the functions of a registered inspector;

(b) that he/she will be capable of conducting inspections competently and efficiently.

To enable HMCI to form a judgement on (b) above, potential registered inspectors will need satisfactorily to complete a training course, part of which will involve participation in an institutional inspection run by HMI. They will, therefore, be invited first to apply for training.

If the training requirements are satisfied, an intending inspector may apply for registration. If successful, he or she will receive the appropriate documentation and the right to enter designated schools for the purpose of inspection. Under Section 10 (5) (c) of the Act, HMCI may impose conditions, either general or specific, on an inspector's registration. Those who fail to abide by any such conditions will be removed from the register. One condition that will be applied to all registered inspectors will be a requirement to use the Inspection Framework set out by HMCI. Other conditions, which would be particular to individual inspectors, may relate to length of registration or phase of inspection. Registered inspectors have the right to appeal to a specially constituted tribunal against the imposition (or variation) of any condition.

The training for potential registered inspectors comprises:

(a) a five-day course (or equivalent) in the use of the Framework for Inspection;
(b) participation in an institutional inspection conducted by HMI.

The course concentrates on:

(a) the scope and conduct of the inspection as set down by HMCI;
(b) the inspection of standards achieved (outcomes) and the quality of a school's educational provision and the factors that contribute to those standards and that quality;
(c) the evaluation criteria for making inspection judgements;
(d) the completion of schedules for the inspection;
(e) the preparation and presentation of reports for governors, parents and the public; and
(f) procedural matters.

Potential registered inspectors will be assessed on their performance during the course. If they are judged satisfactorily to have completed the course, they will be invited to participate in an HMI institutional inspection to take place as soon as can be arranged after the end of the course. Participation in an HMI inspection will provide potential registered inspectors with opportunities:

(a) to observe HMI at work;
(b) to undertake inspection tasks under supervision;
(c) to compare their judgement with those of HMI; and
(d) to present inspection findings in the required ways.

In exceptional circumstances HMI may waive some or all of the requirements for training; for example, if the intending registered inspector can prove to HMI's satisfaction that he/she is already competent to use the FRAMEWORK FOR INSPECTION without further training.

TLK

RELIGIOUS EDUCATION (AND THE BASIC CURRICULUM)
Religious education (RE) is not one of the ten subjects of the National Curriculum. But all pupils aged 4 to 19 in maintained schools in England

and Wales must study religious education, which constitutes part of the 'basic curriculum' under the Education Act (Education Reform Act).

The Education Act 1944 and the ERA form the basis of the legal structure affecting religious education in schools. Under the Education Act 1944 maintained schools cannot attempt to convert pupils or try to impose upon them a specific religion or denomination, although this does not apply to voluntary aided or special agreement schools.

All LEAs must form a Standing Advisory Council for Religious Education (SACRE). This body:

- will advise the LEA on matters relating to religious education and collective worship;
- is empowered to require the LEA to set up an Agreed Syllabus Conference.

This conference comprises representatives from the Church of England, other Christian denominations, other religions, teachers and elected members. RE teaching in maintained schools has to follow the Agreed Syllabus for the LEA produced by the Agreed Syllabus Conference except in the case of aided and special agreement schools.

In drafting an Agreed Syllabus the Conference assumed that a reasonable time can be devoted to RE, which would have equal standing with NC subjects. Conferences can recommend including in the Agreed Syllabus locally agreed ATs, PoS and assessment arrangements. They can also devise and seek approval for their own syllabuses for GCSE (Circular 3/89, Religious Education and Collective Worship).

The content of the Agreed Syllabus should be based on the traditions, practices and teaching of Christianity and other principal world religions. It should extend to morality and a consideration of the effect on people's everyday life of religious beliefs and practices. It would take account of the national and local position and population.

Two broad aims of most Agreed Syllabuses developed since 1988 are that pupils should:

1. Understand the teachings and practices of Christianity and other world religions.
2. Be encouraged to develop their own beliefs and values.

Through balancing these two areas, RE can contribute to the spiritual, moral, cultural and intellectual development of pupils. Many Agreed Syllabuses include ATs and PoS although this is not a statutory requirement. In some syllabuses, ATs are based on content areas such as 'beliefs'. In others there are a few processed-based ATs (e.g. interpretations of expressions of religion) which are applied to all the content in the PoS.

Because Agreed Syllabuses are devised locally, there is variation from one LEA to another in the religions studied and the balance between the teaching of Christianity and other religions. But key concepts and issues appear in most syllabuses (e.g. beliefs about God and sacred texts). RE encourages certain attitudes such as open mindedness and respect for others' views and ways of life. RE in most syllabuses seeks to address questions of universal concern (e.g. Why am I here? or What happens after death?). Addressing these questions, pupils will usually examine the responses of the religions which they are studying.

Where possible, pupils should pursue an RE course to GCSE. Where appropriate, RE work should be assessed and reported. RE teaching should be qualitatively equal to that of other National Curriculum subjects.

It should be remembered that, should the parent request it, a maintained school pupil must be excused religious education. Teachers may also withdraw from teaching RE.

MF

REWARDS (USE OF)

Schools use rewards as one factor in maintaining DISCIPLINE. Some would argue that only intrinsic reward is really valuable: for example, for a student to feel he/she has done well and to be satisfied with a task well done. But few people are genuinely satisfied with intrinsic reward: most need some outward assurance about their performance. Thus most teachers use extrinsic rewards, for example, by putting 'good' on work, giving praise or awarding stars. Sometimes such extrinsic rewards become part of a school's overall strategy of management. Typically, such rewards include announce-ments in assembly, prize-giving, honours boards, or symbols (special ties or coloured braid on jackets to denote sporting 'colours', etc.). These extrinsic rewards may play an important role in setting the SCHOOL ETHOS. Some rewards are better avoided: such as the teacher who awards sweets for good behaviour. Similarly, rewards may give out undesirable messages. A child praised in front of others may become the butt of unwelcome jibes from others. Commonest rewards are praise, or a smile, but teachers should always be conscious of what behaviour is being rewarded and why, and the effect on the recipient and others.

TLK

ROAD SAFETY

The Local Authority has a statutory duty to provide Road Safety Officers as defined in the Road Traffic Acts of 1974 and 1988. Road Safety Officers have a duty towards all sectors of the community and their involvement with schools and school children falls within that remit. With the advent of the National Curriculum many authorities chose to strengthen the ties between Road Safety Officers and teachers by reinforcing Road Safety principles linked to National Attainment Targets and aligned with objectives in National Curriculum Council Curriculum Guidance 5 – Health Education. Road Safety Officers are available to advise teachers on how best to integrate Road Safety into the curriculum, with many local authorities producing excellent teaching aids and packs. Many Road Safety Officers are directly involved with young people through Cycling Proficiency training and testing, and for this and other activities may be contacted at the local County Council offices.

CAK

ROLE
Role is a sociological concept often applied to education. It has its roots in drama, where the actor modifies behaviour to conform with those expected of the character he/she is playing. In the same way, in our social and professional lives we act out roles expected of us: breadwinner, protector, mother, lover, headteacher, student, novice, elder statesman/woman. In any social structure those to whom we are responsible and those for whom we are responsible will have certain expectations of our role, often based on precedent. But, overall, we all play many roles, slipping from one to the other unconsciously most of the time. Similarly, people who share our role – other headteachers, students – may feel we should conform to the (often unwritten) norms of that role: to dress in a dark suit, or to avoid 'sucking up' to teachers. Even within a professional life a teacher will play many roles: instructor, manager, facilitator, adviser, counsellor, nurse etc. When someone is reluctant to fulfil the unwritten norms of his/her role and wishes to act differently (the headteacher coming to school in shorts, perhaps) then role-conflict arises. Social behaviour takes place through the medium of role, and thus it is educationally useful to empathize with others through ROLE-PLAY.

TLK

ROLE OF THE TEACHER
Teachers play many ROLES during a typical career, e.g.:

Instructor
Adviser
Friend

Confidante
Disciplinarian
Counsellor
Referee
Facilitator
Resource
Hero
Judge.

These roles are often played in quick succession and help to define some of the variety of the teaching profession as well as its demanding nature.

TLK

ROLE-PLAY

Teachers sometimes ask pupils to play a ROLE other than their normal ones as a way of educating them in empathy and providing insights into human situations. For example, a rather jejeune example might be that, in order more fully to understand a poem about blindness, the teacher may ask a pupil to be blindfolded and put into a strange environment (with, of course, proper safety precautions). The pupil would then experience and experiment with the sensation of blindness – play the role of a blind person. Afterwards he/she would have a little more empathy with blind people and be able to describe that experience to others. The same technique might be used in the INITIAL or IN-SERVICE TRAINING of teachers themselves. One way to learn about attending a job interview, for example, would be for some members of the group to play interviewers and for one to play the interviewee. By experiencing the process of being interviewed through role-play the teacher would be more prepared for the reality of an actual interview; and by analysing his/her performance he/she might modify performance for the real thing.

TLK

ROTE LEARNING

Rote learning is associated with TRADITIONALIST EDUCATION and is often denigrated as an inferior method of learning which relegates understanding to second place behind the mindless memorizing of facts. However, if the reasons for using rote learning are thought through by the teacher, it can be justified as a method. For example, once multiplication is understood, there is nothing intrinsically wrong with rote learning tables. Indeed such learning can save a great deal of tedious working out for the pupil.

MF

ROUSSEAU, JEAN-JACQUES (1712–1778)

Rousseau was born in Geneva in 1712. He was a man of literature and a philosopher. He was a citizen of Europe, his ideas on government underpinned the French Revolution, and he died in 1778. His importance to education is due to the publication of his book '*Emile*', which was part of a trilogy that aimed to show how the 'natural man' could be formed and educated. The book is divided into five sections. The first, dealing with infancy, emphasized the importance of satisfying natural physical wants and of physical liberty. The second, on boyhood, rings oddly to our ears because it promulgates the view that education of boys should be different from that of girls. The development of speech is emphasized; liberty is still seen as a key concept; there should be a balance between freedom and happiness; but instruction is through direct experience and sensory methods. Early adolescence is dealt with in part three. Attention switches to mental, i.e. cognitive activity, but the medium of learning is still by doing, by active observation, by experience of nature and by tackling problems as they arise. At this stage Rousseau believes that Emile should still be shielded from reading books as from moral instruction. These were held back for adolescence itself (15–20 years), dealt with in part four of the book. Now moral, aesthetic and social issues can be introduced, and a study of history – the realistic portrayal of man – can commence. At this stage, Emile was introduced to polite society and his taste educated through exposure to literature and drama. Thus he shapes up to be a citizen and a head of a household. In part five Emile encounters sex education and marriage; while his partner learns 'female' accomplishments. Of course, *Emile* was written in a context very different from our own; it was extremely controversial and forward-thinking at the time. It contained a series of seminal ideas which have influenced primary education in particular ever since, and can be traced in much more modern documents such as the PLOWDEN REPORT. These ideas included a view of the world as naturally good, but spoiled by humankind. But 'nature wants children to be children before they are men', so that education should be a natural process. A corollary of this view is that education should be child-centred, and what is taught should only be that 'which is befitting his age'. Rousseau's attitude to discipline is one of 'natural consequences' – a view perhaps echoed by pioneers such as A. S. Neill at Summerhill. So education comes through experience and 'work and play are all one' – a key principle of much primary practice today. In Rousseau's view education has to develop the individual into a self-disciplined adult; but that individual must function with society, equipped with appropriate awareness. These ideas echo today's PERSONAL AND SOCIAL EDUCATION, and education for citizenship. Rousseau's significance is two-fold:

first in his influence on the philosophy of education and second in the enduring modernity of many of his ideas.

TLK

SAFETY OF PLAYGROUNDS
(See: PLAYGROUND SAFETY)

SANDWICH COURSES
Training and work experience in industry or commerce or in one of the professions can be 'sandwiched' with courses of study at an institution of higher or further education. One of the benefits of this is that the 'on-the-job' experience can inform the study and vice versa making the study relevant and setting the work experience in a wider context. In the case of technical and vocational courses, the employer may provide financial support for the student.

MF

SCHOOL BROCHURE
Each school has to publish a brochure giving specific information about the school relating to items such as admission procedures, details of the school year and day, names of head and chairperson of governors, curriculum content and homework policy, sex education, examination procedures, how the teaching is organized, arrangements for children with special educational needs, the policy on charging for activities, whether school uniform is required, and details of clubs, societies and other extracurricular activity. The brochure must also include National Curriculum Tests for the school and compare them with local and national results. Secondary school brochures must detail examination results. Rates of unauthorized absence should also be included.

As well as being a statutory requirement, the publication of the School Brochure allows the headteacher and governors to set out in writing their aims and objectives for the future of the school and their aspirations for those pupils who attend.

CAK

SCHOOL DRESS
School dress normally refers to clothing and footwear which are appropriate for wearing in school, but which are not identical from person to person (see SCHOOL UNIFORM). As a compromise between the school dress/school

uniform issue, many schools now take the stance of suggesting a uniform colour.

CAK

SCHOOL ENVIRONMENT

The first impression that a parent or other visitor gains of a school is of the school environment. While the quality of learning is dependent on many factors (e.g. TEACHER EFFECTIVENESS, SCHOOL ETHOS, the INTELLECTUAL CLIMATE and EFFECTIVE MANAGEMENT), the environment of the school repays regular and critical scrutiny. Rather than lay down rules which might not apply in individual cases, this entry provides a useful check-list that can be used by a head, a parent, a governor, to assess the impact of the school's environment.

A guide to looking at a school

Enter the building like a potential visitor would:

- Is it welcoming?
- Are there signs to tell me where to go?
- If there are signs, are they of the 'No parents beyond this sign' variety?
- Is there anyone around to greet/help me?
- Is there a foyer or entrance space?
- Is this space welcoming?
- Is there somewhere for visitors to sit?
- Something for them to do? Look at?
- Is there up-to-date information about the school?

Walk round the corridors:

- Are they clean?
- Free of graffiti?
- Are there notice-boards?
- Are the notices neat? Up-to-date?
- Is there any children's work?
- What about litter?
- How do pupils behave on corridors?
- Are corridors obstruction free and safe?

Look outside:

- Is the playground tidy?
- Are there games pitches marked out?

- Are there seats?
- Is the field in a good state?
- Is there an 'environmental studies' area?

Now try the hall:

- Does it look as if it is used for learning?
- Are storage areas properly used?
- If it has a stage, is this just a 'tip behind curtains'?
- Would *you* want to use it?

TLK

SCHOOL LIBRARY SERVICE (SLS)

A Schools Library Service is run by the Local Education Authority and provides a lending library of additional materials and advice on all aspects of the school library. The aims of the SLS include:

- providing the best resources to enable teachers to deliver the National Curriculum and post 16 courses;
- enabling teachers, school librarians, governors and parents to use the professional expertise of the SLS to develop, maintain and evaluate school libraries at the heart of the curriculum;
- providing a gateway to the vast network of resources outside the school library;
- providing information, advice, practical help and initiatives in the field of learning-resource provision.

Membership of the Schools Library Service is open to all schools within the area of the authority, but many services are now delegated and a charge may be made. Further information about the Service may be obtained from the Local Education Authority for the area in which the school is situated.

CAK

SCHOOL MANAGEMENT PLAN

All schools are required to compile and update annually a school management and development plan. This plan reviews and sets targets for: the available plant; the school's finances; the staffing; the curriculum; the broader issues, e.g. of community and parental relations, etc., The school management plan is best drawn up by the headteacher in consultation with staff, and then presented for discussion to GOVERNORS. LEAS are required to monitor these plans, which must be available during INSPECTIONS.

TLK

SCHOOL MANAGEMENT TASK FORCE

A group of experienced heads appointed by the government to investigate improvements to management in schools. The School Management Task Force reported in 1990:

School Management Task Force (1990) *Developing School Management: the way forward* (DES: London).

TLK

SCHOOL MEALS

School meals were first prepared in 1840 for needy children attending ragged schools (a free elementary school for poor children), but it was not until a century later that they were introduced as a universal right for any child whose parent wished him or her to have them. After World War Two school meals became an integral part of the welfare state, and this reached a peak in the 1970s when school meals provided one-third of the child's daily nutritional needs. This continued until the 1980 Education Act, which allowed LEAs/schools to abandon school meals provision for all except those entitled by law to free school meals. Six years later the Local Government Act (1986) put the school meals service out to competitive tendering, and these two actions combined to introduce a system whereby the availability of hot meals during the day for schoolchildren depends entirely upon the system in operation in the locality in which they live. In authorities where hot meals are available, the aim of the providing agent is to make available to all children at school a varied, wholesome and nutritionally balanced midday meal. Meals may be cooked on or off the school premises, may be at a fixed price or may be cash-cafeteria style. Generally a wide variety of food is provided, with an emphasis lately on vegetarian options being available. For those pupils who do not wish to take advantage of the school meals on offer and who bring a packed lunch, provision must be made for them to eat their lunch. In authorities where school meals still have a high profile, emphasis is placed on relating the provision of midday meals to the school curriculum, and thus, over a period of time, altering some of the children's eating habits. One such project is funded by the East Berkshire Health Authority Health Promotion Unit who work together with local schools on a scheme known as 'The Eating Habit School Meals Project'. Close liaison between the Health Authority, schools and providers has resulted in a pack brim-full of ideas which involves parents, teachers, governors, children and school meals staff. School meals have in the past attracted the attention of authorities looking to make financial cuts in areas not directly involving face-to-face education, and there are fears that, within the next decade, school meals as previously known may disappear altogether.

CAK

SCHOOL MEDICAL STAFF

The school health service is part of the National Health Service. Each District Health Authority has a senior doctor responsible for school health who leads a team which conducts medical inspections in schools. The team includes a school doctor, nurse and dentist.

Parental permission is not required to examine a child showing signs of infection, vermin (e.g. head lice) or abuse. Otherwise parents may refuse to have their child examined or may be present at the inspection.

MF

SCHOOL PHOBIA

School phobia is a somewhat over-used and inaccurately used term. It is not necessarily the sign of a problem (although it may be) that a child is occasionally reluctant to attend school. School phobia is an intense aversion manifested by school refusal. Whereas the term truancy suggests that an informed choice has been made not to attend school, phobia implies an emotional problem. Helping a child with school phobia may involve counselling or psychotherapy, medication or a phased incremental return to school for increasingly longer periods. The close co-operation of home and school is important. Where the difficulties prove insuperable, then home education is an alternative or may be used in the short term while progress is made treating the school phobia.

MF

SCHOOLS' BROADCASTING

In this country there is a good tradition of schools' broadcasting on radio and television. The broadcasting agencies liaise with schools to explore needs, and publish programmes in advance. Most effective use is made of broadcasts where they are taped at the time and then previewed by the teacher as part of his/her lesson preparation, before use with pupils. Like other forms of AUDIO-VISUAL AIDS, broadcasts can add realism to lessons.

TLK

SCHOOLS OF SCIENCE AND TECHNOLOGY

Schools of Science and Technology opened in the early 1990s, the result of joint ventures between local businesses and the LEA (usually). Members of the business community support the schools both financially and through the individual commitment of the managers, engineers and directors. The schools offer the full range of National Curriculum subjects with special emphasis laid upon science, technology and enterprise skills.

CAK

SCHOOL UNIFORM
School uniform is, as the name suggests, an identical form of SCHOOL DRESS worn by all pupils of the same sex. Arguments are presented both for and against a school uniform, those most commonly advanced in favour are:

• it encourages pride in the school;
• it prevents discrimination.

Arguments against school uniform include:

• an excessive and extra cost for many parents;
• a basis of conflict between school and student.

The decision as to whether or not uniform should be worn rests with the GOVERNING BODY. It is expected that the governing body will consult both staff and parents should any change to the current school dress policy be envisaged; in the case of an LEA maintained school, where there is conflict between the governing body and the authority on the issue, the governing body's decision would be final. Information about school dress, whether it be uniform or otherwise, must be included in the SCHOOL BROCHURE which must be made available to all prospective parents.

Schools with ethnic minority pupils must consider the question of school uniform very carefully. Under the Race Relations Act 1976, it is stated that there shall not be less favourable treatment for anyone on the grounds of colour, race, nationality or ethnic origins. A uniform policy that results in the rejection of pupils who cannot comply with it for religious or cultural reasons is generally (albeit indirectly) discriminatory. Thus sensible arrangements for Muslim girls who require to wear trousers, for example, must be agreed in advance of any policy being formulated.

CAK

SCIENCE (IN THE NATIONAL CURRICULUM)
If you are not familiar with National Curriculum terminology, before reading this subject entry you may find it helpful to first read the entries on:

Attainment Targets
National Curriculum

Programmes of Study
Standard Assessment Tasks

Attainment targets (ATs) in the science National Curriculum are each composed of strands which describe how the main scientific ideas develop through National Curriculum levels. These are shown below.

AT1	Scientific investigation	(i)	Ask questions, predict and hypothesize
		(ii)	Observe, measure and manipulate variables
		(iii)	Interpret their results and evaluate scientific evidence
AT2	Life and living processes	(i)	Life processes and the organization of living things
		(ii)	Variation and the mechanisms of inheritance and evolution
		(iii)	Populations and human influences within ecosystems
		(iv)	Energy flows and cycles of matter within ecosystems
AT3	Materials and their properties	(i)	The properties, classification and structure of materials
		(ii)	Explanations of the properties of materials
		(ii)	Chemical changes
		(iv)	The Earth and its atmosphere
AT4	Physical processes	(i)	Electricity and magnetism
		(ii)	Energy resources and energy transfer
		(ii)	Forces and their effects
		(iv)	Light and sound
		(v)	The Earth's place in the Universe

The key stages (KS) relate to levels of attainment in the following way:

> KS1 – Levels 1–3
> KS2 – Levels 2–5
> KS3 – Levels 3–7
> KS4 – Levels 4–10

Regarding programmes of study (PoS), there is a PoS for each AT in each key stage. In the Statutory Order, the PoS are displayed on the same pages as the SoA for a particular AT.

The PoS for ATs 2 to 4 cover knowledge and understanding. The PoS for AT1 describe the processes and skills of scientific investigation which allow pupils to explore the contexts provided in AT 2 to 4. AT1 should be taught in relation to the PoS for other ATs.

The majority of pupils in KS4 will follow a course of study covering all the ATs and all the strands. This will, for most pupils, lead to a double GCSE in science. Some pupils may wish to study a reduced course – single science, leading to a single GCSE. Pupils may also study three separate science GCSEs.

Further reading

DES/WO (1992) *Science in the National Curriculum* (HMSO).
Ryles, A. (1994) 'The Science Curriculum' in the series *Education for Teaching* (HMSO).

MF

SCOTLAND: EDUCATION SYSTEM
In Scotland, the Secretary of State for Scotland is responsible for education. Education authorities are responsible for administering public (state) education. Statutory controls are administered by the Scottish Education Department, which is answerable to the Secretary of State for Scotland.

MF

SECONDARY SCHOOLS/SECONDARY EDUCATION
Secondary schools provide education for pupils aged between 11 and 18 (12 and 18 in Scotland). While the NATIONAL CURRICULUM aims to provide consistency between schools, including secondary schools, at other levels there is much diversity in secondary education. Some schools still maintain the comprehensive principles encouraged by the Education Act 1976. Under the provisions of the Education Act 1979, which repealed the earlier Act, other secondary schools have remained selective or returned to being selective. Grant Maintained schools and CITY TECHNOLOGY COLLEGES both directly funded by central government have profoundly altered the landscape of secondary education. In the independent sector, academic pupils who secure a place can apply under the assisted places scheme to have fees paid by the Department for Education. SIXTH-FORM COLLEGES educate pupils aged 16 to 18/19.

MF

SECRETARY OF STATE FOR EDUCATION
The Secretary of State for Education has a duty to 'promote' the education of people of England and Wales and to ensure that LEAs provide an

educational service which is 'varied and comprehensive' (Education Act 1944, section 1). In order to fulfil these duties the Secretary of State can give grants, make regulations, give directions, demand information, set up enquiries, cause inspections to be made and give guidance. The Secretary of State has to ensure that there are adequate facilities for training teachers (Education Act 1944, section 62).

The Secretary of State for Wales assumed responsibility for primary and secondary education in Wales in 1970. Previously these responsibilities had been those of the Secretary of State for Education and Science (as the Secretary of State for Education was then called). The Secretary of State for Education and Science was left with responsibility for the following in Wales:

- further and higher education;
- the youth service;
- teacher supply, training, qualifications, remuneration, superannuation and misconduct;
- grants to community centres, village halls and adult education;
- the appointment of Her Majesty's Inspectors.

MF

SELECTION ACCORDING TO ABILITY
A tendency among state secondary schools towards selecting pupils for admission according to ability is developing because of three factors:

1. The increase in the number of Grant Maintained schools which may apply to become selective.
2. The right of parents to choose their child's school.
3. The publication of National Curriculum assessment results.

The results of assessment at the end of Key Stage 2 when pupils are 11 years old coincides with the age of transfer to most secondary schools and these results could be used to aid selection.

In the independent sector, selection for secondary school is made through the results of the Common Entrance examination.

MF

SETTING
A system of organizing children into classes. It is a form of streaming by subject. Thus in any year group the best children at French join French group A (and so on); the best in maths join maths group A (etc.). Any

individual child may have a profile which puts them in Group A for French, B for English, E for maths, C for history.

TLK

SEX EDUCATION

In county, controlled and maintained special schools it is the duty of the GOVERNING BODY to consider separately whether sex education should form part of the secular curriculum. A written statement should be provided detailing content and organization of that part of the curriculum if sex education is to be given, or of their decision if their conclusion is that it should not form part of the curriculum. Once a policy has been formulated, it must be updated as necessary and published in the SCHOOL BROCHURE.

Generally a child attending a school where the LEA guidelines on sex education are followed, will expect to start sex education early in the primary school, and it will continue through junior and into secondary schooling. Sex education is handled sympathetically, throughout the child's school years and may form part of a personal, social and health education programme.

Human and animal reproduction are part of the programmes of study in National Curriculum science and form part of GCSE courses. In secondary schools additional sex education must be provided under the GOVERNORS' policies and must include information about HIV and AIDS; however, parents may legally withdraw their children from those lessons which do not form part of the National Curriculum. From September 1994, under the Education Act 1993, the right to withdraw children from sex lessons other than those prescribed by the National Curriculum will be extended to cover the primary school age. Many schools provide opportunities for parents to see for themselves the teaching materials that are used in the school, and the context within which they are used, and usually headteachers and governors are happy to discuss both their policies and approaches.

In LEA maintained schools both the governors and head share with the authority the responsibility of taking 'such steps as are reasonably practicable to secure that where sex education is given . . . it is given in such a manner as to encourage . . . pupils to have due regard to moral considerations and the value of family life'. In Grant Maintained schools this is the responsibility of the governing body and the headteacher.

CAK

SILENCE (USE OF)

There are probably two main ways in which silence impinges on the educational process. First is in relation to the TEACHING SKILLS of the teacher, in the context of COMMUNICATING IN THE CLASSROOM. Silence can be used as a punctuation to verbal language and as a cue to pupils to think or contribute; or to emphasize a point. Likewise when QUESTIONING a class, a pause (= silence) gives students an opportunity to answer. Second, a silent class may be viewed as a measure of effective CLASS MANAGEMENT. However, silence in this context is ambiguous. There are some CLASSROOM TASKS which require silence: silent reading, answering mock examination questions, etc. Other tasks, such as GROUP WORK or DISCUSSION, require participation by the pupils: so a silent class would be inappropriate. Good advice to novice teachers would, nevertheless, be always to gain silent attention before starting a lesson or addressing the class. Teachers should also establish ground rules of good behaviour, so that when one pupil is speaking others remain silent and do not interrupt.

TLK

SIXTH FORM/SIXTH-FORM COLLEGES
Sixth forms in secondary schools offer mainly A levels and AS level courses, although (General) National Vocational Qualifications are playing an increasingly important part in the curricula of sixth forms.

Sixth Form Colleges provide exclusively for pupils aged 16 to 19. In areas where they exist, these colleges essentially gather together from several schools pupils that would otherwise have been in a school sixth form. By doing this the college has more pupils than any individual school sixth form would have and can therefore offer a wider range of courses.

Further reading

Compendium of Tertiary and Sixth Form Colleges, available from: Standing Conference of Tertiary and Sixth Form College Principals, King George V College, Southport, Merseyside PR8 6LR
tel: 0704 30601

MF

SKILLS
In psychology, the expression 'skill' relates to muscular action, usually concerning the accuracy, speed and ease with which a person performs an action or task. In education, the term has similar connotations, usually referring to a facility in physical activities or tasks. Skills are demonstrable and therefore comparatively easy to assess.

MF

SKINNER, B. F. (1904–90)

An American psychologist and advocate of Behaviourism, Skinner's influence on education includes the development of programmed learning techniques. This individualized approach to teaching reinforces learning by giving immediate 'feedback'. His techniques have been applied to the social training of people with severe learning difficulties.

MF

SMOKING

(See: DRUG ABUSE)

SOCIAL INFLUENCES (ON EDUCATION)

There can be little doubt that some degree of influence on the education of the pupil is exercised by the background from which he or she comes. Many would argue that social influences have a massive effect on the ability of a child to benefit from schooling (see NURSERY EDUCATION). A teacher of a reception class, receiving pupils into school for the first time, may need to be aware of a large variety of social factors which could be at work on the individual:

- complete or disrupted family;
- relatively high or relatively low family income;
- good or poor housing conditions and facilities;
- large or small family;
- extended or nuclear family;
- affluent or impoverished neighbourhood;
- good or poor health of child or parents;
- genetic characteristics inherited from parents;
- father working or not employed;
- mother working or not employed;
- urban, suburban or rural environment;
- parents with good knowledge/little knowledge of education system;
- psychologically secure/insecure family climate;
- opportunities for peer-group social relationships available/lacking in the home;
- whether or not the child attended nursery school/playgroup, etc.

This list is exemplary not exhaustive; and social influences remain with the student through his/her education (and beyond). Teachers in the secondary sector have to be equally aware of these issues, and of others such as the parental attitudes to education (aspiring, hostile), the effect of divorce in the family, or events such as CHILD ABUSE. Social influence also operates through the PEER GROUP, and through the broader values of society especially as these are reflected in the media.

TLK

SOCIOLOGY OF EDUCATION

Sociology is a social science of society. It is concerned with social organization, its development and principles, and with group behaviour (rather than the behaviour of the individual members of a group). The sociologist is interested in the 'facts' of society and social relationships and in developing an understanding of them using statistical and scientific methods of analysis. Sociology may be able to predict, using statistical information. But it may also provide information which can be used prescriptively in a way which for example improves matters for people.

Sociology attempts to develop theories from its data concerning society in general or a specific society in particular. It develops theories of 'macro-society' and its evolution by using comparative analysis. Sociology concerns itself with such phenomena as social institutions, social class structure and family.

The sociology of education deals with:

(a) applying sociology's general principles and findings to the adminis-tration and process of education; and
(b) analysing sociological processes within an educational institution.

The sociology of education considers the context in which education takes place, comparing this context within a society and across one society and another. It studies the relations between education and society focusing on concepts such as society, culture, community, social class, status and role. It is concerned with such issues as the effect of the economy on the sort of education provided by the state, the social institutions (e.g. family) involved in the process of education, the school as a formal organization, and social change and education.

Further reading

Morrish, I. (1978) *The Sociology of Education: An Introduction* (second edition) (George Allen and Unwin).

MF

SPEAKING

Much COMMUNICATION IN THE CLASSROOM is dependent on the process of speaking: often a teacher speaking to pupils; but also pupils addressing the teacher and each other. Speaking is a physiological process involving the speaker in breathing quickly and deeply and then outputting the air in a slower controlled way through the larynx. This process can be controlled to produce a variety of speech effects which make the voice more varied and interesting to listen to. Rhythm is particularly important in sustaining the listener's interest; and this is achieved through the use of stress (e.g. for emphasis), intonation, the length for which syllables are held, pace, the use of pausing and phrasing, and articulation (i.e. enunciation or diction). Beginning teachers may need to work quite consciously on improving speaking skills. For example, classrooms are often large with distracting noise a problem; so audibility has to be achieved. In the process of raising the voice, the student teacher may raise its pitch or become strident so that he/she becomes uncomfortable to listen to. It is helpful if a teacher can adopt a less formal style, and become more conversational with resulting improvement in voice control. A very common problem is monotony of tone, which often includes too consistent volume, poor intonation, unvaried pace, failure to use pausing, and too regular phrase-length among the components. Other problems may relate to poor ability by the speaker to make clear sounds, and this can be aided by practice using a tape-recorder (see also LISTENING).

TLK

SPECIAL EDUCATIONAL NEEDS

Following the Warnock Report of 1978 the Education Act 1981 widened the definition of special needs. Previously the focus had been primarily on obviously disadvantaged children such as those with physical disabilities and children with emotional and behavioural difficulties. The 1981 Act widened the definition to children who have a significantly greater difficulty in learning than their peers. As many as one child in five it was accepted could at some stage in their school career have special needs. The Act placed a duty on LEAs to identify and assess children with special needs.

A phased system on intervention is followed which if necessary can lead to the Local Education Authority making a 'statement' of special educational needs. In Scotland this is a 'record of needs'. The statement is a legally-binding document which sets out the observations of various parties including the school and the parents. It summarizes the particular special needs and sets out the steps which need to be taken to ensure that help is provided.

School governors have a statutory duty to provide help for pupils with special needs.

Under the Education Act 1993, a Cod of Practice has been issued to which LEAs, schools and others must 'have regard'.

(See also: SPECIAL SCHOOLS AND UNITS; STATEMENTING)

Address

National Council for Special Education, York House, Exhall Grange, Wheelwright Lane, Exhall, Coventry CV7 9HP
tel: 0203 362414

Further reading

Weiner, G. and Hackney, A. (1994) 'Valuing the Individual: Equal Opportunities and Special Needs' in the series Farrell, M. (Ed.), *Education for Teaching* (HMSO).

MF

SPECIAL PURPOSE GRANTS
Special Purpose Grants are payable to Grant Maintained schools to cover the costs of specific needs of the school over and above those needs which are catered for by the ANNUAL MAINTENANCE GRANT. Given that the Department for Education agrees with the school's proposals for its in-service training of staff, it is intended that a Special Purpose Grant should cover Curriculum and Staff Development in such a way that it is commensurate with the level provided by the LEA to county schools through its GEST funding. Other Special Purpose Grants are available for VAT and rate relief, premises insurance and staff restructuring. This last grant is available (subject to a satisfactory bid) during the first year of grant maintained status; it is designed to help with the costs of restructuring teaching staff, and to help with any necessary early retirement, voluntary redundancy or severance costs. In the case of early retirement, the grant is designed to help with both the immediate situation and the costs of pension enhancements in subsequent years.

CAK

SPECIAL SCHOOLS
Special schools educate children with special needs who cannot benefit from education in a mainstream school. Special schools must follow the National Curriculum although special provision can be made to 'disapply' the National Curriculum in the case of individual pupils for a period of time.

There are some residential special schools but the majority are day schools. They tend to be smaller than mainstream schools and have a higher teacher: pupil ratio. Some special schools take a very wide age range of pupils, perhaps from 4 to 16 years old or over. This may be necessary where, for example, a school specializes in meeting a comparatively rare special need such as those associated with autism. In order for the specialist help to be available to the widest number of children in a locality, it may be thought necessary to accept pupils from a wide age range.

MF

SPECIAL UNITS

Special units are provided by some mainstream schools to educate pupils with special educational needs. The use of such units represents varying degrees of integration with the school. Pupils may attend the unit in the long term or the short term; for a lesson or two a week or for the whole week. Positive aspects of special units include the specialized help they can offer; a better teacher:pupil ratio, the opportunity to build relationships between teachers and pupils and greater opportunity for individualized work. Among the potential disadvantages are that long-term, full-time education in a unit may limit curriculum breadth and depth offered and that such units can become exclusion zones for difficult pupils.

MF

SPELLING

Improving a child's spelling can be achieved in several ways. Word games which encourage paying attention to correct spelling can be an enjoyable way of developing an ability which is all too often fraught with anxiety for a child. Word dominoes, word lotto and various word matching games, and the use of appropriate computer software, can be motivating as well as being of practical help.

Visual as well as auditory aids can be encouraged, that is the teacher can encourage a child to break up appropriate words phonetically but to visualize others. School marking of spelling mistakes tends to be more effective if it is selective, perhaps involving highlighting three misspelled words in each piece of written work.

Picture dictionaries and, later, formal dictionaries can encourage the habit of checking words about which the pupil is unsure. A to Z booklets of words which a child commonly misspells can be kept but it is also helpful to group misspellings such as words with the same beginning or ending (*ph*ysics, *ph*osphorus, *ph*ilately; ri*ght*, ni*ght*, bri*ght*).

Key factors in improving spelling are observation (noticing how a word is spelt rather than glossing over it) and confidence, which can be built by emphasizing progress as well as pinpointing mistakes.

MF

SPORT

Physical education is a foundation subject of the National Curriculum. While sport complements the aims of physical education, there has been a decline in time spent on sport and facilities for it in state schools in recent years. School sport is supplemented by after school activities, which may have to be paid for by parents, and by activities offered at local sports clubs.

Addresses

Sports Council, 16 Upper Woburn Place, London WC1 OQP
tel: 071 388 1277
Scottish Sports Council, 1 Colme Street, Edinburgh EH3 6AA
tel: 031 225 8411
Sports Council for Northern Ireland, House of Sport, Upper Malone Road, Belfast BT9 5LA
tel: 0232 381222
Sports Council for Wales, Sophia Gardens, Cardiff CF1 9SW
tel: 0222 397571

MF

STANDARD ASSESSMENT TASKS (SATs)

SATs are a part of the procedures for ASSESSMENT IN THE NATIONAL CURRICULUM. SATs were originally intended as a range of tasks which fitted into the classroom context and could be given fairly unobtrusively where appropriate. Streamlining and simplifying the administrative arrangements for SATs is tending to slant them more towards pencil and paper tests.

MF

STANDING ADVISORY COUNCILS ON RELIGIOUS EDUCATION – SACRE

SACRE is a local statutory body which must be convened by each LEA to advise on religious education (RE). It has to agree the production and acceptance of a local syllabus for RE. The members of each local committee represent the Church of England, Christian Groups and faiths other than the Church of England, teachers and the LEA. Under the Education Act 1993, the main criteria for a religious representative being a member of the local SACRE is that there is a sufficient number of adult members of that faith in the local area to justify having representation. However, there is diversity (and perhaps confusion) among LEAs concerning such representation.

MF

STARTING SCHOOL

By law children are required to receive education from the beginning of the school term *after* they reach the age of 5. However, admissions policies across the country vary greatly, and these may be dictated by the kind of area in which one lives (i.e. rural or inner city), the political persuasion of the ruling authority of the local council, or the stance of the government of the day. First admissions fall into one of the following categories:

- *Nursery education (3 and 4 year olds)* – nursery education is, at best, patchy. Demand for nursery education is usually high and outstrips places available. Nearly every authority has a waiting list, for some it will be on a 'first come, first served' basis; for others priority will be given to children who have special social or educational needs, children who are on the child protection 'at-risk' register, or who are recommended for admission by a medical officer. Attendance may be on a part-time basis in the first instance.
- *'Rising Fives'* – pupils are admitted at the beginning of the term in which they attain the age of 5. For this term only, pupils may be offered part-time education, generally not less than 40 per cent of the whole week. In effect, part-time education means attending for either the morning or the afternoon sessions, gradually building up to full-time attendance. Some authorities admit on a full-time basis from the first day.
- *Statutory* – pupils must attend school at the beginning of the school term after they attain five years. Education is on a full-time basis.
- *Admission of other 4-year olds* – provided that there are places available within the planned admission limits, and that the school has sufficient staff, accommodation and other resources to meet the needs of non-statutory age children, 4-year olds other than those whose birthday falls in the term in which they are admitted, may be offered places at an infant or primary school. These differences are very local, and any approaches should be made to the headteacher of the relevant school.

CAK

STATEMENTING

A statement of special educational needs is a document written by the LEA which sets out the nature of a child's special needs and specifies the support which the LEA can provide. It is a legally binding document. (In the case of non-statemented children, schools are not legally obliged to provide extra help.)

Statementing is the process of preparing a statement and involves gathering the views and recommendations of parents and various professionals. Appendices to the statement includes parents' evidence; education, medical and other advice and information given by the District Health Authority, the Social Services Department and other bodies or individuals as appropriate.

MF

STATEMENT OF ATTAINMENT

(See: NATIONAL CURRICULUM)

STATUTORY INSTRUMENTS (SIs)

SIs are the vehicle of much specific direction of educational policy. SIs have to be put before parliament (Education Act 1944, section 112) and if successfully passed, become law. Policy and guidance is also set out in administrative memoranda and circulars issued by the Secretary of State but these lack the force of law. Before 1946, SIs were called Statutory Rules and Orders.

MF

STEINER, RUDOLPH (1861–1925)

The Austrian philosopher and educator Rudolph Steiner founded a school in Stuttgart in 1919 for children of workers at the Waldorf Astoria cigarette factory. Hence it was called the Waldorf School.

Steiner founded the spiritual doctrine of anthroposophy. He saw education as the way of retraining the human faculty for spiritual perception which had been dulled by the demands of the modern world. STEINER SCHOOLS have developed world-wide.

MF

STEINER SCHOOLS

Steiner or Waldorf Schools build on the work and ideas of RUDOLPH STEINER. World-wide there are about 250 such schools, while in Britain there are 16 schools which are all in the independent sector. The ethos of these schools is non-denominational Christian. The schools are co-educational and cater for pupils aged 4 to 18 who are grouped according to age. Artistic and practical activities as well as academic pursuits are encouraged to give a broad education which does not guide the child into specializing too early, Eurhythmy, drama, myths and art are important. Steiner teachers are specially trained in the Steiner approach.

Address

Rudolph Steiner Bookshop, 35 Park Road, London NW1 6XT
tel: 071 723 4400

MF

STENHOUSE, LAWRENCE

Lawrence Stenhouse was Professor of Education and Director of the Centre for Applied Research in Education at the University of East Anglia from 1970 until his death in 1982. Stenhouse was best known as Director of the Schools Council–Nuffield Foundation Humanities Curriculum Project, a project which was to have a lasting effect on the theory and practice of teaching. Stenhouse and his colleagues introduced the controversial concept of the teacher as 'neutral chairman'.

CAK

STORY READING

The use of story reading or STORY TELLING is widely believed by teachers to be a valuable part of a child's education into language and LITERACY. The value of story can be significantly enhanced if the teacher is aware of a range of skills and techniques for increased effectiveness. Without these, teachers may reduce story to little more than oral comprehension, thus making literature act like a reading scheme. Many experts argue for a more reflective approach, which includes such features as the teacher:

- providing a suitable environment within the classroom (e.g. a carpeted area with appropriate displays) for story-reading;
- being knowledgeable about and enjoying the stories they want to share with pupils;
- building up a literature-rich environment in the classroom and in learning generally;
- encouraging children to articulate to each other their own insights and enjoyment of books;

- focusing, and encouraging pupils to reflect, on characters and incidents in a text;
- making links between literature and the pupil's own experiences and life;
- planning variety into the pupils' literary experiences.

With young children in particular, the encouragement of the use of story in the home is important; and so the HOME-SCHOOL RELATIONS are important. Story reading is not merely an exercise in the COGNITIVE DOMAIN, but also in the AFFECTIVE.

TLK

STORY TELLING

The principles of story telling are very similar to those of STORY READING. The distinction is that, whereas read stories usually come from a body of literature, stories which are told may be taken from oral tradition or simply made up by the teacher. Such an approach to story will give teachers an opportunity to use their own creative skills; and it may lead itself to promoting pupils' imagination, too. For example, pupils may be actively involved in suggesting 'what happened next', fresh episodes or possible endings. Many different outcomes are possible from a single beginning. This technique is particularly useful in promoting written follow-up to a story to pupils of suitable age-groups.

TLK

STRANDS (IN THE NATIONAL CURRICULUM)

Strands are a way of describing ATTAINMENT TARGETS and their related PROGRAMMES OF STUDY which illustrate how important ideas concerning a subject develop through the NATIONAL CURRICULUM levels. In MATHEMATICS, for example, for AT1 the strands are: applications; mathematical communication; and reasoning, logic and proof. In SCIENCE, AT1 comprises the strands: ask questions, predict and hypothesize; observe, measure and manipulate variables; and interpret their results and evaluate scientific evidence.

MF

STREAMING

A form of organization in which all the ablest children are put in one class (the A stream), the next ablest in the next class (the B stream), and so on. Sometimes advocated (as against MIXED ABILITY CLASSES) for encouraging

ABLE CHILDREN; but likely to produce 'sink groups', characterized by poor performance, morale and behaviour, at the lower end. Preferred by some politicians, but discredited in the view of many educationists.
(See: ABILITY GROUPING)

TLK

STRESS (TEACHER AND PUPIL)

Stress is a level of physiological arousal at which performance begins to decline and symptoms such as poor concentration, palpitations and tension headaches may develop.

For teachers, stress can be produced by such factors as poor SCHOOL ETHOS, unreasonable demands upon their time, unco-operative pupils and insufficient resources. Other stressors include a teacher's lack of control over how much of his or her time is allocated and the many changes to teaching brought about by legislative changes in the 1980s and 1990s, such as the requirements of the National Curriculum. For pupils, stress is most commonly associated with the demands of preparing for examinations.

Among ways of tackling stress are counselling, improved time management (especially prioritizing), physical exercise, recreation which helps 'switch off' pressures of the day, and sufficient sleep.

MF

STUDENT CHARTER

As part of the government's strategy to bring total quality management (TQM) techniques to education, the student charter sets out what a student as consumer can expect from his/her education institution, mainly in terms of efficiency targets.

MF

STUDY SKILLS

The acquisition of study skills allows pupils to become INDEPENDENT LEARNERS operating in an appropriate INTELLECTUAL CLIMATE. Typical study skills which need to be acquired by all pupils/students from an early age are as follows. Classroom work requires pupils to acquire the skill of concentration for reasonable periods of time and to listen closely. Older pupils/students need to be able to take concise notes in a readable form for later reference. In written work, learners have to be able to plan and draft material, as well as to write in appropriate styles (notes, essays, letters, etc.). Increasingly learners have to access non-book information using information technology, or analysing a videotape.

Much learning takes place between peers, so learners need to use DISCUSSION and to value the contributions of others. As learners become more responsible for their own learning, they need to acquire skills of planning study programmes (e.g. for revision purposes) and to prioritize (e.g. to concentrate on weaknesses). Practical work must be reflected upon and used as EXPERIENTIAL LEARNING. Learners need to be able to articulate what they have learned to a variety of audiences (the teacher, potential employers, examiners). They need specific investigational skills: to use a contents page or an index; to use a library catalogue; to work a word-processor. Effective learners will ask questions when things are not clear and will work neatly in sequence. Two important skills are to be able to meet deadlines by working to a time scale, and to be able to work alone (e.g. at home or in a public library). Independent learners will acquire the self-critical ability to make accurate judgements of their own levels of performance without frequent supervision. They will also understand when to take a break or stop studying. Study skills are best practised from the earliest days of the primary school. They are especially important in MIXED ABILITY CLASSES, when INDIVIDUALIZED LEARNING is in progress, or when INFORMAL teaching styles are adopted. They are a fundamental requisite for TOPIC WORK and PROBLEM-SOLVING.

TLK

TAPE RECORDER
Video and audio tape recorders allow a wide range of AUDIO-VISUAL AIDS to be used to enhance lessons. They also have a role to play, e.g. through MICROTEACHING, in initial training and professional development. They play an integral role in OPEN AND DISTANCE LEARNING.

TLK

TASKS
A task is any piece of work set to students by a teacher. This would include work done in class and for HOMEWORK. Task outcomes could be written (such as an essay, or test paper, or a set of problems in maths), or practical (to make up and perform a play, to swim a length). Tasks make varying levels of cognitive demand on students. Thus teachers can achieve DIFFERENTIATION in the class by subtle use of task-setting skills. Research has tended to show, however, that teachers are often not sufficiently flexible in the use of classroom tasks, relying too much on WHOLE CLASS approaches, rather than GROUP TASKS or INDIVIDUALIZED LEARNING. Task performance is an efficient form of FEEDBACK to teachers, which may inform the ASSESSMENT and EVALUATION processes.

TLK

TEACHER APPRAISAL

The appraisal of teacher performance is foreshadowed in the Miscellaneous Matters of Education Act 1986 (section 53, part 4). This empowers the Secretary of State to require LEAs, school governors and others to see that arrangements are made for regular teacher appraisal.

A plan for national teacher appraisal was implemented by the Secretary of State in 1990 which should lead to all teachers having been appraised by the mid-1990s.

MF

TEACHER EFFECTIVENESS: THE PUPILS' VIEWS

When pupils are interviewed about the characteristics they most value in EFFECTIVE TEACHERS these are the most frequent outcomes:

Fairness	Pupils dislike teachers who show bias or favouritism. They have a well-developed sense of justice which can judge adults quite harshly.
Consistency	Pupils need to know that today's decisions will be tomorrow's policy, too. They don't mind 'strict' teachers provided they know the rules won't change.
Friendliness	Pupils like teachers who, without losing authority, can keep up good personal relations with each class member. Friendliness includes a sense of humour.
Kindness	A caring attitude and understanding of individual needs and problems is always valued by pupils.
Being interested	Pupils value teachers who put work over in ways which show thought, planning and an attempt to make it relevant.
Being a 'good teacher'	By which youngsters usually mean 'knowledgeable'.
Being well organized	Pupils generally loathe chaos, even if a few will capitalize on the opportunity to be deviant.

Words and descriptions which occur often in lists of dislikes include:

- favourites;
- allowing pupils to 'mess about';
- teachers not knowing the answers themselves;
- 'stuck up';
- 'doesn't get on with the work';
- boring.

TLK

TEACHER GOVERNORS

Teacher governors must be employed at the school, and will cease to be governors upon leaving. Both part-time and full-time teachers may stand for election, and have full and equal rights upon the governing body. The only constraint against teacher governors is that they may not chair the governing body or any of its committees, and may not take part in any discussion that relates to either their own post or conduct.

(See: ELECTION OF PARENT AND TEACHER GOVERNORS)

CAK

TEACHER AS A RESOURCE

Considering the teacher as a resource can help managers and teachers themselves appreciate the finite nature of a teacher's time and talents and allocate them more effectively.

Among the many implications of this perspective is that care is needed to ensure that the teacher's time is equitably distributed when teaching pupils. What amount of time should be spent with pupils who are capable of working on their own but would benefit from some extra input from the teacher? How should time be allocated to pupils who would progress very little without a great deal of the teacher's help? Are disruptive pupils able to get an unfair share of teacher attention?

Time management is a further implication. Teachers may feel that there is little room for manoeuvre regarding their time as so much of it is allocated to timetabled teaching. However, the use of non-teaching time often involves difficult decisions reflecting the notion of the teacher as a resource. Time spent on lesson preparation can leave the teacher's hands freer in the subsequent lesson but too much time spent on lesson preparation in out of school time can drain the energy to such an extent that teaching performance begins to suffer.

If the teacher's central skill is to teach then it may be worth reviewing the amount of time a school asks a teacher to spend on other tasks at the expense of teaching, especially if these tasks could be appropriately delegated to non-teaching staff.

MF

TEACHER TALK

(See: COMMUNICATION IN THE CLASSROOM; EXPLAINING)

TEACHERS' CENTRES

The Teachers' Centre movement had its heyday in the late 1960s and early 1970s, when LOCAL EDUCATION AUTHORITIES, in an attempt to promote and improve the IN-SERVICE TRAINING of teachers, often made accommodation available for the purpose. At root, the concept of a Teachers' Centre was of a location and a community of professionals where professional learning took place. The 'ownership' of the learning was held by the professional community, which often arranged more or less formal events of programmes of in-service activity. Often, a senior teacher was employed as a leader, warden or head: the terminology reflected rather different conceptual formulations of what the Centre was. Most centres were housed in school buildings which were (partially) surplus to requirements. However, already by the late 1970s the costs of running such centres were proving a stumbling block. Too many elected members on EDUCATION COMMITTEES failed to discern their purpose; and centres were often – from this time until now – the casualties of crises over cash. Alongside these hazards, various changes in approach and philosophy altered the structure of centres; and these changes are reflected in the terminology used. Some centres became Professional Development Centres, where the ownership of teachers tended to be shared with the need of LEA ADVISERS to promote their own, and the Government's, agendas of in-service training. Other terminology included: In-service Centre, and Resource Centre.

Whilst most centres initially saw it as their role to carry a range of curriculum support materials and equipment for teachers to borrow or the latest publications for them to consult, this role had to be seen as a secondary and peripheral one of an ideas forum for professional development. Indeed, it has been the role most rapidly shed when money has become tight. Under the control of LEA advisers, the centres have often become the 'home-base' of skilled personnel, such as advisory and support teachers with specialist skills. Over the last few years the Government has increasingly laid down the training agenda for teachers, with ever tightening strictures on, and devolution of, GEST funding for in-service work. In this climate centres have frequently been financial casualties or have lost sight of their original purpose. Where they do exist, the emotional ties of teachers to them is often very powerful – a positive commitment to PROFESSIONAL DEVELOPMENT. The work of centres is promoted by the National Association of Teachers' Centres and Professional Development Centres (NTCPD) which acts as an association for heads of centres nationwide. Ironically, England has tended to be exporting the concept of Teachers' Centres to Europe and developing countries across the world at precisely the moment when Government funding is squeezing them out of existence here.

TLK

TEACHERS' CERTIFICATE

A qualification formerly awarded to non-graduate teachers who had attended training colleges and obtained QUALIFIED TEACHER STATUS thereby. Superseded by the B.ED. DEGREE and the PGCE routes for INITIAL TEACHER TRAINING.

TLK

TEACHER TRAINING AGENCY

Amongst the proposed reforms for INITIAL TEACHER TRAINING (ITT) following the Education Act 1993, was the setting up of the Teacher Training Agency. The Agency is to take over responsibility for funding of all ITT and most education research from the Higher Education Funding Council.

Its brief includes:

* determining the overall distribution of Initial Teacher Training places between different providers;
* determining the balance of grant support between different types of courses and subjects and different areas of the country;
* allocating the grant to the providers;
* administering grants for LICENSED TEACHERS and overseas trained teachers;
* acting as a focal point for information giving and advice about routes into teaching for those considering it as a career;
* promoting school involvement in ITT;
* accrediting schools and INSTITUTES OF HIGHER EDUCATION;
* awarding QUALIFIED TEACHER STATUS (QTS) to students successfully completing an ITT course at an accredited institution.

The Bill allows the Secretary of State to appoint all the members of the Teacher Training Agency; it is anticipated that the TTA will comply with the code of practice on open government, and its accounts will be audited by the National Audit Office.
Source: Teaching as a Career.

CAK

TEACHING METHOD

A blanket term to indicate one of many available strategies: see ACTIVE LEARNING, INDIVIDUALIZED LEARNING, GROUP-WORK, DISCUSSION, AUDIO-VISUAL approaches, WHOLE CLASS TEACHING, TEAM TEACHING, USE OF TOPIC WORK, DIDACTIC TEACHING, etc.

TLK

TEACHING MODE

A phrase used to describe the ways in which a class can be divided for teaching purposes (not to be confused with teaching methods). There are three basic teaching modes: WHOLE CLASS TEACHING, GROUP WORK and INDIVIDUALIZED LEARNING..

TLK

TEACHING SKILLS

The traditional skills of the teacher include CLASS MANAGEMENT and DISCIPLINE, SPEAKING, EXPLAINING, QUESTIONING, TASK-SETTING and ASSESSING. All these are fundamental to EFFECTIVE TEACHING. The word skill has fallen out of favour recently and given way to the vocational term COMPETENCE.

TLK

TEAM TEACHING

A technique whereby several teachers work together to deliver a piece of curriculum, usually to a pooled group of pupils. It contrasts with more traditional class teaching (either in the primary or secondary sector). The advantages of team teaching can be significant. A group of three or four teachers from different subject disciplines might get together to deliver work around a TOPIC or theme; or more informally, might use broader expertise (in IT or special needs) in the same way. So pupils gain a cross-section of expertise. Teaching teams may also use time management techniques to, say, free up one member to organize a visit or do the group's admin, while the others have pupil contact. Often, time freed in this way is used to develop curriculum or produce worksheets or other AUDIO-VISUAL AIDS to learning. Team teaching provides variety as one of a range of TEACHING METHODS.

TLK

TECHNICAL AND VOCATIONAL EDUCATION INITIATIVE (TVEI)

TVEI is a government scheme under which LEAs are awarded grants from central government through the local TRAINING AND ENTERPRISE COUNCIL. In order to improve co-operation between the education system and the vocational sphere, these grants are used for technical and vocational programmes perhaps involving paying for extra teachers and buying technology equipment for schools.

MF

TECHNOLOGY (IN THE NATIONAL CURRICULUM)

If you are not familiar with National Curriculum terminology, before reading this subject entry, you may find it helpful to first read the entries on:

Attainment Targets
National Curriculum
Programmes of Study
Standard Assessment Tasks

Attainment targets (ATs) for technology are related to key aspects of design and technology (AT1 to AT4) and 'strands' (AT5) in the following way.

Design & technology capability		Aspect of design & technology
AT1	Identifying needs and opportunities	• Exploring and investigating contexts • Identifying and evaluating opportunities • Recognizing issues and implications
AT2	Generating a design	• Exploring and developing ideas • Evaluating ideas and making decisions • Modelling and communicating ideas
AT3	Planning and making	• Organizing and planning • Using materials, equipment and processes • Making things work
AT5	Evaluating	• Evaluating the outcomes and processes of one's own work • Evaluating the technological activity of other people, including those from other times and cultures

Information technology capability		Strands
AT5	Information technology capability (this will usually be developed through using IT to support learning in other subjects)	• Communicating ideas and information • Handling information • Designing, investigating, developing, exploring and evaluating models of real or imaginary situations • Measuring and controlling physical variables and movement • Understanding and evaluating the applications and effects of information technology

ATs 1 to 4 describe four complementary aspects of design and technology capability. Although the ATs appear to describe a sequential development, several aspects may be operating simultaneously at any time in a design and technology activity. Regarding the strands within AT5, the applications and effects of an information technology strand draws on the knowledge developed in the other four strands of information technology capability.

The key stages (KS) relate to levels of attainment as follows:

KS1 – Levels 1–3
KS2 – Levels 2–5
KS3 – Levels 3–7
KS4 – Levels 4–10

The Programmes of Study (PoS) for ATs 1 to 4 are in three parts.

1. *For pupils in every key stage* (requirements include):
   * designing and making artefacts, systems and environments;
   * working in a range of contexts which includes home, school, recreation, community, business and industry;
   * being careful for the safety of themselves and others;
   * working with a range of materials, including textiles, graphic media, construction materials and food.

2. *For pupils in a particular key stage* (requirements which apply to all pupils in that particular key stage are arranged in the following categories):
   * developing and using artefacts, systems and environments;
   * working with materials;
   * developing and communicating ideas;
   * satisfying needs and addressing opportunities.

3. *For pupils working towards a particular level*: (additional requirements to 1 and 2 above which apply to pupils working towards a particular level are arranged in the same categories as 2, above).

The PoS for AT5 are in three parts:

1. General requirements for all key stages.
2. Requirements for pupils in a particular key stage.
3. Requirements for pupils working towards a particular level.

A revised order of technology including IT will take effect for pupils in KS1 to 3 from August 1995 and for pupils beginning KS4 from 1996.

MF

TERTIARY EDUCATION

Tertiary education in a general sense encompasses all education after the age of 16. In a more specific sense, it is associated with education delivered at tertiary colleges. These cater for students aged from 16 to 19 years. Bringing together the functions of a College of Further Education and a Sixth-Form College, Tertiary Colleges offer full-time and part-time academic and vocational courses.

Address

Tertiary Colleges Association, Accrington and Rossendale College, Sandy Lane, Accrington BB5 2AW
tel: 0254 35334

MF

THEORY AND EDUCATION

The power of a theory is that it enables predictions to be made so that every occasion need not be treated as if it was unique.

The term theory is used in several ways.

1. In pure mathematics, theories begin with certain premises from which theories are derived by a process of deductive reasoning.
2. In the physical sciences, observation, hypothesis and experiment contribute to theories such as the theory of gravity.
3. In the social sciences an attempt is made to apply the discipline of physical sciences to human behaviour.
4. In philosophy, theorizing is characterized by examining the meaning of words and logically thinking issues through.

Educational theory draws on points 3 and 4 above. From the social sciences, for example, various learning theories contribute to education (e.g. behaviourist, Gestalt theory). Philosophically-oriented theorizing, though sometimes dismissed as being distant from practice, should intimately interact with practice. A teacher who does not coherently think through the concepts and approaches of education, and examine school procedures, may be losing valuable insights into practice.

MF

THINKING SKILLS

An approach whereby students are encouraged not merely to regurgitate previously-supplied factual information, but to use creative approaches to devise innovative solutions to problems.

(See also: COGNITION; CREATIVITY)

TLK

TIMES EDUCATIONAL SUPPLEMENT

The Times Educational Supplement (*TES*) was founded in 1910 as a paper for teachers. By far the most widely read paper specializing in education, it now has an average weekly readership of over 500,000. It is read by teachers in the state and independent schools, colleges of further and higher education, educational administrators and, increasingly, school governors and parents.

Adresses

Patricia Rowan (Editor), *Times Educational Supplement*,
66–68 East Smithfield, London E1 9XY
tel: 071 782 3000   fax: 071 782 3200
Scottish Edition (founded 1965), Willis Pickard (editor),
37 George Street, Edinburgh EH2 2HN
tel: 031 220 1100   fax: 031 220 1616

TIMES HIGHER EDUCATION SUPPLEMENT

Published weekly since 1971, The *THES* is the newspaper of UK higher and further education and has a circulation of about 25,000. Its main areas of coverage are UK news, provided by reporting staff in London and Edinburgh, overseas news, opinion and leaders – including views from the world's top academics and intellectuals, features and scholarly book reviews. The *THES* also includes advertising for the vast majority of higher education posts. It is published each Friday.

Address

THES, Admiral House, 66–68 East Smithfield, London E1 9XY
tel: 071 782 3000   fax: 071 782 3300

MF

TOPIC WORK

Teachers use a variety of labels to describe what might be called 'topic' work (e.g. project, themes). But several basic characteristics emerge:

• most topic work is in fact interdisciplinary, not simply thematic;
• topic work involves active learning (visits, finding out from reference material);
• the learning is likely to be in pairs or groups rather than in individual or whole-class contexts;

- end products in the form of presentations or displays may be typical of this approach;
- the implicit role for the teacher is that of wise facilitator rather than of instructor.

The child-centredness of topic work has its roots with ROSSEAU and DEWEY, both of whom valued DISCOVERY LEARNING. The method was documented in the PLOWDEN REPORT.

Key reasons for using topic work approaches would include:

- to cater for varying levels of ability at the same time;
- to promote environmental awareness;
- to encourage curiosity;
- to provide a forum for interdisciplinary approaches;
- to practise basic skills, concepts;
- to give breadth of knowledge and a context in which to apply knowledge;
- to encourage pupils to speculate and hypothesize;
- to promote STUDY SKILLS;
- to foster CREATIVITY;
- to promote collaborative learning among pupils.

The precise status of topic work in a NATIONAL CURRICULUM context is ambiguous, being favoured by teachers and less so by politicians. The NCC's document 'A Framework for the Primary Curriculum' (1989) suggested that primary schools might need to plan their curriculum in an 'integrated' or 'topic-based' way. More recently the NCC Circular 6, 'The National Curriculum and Whole Curriculum Planning: Preliminary Guidance' (October 1989), has given teachers help in exploring some of the issues around cross-curricular approaches.

A useful way of incorporating topic work into lessons is to study the curriculum in an interdisciplinary way. Many of the National Curriculum atttainment targets can be achieved by careful planning. It is useful, in LESSON PLANNING, for example, to list the intentions of the pupils' learning in terms of the verbs which describe their activities e.g.:

- pupils will *guess* (= hypothesize) which will float;
- pupils will *estimate* the weight of the blocks;
- pupils will *compare* the two sizes;
- pupils will *imagine* they are alone on a desert island;
- pupils will *discover* what life was like here in 1890;
- pupils will *tell* each other a short story of their own;

- pupils will *co-operate* to build a cardboard bridge for the experiment.

Further information about topic work can be found in Kerry, T. and Eggleston, J. (1986) *Topic Teaching in the Primary School* (London: Routledge).

TLK

TOPIC WORK: CRITERIA FOR SUCCESS
While topic work is an approach often favoured by teachers and pupils, topics vary in their success. Research suggests that teachers use a number of criteria to decide whether or not a topic has been worthwhile. These include:

- it uses the knowledge, skills and understanding to meet appropriate National Curriculum requirements;
- the pupils are interested, enthusiastic, motivated and enjoy it;
- the quality of work produced is high;
- the pupils bring items of interest from home, etc.;
- the pupils talk informally about it;
- the pupils have gained in knowledge or information;
- the pupils' interest is sustained at a high level for a long time;
- the pupils can remember the work some weeks/months after it has finished;
- good display materials are produced;
- the pupils follow the interest outside school or timetable time;
- parents comment favourably;
- there is a feeling of job satisfaction for the teacher;
- the quantity of work done is acceptable/large;
- the pupils have acquired and progressed in (unspecified) skills;
- the pupils offer ideas and ask questions;
- the pupils have gained in experience and understanding;
- the teacher's original aims have been fulfilled;
- the pupils have produced creative work;
- the pupils look forward to topic lessons;
- the pupils remember what they have learned;
- the topic itself expands in scope spontaneously.

TLK

TOPIC WORK: TEACHER PREPARATIONS FOR
TOPIC WORK, like other TEACHING METHODS, requires careful preparation. Research has shown that teachers approaching the teaching of a new topic follow these stages in their preparation:

- make a display of related charts, reference books etc.;
- prepare a display area;
- prepare resource collections;
- decide on the layout of the furniture;
- check that any software or apparatus required is readily available;
- provide suitable folders or storage for pupils' work;
- organize outside or ancillary help;
- explore the potential of school-based facilities (such as rain gauges).

TLK

TRADITIONALIST EDUCATION

A traditionalist view of education may be contrasted to CHILD-CENTRED EDUCATION. Traditionalist education emphasizes moulding the child through education ('Give me a child until he is seven and he is mine for life', as Jesuits are caricatured as saying). The teacher's view of what the content and method of education should be takes precedence over that of the child. Education is according to adult values and attitudes, and the child has to move toward and into the adult world, including that of work. The curriculum is subject centred.

Traditionalist education is often associated with the teaching method of ROTE LEARNING.

MF

TRAINING ENTERPRISE COUNCILS (TECs)

In 1989, TECs were established by the Department for Employment. They took over responsibility for:

(a) the Youth Training Scheme, a part-time vocational scheme for 16-to-18-year olds;
(b) the Department for Employment's Training Agency programme for stimulating small businesses and enterprise. (The Training Agency was disbanded.)

TECs also have partial responsibility for the TRAINING AND VOCATIONAL EDUCATION INITIATIVE. The 80 local TECs in England and Wales receive administrative support from the 49 Training Agency area offices whose staff were divided among the TECs.

TECs are controlled mainly by a board of about 10 to 15 people, including local business people, members of local authority groupings such as the chief education officer, union members and others. Board members serve in a personal capacity not as representatives of their 'constituency' group.

Each TEC is accountable through a contract with the Department of Employment based on performance targets.

Training credits are part of a scheme run by TECs working with the local education authority for 16 and 17 year olds. On leaving full-time education, young people receive a voucher ('credit') which they present to a prospective employer. Employer and employee work out a programme of part-time education and training up to an agreed standard to be bought with the credit.

The aim of credits is to:

• expand and improve the skills of young people already in work;
• motivate young people to train to higher standards;
• make training better fit the requirement of employers and young people;
• produce a more efficient and adaptable training market.

Careers officers and school careers teachers advise young people of the opportunities available. Building on their school record, the pupil should be able to agree an action plan for their future training and career to enable them to negotiate with any prospective employer.

MF

TRANSFER BETWEEN SCHOOLS

When an under-five child who has been attending school moves to another area, attempts are usually made to ensure continuity in education. However, rising-five and under-five education is not yet statutory, and local differences will occur. Advice should be sought from the LEA.

Transfer of pupils of statutory school age within a county or borough

When parents move house and a change of school becomes necessary, the child will usually be allocated a place at the school in whose catchment area he or she lives, provided the appropriate year group has available places. Parents who move house but wish their child to remain at his or her existing school must ensure attendance at school and meet the costs of transport from home to school if their new home is outside the catchment area of that school.

Parental preference

When a change of school is requested because of parental preference, parents must accept full responsibility both for making travel arrangements and for meeting the cost of transport.

Transfer from one authority to another

Parents should contact the LEA of the area in which the new home falls to obtain a list of schools. The LEA will advise which school is deemed appropriate, and whether a place is available within the year group. Admission to a school other than the one in whose catchment area the new home falls may be granted if the school is appropriate to the child's needs and has enough resources for the admission. In this latter case, parents will be required to agree to meet the costs and responsibility for transporting the child.

CAK

TRANSITIONAL GRANT

A transitional grant is given to schools to enable them to prepare for GRANT MAINTAINED STATUS. It is a one-off payment intended to meet the essential extra spending that goes with the school's newly acquired status. From October 1992 all secondary schools and primary schools with 200 or more pupils have been eligible to receive £30,000 plus £30 for each pupil, subject to a maximum of £60,000. For a primary school with fewer than 200 pupils the allocation is £20,000 plus £30 for each pupil.

CAK

TRANSPORT (SCHOOL)

Parents are required to make whatever arrangements are necessary to ensure that their child attends school regularly. Education authorities are required to provide free transport for pupils who attend the school designated as appropriate by the LEA, but who live more than the walking distance away. Walking distance is defined in law as being two miles for a pupil under 8 years of age, and three miles for pupils 8 years and over. Some education authorities adopt a policy of shorter distances for some age groups, and details of any local difference may be obtained from the County Education Officer.

Parents choosing a different school from the designated school are responsible for making their own travel arrangements and for meeting the cost.

Pupils attending denominational schools

Assistance with transport may be provided for pupils attending their nearest church school on denominational grouds provided:

(a) they do not live within the walking distances adopted by the local authority;

(b) in the case of pupils under 11 that the daily total travelling time does not exceed 90 minutes;

(c) and in the case of pupils over 11 that the daily total travelling time does not exceed 2 hrs 30 mins.

Local differences may occur with regard to the actual assistance provided. Where public transport is available the provision of a ticket may be made; where public transport is not available assistance in the form of an allowance may be made. Details may be obtained from the County Education Officer.

Transport may be provided for certain pupils with special educational needs attending the school designated as appropriate by the LEA.

Pupils attending Grant Maintained schools

The LEA is responsible for providing home to school transport for those pupils who attend Grant Maintained schools and for whom it is the designated appropriate school. The same criteria regarding walking distances apply.

CAK

TRAVELLER CHILDREN

Traveller children are children of the families variously described as travellers, tinkers, gypsies, Romanies, or showmen. Definition is difficult because these families may be temporarily or permanently travelling, and may spend part of the year only as travellers. Culturally the groups may be very different, and may include not only traditional groups but others such as so-called New Age Travellers. The education of traveller children may be substantially disrupted by significant periods away from a home-base. Their education is often seen as part of a LOCAL EDUCATION AUTHORITY's provision for SPECIAL EDUCATIONAL NEEDS. Every child is entitled to, and statutorily required to attend, schooling. Since by definition traveller children find this difficult many LEAs set up Traveller Support Units to try to bring this about. The staff of these units may use a range of methods such as direct teaching on a traveller site, the escorting of children to local schools, or postal lessons sent to pupils (often by quite devious routes) while they are on the road. Some traveller families value these services, though studies suggest that many are selective in their view about the value of education. There is a prevalent view that, since education is for employment, the best education for children is working on-the-job with their elders, for example in the scrap business or with horses. Some feel the traveller culture may be under threat unless the communities remain closed to a large extent from outside influences. Traveller children may meet prejudice when they attend school, and so part of the role of Traveller Support Unit staff is to train teachers and to educate the public into traveller culture and to suggest ways in which this can be better integrated into school life.

TLK

TRUANCY

Truancy is accepted as being an important issue but there is not yet agreement between schools, administrators, parents and Government about how to tackle it. School records of truancy are difficult to interpret because there is inconsistency about what constitutes truancy (although attempts are being made to address this).

LEAs can deal with persistent truants by applying for an educational supervision order to be served on parents. This requires parents to work with a supervisor (usually an EDUCATIONAL WELFARE OFFICER) to tackle the issue. Fines can be imposed on parents if they do not co-operate. Alternative approaches place greater emphasis on tackling underlying causes of truancy, for example, some pupils perceive school work as irrelevant to what they intend to do in later life. In any event, truancy is unlikely to be curtailed without close co-operation between home and school. This might involve helping parents with the disciplining of their children if staff and funds are available.

In 1994, in the wake of the James Bulger case in which a child was abducted and murdered by two truanting schoolboys, the then Education Secretary, John Patten, called for a Truancy-Watch scheme.

MF

TUITION

Often used to refer to one-to-one teaching between a student and teacher. For example, an individual student attending for a piano lesson with a private teacher would refer to the process as tuition and the teacher as a TUTOR.

TLK

TUTOR

A teacher undertaking a specialized role of one of the kinds listed:

- one-to-one teaching (see TUITION);
- PASTORAL CARE or COUNSELLING;
- VOCATIONAL and related education guidance at a TUTORIAL.

TLK

TUTORIAL

A one-to-one weekly meeting between a school or college teacher and a student, usually for the purpose of giving vocational guidance and assessing progress.

TLK

UNDERACHIEVEMENT

Underachievement may be a feature which affects the ABLE, the AVERAGE PUPIL or those with LEARNING DIFFICULTIES (see: SPECIAL EDUCATION NEEDS). In other words, any child may fail to live up to his/her potential either temporarily or for a sustained period of time. The phrase is, however, most commonly used as a quasi-technical term to describe able pupils who deliberately and systematically fail to achieve. A number of research studies have provided profiles of the underachiever, which agree about the main characteristics, while differing in detail and emphasis. Typically the underachiever is anti-school and may not accept its values. He/she may be good orally, but produces poor written work, avoids teacher approval and may be outwardly hostile to achievement. He/she may be apparently bored and unmotivated, easily distracted, absorbed in a private world, friendly with older pupils outside his/her immediate class. Underachievers are sometimes emotionally unstable, frustrated or moody. By contrast, such pupils may be very interested and inventive when motivated, quick to learn, and able to ask 'difficult', i.e. insightful, questions. Sometimes such pupils display one or two all-consuming interests in which they achieve quite noticeably. No individual pupil will exactly match all the characteristics of any such check-list, but it is often estimated that up to 20 per cent of all pupils may underachieve consistently. In the case of able pupils a common motivation for underachievement is often social pressure. In some schools teachers and head teachers are reluctant to admit the presence of able pupils because of the implication for teaching them; so the teachers contribute to the underachievers' deliberately depressed self-image. In rather more cases peer-pressure discourages pupils who always get the right answers, show enthusiasm, behave or are seen as 'swots' or 'teacher's pet'. In extreme cases a few examples of suicide by school pupils have been attributed to this cause. Where a teacher suspects underachievement for any cause, careful but sensitive investigation should be undertaken to ascertain the cause, and a programme of remedial action sought.

(See also: OVERACHIEVEMENT)

TLK

UNDERSTANDING

Barrow and Woods (1988) distinguish between two types of understanding:

1. Mechanical understanding centres on knowing what to do, as when we speak of someone knowing how to operate a video recorder.
2. Reasoned understanding involves explanation and theoretical rationale, as when we refer to someone understanding calculus.

In 'teaching for understanding', it is reasoned understanding which is the aim. Such reasoned understanding involves the notions of connecting, relating and fitting in, so that EXPLANATIONS involve drawing on related issues, getting a topic in context or showing links with other topics. It makes sense to speak of partial understanding. A fuller understanding develops when generalities or principles are balanced with an understanding of particular cases. In teaching, if the balance tilts too much towards encouraging an understanding of generalities, the pupil may have insufficient examples of particulars to draw on to make the generalities meaningful. This might be the case if general principles of mathematics were drawn before a sufficient grasp of exemplars was reached. On the other hand, if the balance goes too far towards encouraging understanding of particulars, the learning can degenerate into rote learning of facts without the necessary general structures to enrich and give full meaning to them. An example of this would be memorizing the names of kings and queens and dates in history as though they were, in themselves, of value.

While cognitive understanding springs to mind readily, we can also speak of a more emotional understanding. Being able to sympathize with someone or seeing the justification for their views or actions constitutes this kind of understanding. Such understanding forms part of moral learning.

When a teacher wishes to check a pupil's rational understanding, the evidence that would contribute towards deciding that a pupil possessed understanding would centre on pupil responses to probing questions which revealed the pupil's ability to connect and relate information, issues, ideas, etc.

Further reading

Barrow, R. and Woods, R. (1989) *An Introduction to Philosophy of Education* (Routledge).

MF

UNEMPLOYMENT (AND SCHOOL LEAVERS)

Not surprisingly, the better qualified a school leaver, the better the chances of employment. Those with even minimal school-leaver qualifications are more successful in finding work than the completely unqualified.

Youth training eligibility rules give school leavers the right to:

- training of up to a year to the level of a National Vocational Qualification (including GCSE);
- training up to the age of 18;
- concessions for the disabled and people whose first language is not English.

MF

UNIVERSITY

Universities form the most prestigious provision in higher education. Financed mainly through Government funding via the Universities Funding Council, universities are independent self-governing institutions. A Royal Charter gives universities their rights and privileges and they can apply to the Crown, represented by Privy Council, for amendments to their charter or statutes. Universities independently decide:

- the degrees they award and the conditions under which degrees are conferred;
- student admissions;
- staff appointments.

As well as their teaching role, universities have a commitment to research.

MF

VERTICAL GROUPING

A system of organizing pupils into classes adopted mainly in small primary schools where there are insufficient staff to allow a single class to each year-group. Thus in vertically grouped classes (sometimes called 'family groups') there will be children whose ages span several school years. Those in favour of this kind of grouping argue its social values: older pupils learn to assist younger ones, both in learning and in practical tasks such as tying shoelaces. Nevertheless research suggests that, in well over half of the schools where vertical grouping occurs, this form of organization arises not out of educational imperative but simply as response to falling rolls or other external circumstances. Some possible problems associated with this kind of mixed-age schooling include the following:

- difficulties in delivering the National Curriculum;
- some staff may not be sufficiently experienced or committed to cope with it;
- parents may be suspicious of its effects on their children's progress;
- it may be a way of increasing class size or of sustaining over-size classes;
- this form of organization may be thought to be based on political or economic criteria rather than educational ones;
- it may increase the need for the quantity and range of resources available in individual classrooms;
- it may demand more individual attention for pupils than teachers have time to give;
- less able children may just sink through lack of individual attention;
- brighter/older pupils may be insufficiently stimulated;
- the school buildings may be unsuitable;
- staff may not have a sufficient range of teaching methods at their fingertips to work effectively in this context;
- there may be increased behaviour problems;
- it may cause stress to staff;
- there may be an increased administrative demand on staff, e.g. to keep records of pupil progress;
- the pupils may not like it.

TLK

VIDEO RECORDER
(See: TAPE RECORDER)

VOCATIONAL EDUCATION AND TRAINING
Among contributors to the wide area of vocational education and training are TRAINING ENTERPRISE COUNCILS (TECs) established by the Department for Employment; COLLEGES OF FURTHER EDUCATION; and COMPACTS, which are schemes to bring together schools and industry and the TRAINING AND VOCATIONAL EDUCATION INITIATIVE providing courses for 14 to 18 year olds. APPRENTICESHIP is being given new impetus by the government.

MF

VOCATIONAL GUIDANCE/VOCATIONAL EDUCATION
Vocational guidance tends to be less specific than careers guidance or careers education. It looks at broad abilities and skills and attempts to match these with broad areas of work such as clerical, manual or technological.

Vocational education leads to qualifications such as one of the National Vocational Qualifications, which provide a prospective employer with evidence that the person holding the qualification has skills which may be useful in industry or commerce.

MF

VOLUNTARY AIDED SCHOOLS
Voluntary Aided (VA) schools were defined following the 1944 Education Act. The 1944 Act established statutory education for secondary pupils but recognized the difficulty the church (and other providing bodies) could face in the light of the new needs. Two categories of voluntary schools were defined – Voluntary Aided and VOLUNTARY CONTROLLED. Voluntary aided schools received grant-aid from central government, and, unlike Voluntary Controlled schools, religious instruction could be given in accordance with the principles and doctrines of the providing body. To assist VA schools with this provision, Diocesan syllabuses have been developed by most of the Diocesan Boards of Education and Training. In VA schools, church governors are in a majority on the GOVERNING BODY.

CAK

VOLUNTARY CONTROLLED SCHOOLS
Voluntary Controlled (VC) schools were defined following the 1944 Education Act. The 1944 Act established statutory education for secondary schools but recognized the difficulty the church (and other providing bodies) could face in the light of the new needs. Two categories of voluntary schools were defined – VOLUNTARY AIDED and Voluntary Controlled. Voluntary controlled schools were entirely paid for by the LEA but the original providing body retained some rights. In VC schools religious education was taught according to the Agreed Syllabus of the LEA, with the provision to allow parents to ask for denominational instruction. In VC schools church governors are in a minority on the GOVERNING BODY.

CAK

VYGOTSKY, LEV (1896–1943)
The Russian psychologist Vygotsky conducted studies of cognitive development which indicated that learning and knowledge were acquired through social contacts with others who had more knowledge and greater skills. When children attempted tasks while working with others who were more competent they were more likely to succeed than if they tried the task alone. Pointers and directions were given by the more competent pupils which

helped the child view the task more clearly and focus on possible routes to understanding. Vygotsky also investigated the sequence of actions which led to understanding and the relationships between thought and language.

Further reading

Van Der Veer, R. and Valsiner, J. (Eds) (1994) *The Vygotsky Reader* (Blackwell).
Van Der Veer, R. and Valsiner, J. (1993) *Understanding Vygotsky: A Quest for Synthesis* (Blackwell).

MF

WALES
In Wales, the Secretary of State for Wales is responsible for education. Aspects of education coming outside the remit of the Secretary of State include universities, teacher qualifications, salaries, pensions and conduct.

MF

WELSH LANGUAGE
Education through the medium of Welsh is available throughout the statutory years of schooling in all Welsh LEAs. However, this does not apply to all areas within each LEA.

In Welsh schools where the medium of teaching is the English language, Welsh is offered as a first or a second language in primary and secondary schools.

Address

Welsh Office, Education Department, Phase 2 Government Buildings, Ty Glas Road, Llanishen, Cardiff CF4 5WE
tel: 0222 825111

MF

WHITE PAPER – EDUCATION AND TRAINING FOR THE 21ST CENTURY, MAY 1991
This White Paper provided two volumes of substantial reform to the post-16 sector. The intentions of the White Paper were set out as follows:

1. To introduce NATIONAL VOCATIONAL QUALIFICATIONS as fast as possible, with more general NVQs for young people. A level and AS level syllabuses to be strengthened.

2. To develop new Diplomas, recording achievement in academic and vocational qualifications. Schools to be allowed to admit part-time and adult students to their sixth forms.
3. To extend employer influence in the education system through TRAINING AND ENTERPRISE COUNCILS (TEC).
4. To offer every 16 and 17 year old leaving full-time education a training credit within the life of the next Parliament.
5. To strengthen careers advice and vocational work in schools, and to legislate to allow a variety of local options about how the Careers Service is run.
6. Levels of attainment to be raised by:

   • ensuring that all pupils aged 16 stay to the end of the summer term;
   • extending the COMPACTS approach nation-wide;
   • increasing achievement of higher level vocational qualifications;
   • providing more places in higher education for the increasing numbers who can benefit from them.

7. To legislate to give further education and sixth-form colleges independence to expand and respond to their markets.

TLK

WHOLE CLASS TEACHING

Whole class teaching is the most common TEACHING MODE. It consists fundamentally of the teacher either delivering the same information to all pupils simultaneously (what we have called the DIDACTIC MODEL of teaching) or setting the whole class the same task at the same time. Research has shown that more than 75 per cent of a pupil's experience, especially in secondary schools, may be of this type of teaching.

The advantages of whole class teaching are seen to be that:

• it gives all pupils in the class shared information or knowledge;
• it is an economic method of putting knowledge across in a short space of time;
• it helps to give a shared experience;
• it keeps pupils close together in covering the syllabus;
• it can ensure (e.g. in examination work) that at least a minimum of course work is covered;
• it may be a good way of giving a skill or set of instructions (e.g. how to conduct an experiment) before group or individualized work;
• it helps pupils respect each other's strengths and weaknesses;

- it may allow more access to apparatus which is in short supply;
- it enables teachers to tailor a range of tasks more appropriately to children's needs and abilities;
- it is a useful way of beginning a topic;
- it can be a useful way of pulling pupils at different stages in a task together;
- it can be a vehicle for revision or reinforcement;
- it can provide feedback to the teacher on pupils' progress.

Some examples of its appropriate use:

Miss Smith uses whole class teaching to start off a topic on 'colour' with her primary class. She wants them to begin from shared materials, ideas and working patterns, and later to branch out on ideas of their own.

Mr Jones is a science teacher. He uses the whole class to demonstrate how to carry out a scientific experiment to manufacture oxygen gas.

Mrs Williams teaches music. She uses the whole class to build up a picture of how different sections of an orchestra come together to make harmonious sound.

Mr French is a linguist. He uses the whole class for rapid-fire question and answer revision of grammar and vocabulary.

Teaching skills required for whole class teaching:

- the ability to give clear instructions;
- good EXPLAINING SKILLS;
- CLASS CONTROL skills;
- sound preparation.

The role of the teacher is fundamentally that of an instructor.

TLK

WHOLE CURRICULUM
(See: NATIONAL CURRICULUM)

WORK EXPERIENCE
Work experience is allowed for school pupils aged 14 to 16 so long as it is seen as a general broad introduction to the world of work and not a training in a specific job or career. Up to two weeks per year is permitted. To be effective, work experience requires appropriate preparation and follow-up

work at school and needs to be carefully planned and monitored. It may involve pupils making a range of visits to places of work, 'shadowing' an employee to learn about the work or some form of participation in the job itself.

MF

WRITING (PUPILS)
(See: ENGLISH)

YEARS OF SCHOOLING (NOMENCLATURE)
The nomenclature for the years of schooling encompassed by statutory education is as follows: (Y = year)

Age	Description	Key Stage
5 or below	reception (R)	
5 to 7	Y1 and 2	1
7 to 11	Y3 to 6	2
11 to 14	Y7 to 9	3
14 to 16	Y10 and 11	4
16 to 18	Y12 and 13	(5)

MF

YOUTH WORK
LEAs provide youth work staff, buildings and other resources for young people and there is a wide range of national and local voluntary youth organizations. This includes youth clubs, uniformed organizations, school-based youth centres, residential centres and specialized youth centres (e.g. for sport). Special projects have developed to target specific groups such as the unemployed or young people from minority ethnic communities. 'Outreach' workers strive to involve young people who are not involved in the more formal organizations. Counselling and advice services are also offered on such issues as drugs and sexual behaviour.

MF

Section 2 – Acronyms and Abbreviations

Michael Farrell

AACE	Association for Adult and Continuing Education
AAI	Association of Art Institutions
AASSH	Anglican Association of Secondary School Heads
ABAPSTAS	Association of Blind and Partially Sighted Teachers and Students
ABE	Adult basic education
ABRC	Advisory Board for the Research Councils
ACACE	Advisory Council for Adult and Continuing Education
ACACHE	Association of Career Advisers in Colleges of Higher Education
ACC	Association of County Councils
ACE	Advisory Centre for Education
ACFHE	Association of Colleges of Further and Higher Education
ACG	Annual Capital Grants
ACOST	Advisory Council on Science and Technology
ACP	Associate of the College of Preceptors
ACU	Association of Commonwealth Universities
ADAR	Art and Design Admissions Registry
ADE	Association of Directors of Education
ADES	Association of Directors of Education in Scotland
AEAS	Association of Educational Advisers in Scotland
AEB	Associated Examining Board
AEC	Association of Education Committees
AEP	Association of Educational Psychologists
AGCAS	Association of Graduate Careers Advisory Services
AGMAS	Association of Grant Maintained and Aided Schools
AHMPS	Association of Head Mistresses of Preparatory Schools
ALBSU	Adult Literacy and Basic Skills Unit
ALL	Association for Language Learning
AMA	Association of Metropolitan Authorities
APA	Accreditation of Prior Learning
APC	Association of Principals of Colleges
APER	Association of Publishers' Educational Representatives
APFO	Association of Playing Fields Officers
APHE	Association for Part-Time Higher Education
APL	Accreditation of Prior Learning

APLET	Association for Programmed Learning and Educational Technology
APRE	Association for Recruitment and Retention in Education
APS	Assisted Places Scheme
APU	Assessment of Performance Unit
APVIC	Association of Principals in Sixth Form Colleges
ARE	Association for Recurrent Education
ARELS	Association of Recognised English Language Schools
ASE	Association for Science Education
	Association for Special Education
ASLIB	Association of Special Libraries and Information Bureaux
AT	Attainment targets
ATCODE	Association of Teachers in Colleges and Departments of Education
ATD	Art Teachers Diploma
ATDS	Association of Teachers of Domestic Science
ATL	Association of Teachers and Lecturers
ATM	Association of Teachers of Mathematics
AUT	Association of University Teachers
AVA	Audio-visual aid
BA	Bachelor of Arts
BAALPE	British Association of Advisers and Lecturers in Physical Education
BAAS	British Association for the Advancement of Science
BAAT	British Association of Art Therapists
BAC	British Association for Counselling
BACIE	British Association for Commercial and Industrial Education
BAECE	British Association for Early Childhood Education
BALT	British Association for Language Teaching
BATOD	British Association of Teachers of the Deaf
BDA	British Dyslexia Association
BEAS	British Educational Administration Society
B.Ed.	Bachelor of Education
BEEA	British Educational Equipment Association
BEMAS	British Educational Management and Administration Society
BERA	British Education Research Association
BFES	British Families Education Service
BIM	British Institute of Management

BL	British Library
BPS	British Psychological Society
B.Sc.	Bachelor of Science
BSS	Broadcasting Support Services
BTEC	Business and Technology Education Council
BYC	British Youth Council
CAD	Computer-assisted design
CAL	Computer-assisted learning
CAM	Computer-assisted manufacture
CASE	Campaign for the Advancement of State Education
CATE	Council for Accreditation of Teacher Education
CATS	Credit Accumulation and Transfer System
CBT	Competency-based teaching
CCETSW	Central Council for Education and Training in Social Work
CCPR	Central Council of Physical Recreation
CCT	Compulsory competitive tendering
CDP	Committee of Directors of Polytechnics
CEA	Council for Educational Advance
	Community Education Association
CEDC	Community Education Development Centre
CEDO	Centre for Educational Development Overseas
CEE	Centre for Environmental Education
CEO	Chief Education Officer
CEP	Community Enterprise Project
CERI	Centre for Educational Research and Innovation
CET	Council for Educational Technology
CEWC	Council for Education in World Citizenship
CFE	College of Further Education
CFF	Common funding formula
CGLI	City and Guilds of London Institute
CHC	Community Health Council
CHE	College of Higher Education
CI	Chief Inspector
CILT	Centre for Information on Language Teaching and Research
CLASP	Consortium of Local Authorities Special Program
CLAW	Consortium, Local Authorities Wales
CLEA	Council of Local Education Authorities
CLEA/ST	Council of Local Education Authorities/School Teachers' Joint Committee

CLEAPSE	Consortium of Local Education Authorities for the Provision of Science Equipment
Cmnd	Command paper
COIC	Careers and Occupational Information Centre
COPS	Committee of Polytechnic Secretaries
COSLA	Convention of Scottish Local Authorities
CPVE	Certificate of Pre-Vocational Education
CRAC	Careers Research and Advisory Centre
CRE	Commission for Racial Equality
CSIE	Centre for Studies on Integration in Education
CSV	Community Service Volunteers
CTC	City Technology College
CTF	Catholic Teachers Foundation
CVCP	Committee of Vice-Chancellors and Principals
CYSA	Community and Youth Service Association
DE	Department of Employment
DENI	Department of Education for Northern Ireland
DFE	Department For Education
DHSS	Department of Health and Social Security
DipHE	Diploma in Higher Education
DMS	Diploma in Management Studies
DoE	Department of the Environment
EBD	Emotional and behavioural difficulties
Ed.D.	Doctor of Education
EDU	Educational Disadvantage Unit
EFL	English as a Foreign Language
EFVA	Educational Foundation for Visual Aids
EIS	Educational Institute of Scotland
ELAS	Education Law Advisers Service
EMIE	Education Management Information Exchange
EnTra	Engineering Training Authority
EOC	Equal Opportunities Commission
EPC	Educational Publishers Council
EPIC	Educational Policy Information Service
ERA	Educational Recording Agency
	Education Reform Act
ESAC	House of Commons Education, Science and Arts Committee
ESG	Education Support Grants
ESHA	European Secondary Heads Association

ESL	English as a Second Language
ESRC	Economic and Social Research Council
ETUCE	European Trade Union Committee on Education
FAS	Funding Agency for Schools
FCP	Fellow of the College of Preceptors
FE	Further education
FEFCE	Further Education Funding Council for England
FETT	Further Education Teacher Training
FEU	Further Education Unit
FSA	Foundation for Sport and the Arts
FTE	Full-time equivalent
GBA	Governing Bodies (of Boys Public Schools) Association
GBGSA	Governing Bodies of Girls' (Public) Schools Association
GCSE	General Certificate of Secondary Education
GEST	Grants for Education Support and Training
GM	Grant Maintained (Schools)
GNVQ	General National Vocational Qualification
GPDST	Girls Public Day School Trust
GRE	Grant Related Expenditure
GSA	Girls' Schools Association
GTC	General Teaching Council
GTTR	Graduate Teachers Training Registry
HAPA	Handicapped Adventure Playground Association
HE	Higher Education
HEFC	Higher Education Funding Council for England
HEFCW	Higher Education Funding Council for Wales
HEIST	Higher Education Information Services Trust
HEQC	Higher Education Quality Council
HMC	Head Masters' Conference
HMI	Her Majesty's Inspectorate/Inspectors
HMSO	Her Majesty's Stationery Office
HNC	Higher National Certificate
HND	Higher National Diploma
IAC	Interim Advisory Committee on School Teachers' Pay and Conditions
IAPS	Incorporated Association of Preparatory Schools
IBA	Independent Broadcasting Authority

IBO	International Baccalaureate Organisation
ICA	Institute for Contemporary Arts
ICCS	International Centre for Child Studies
ICEd	Institute of Craft Education
ICO	Institute of Careers Officers
ILEP	International Institute for Educational Planning
INSET	In-service training of teachers
INTO	Irish National Teachers' Organisation
IPPR	Institute for Public Policy Research
IQ	Intelligence quotient
ISIS	Independent Schools Information Service
IT	Information Technology
ITB	Industrial Training Board
ITT	Initial teacher training
IVS	International Voluntary Service
JCR	Junior common room
JNC	Joint Negotiating Committee
KS	Key Stage(s)
LACSAB	Local Authorities' Conditions of Service Advisory Board (Burnham Secretariat)
LAMSAC	Local Authorities' Management Services and Computer Committee
LCCI	London Chamber of Commerce and Industry
LCP	Licentiate of the College of Preceptors
LEA	Local Education Authority
LEAP	LEA Project for School Management Training
LETGS	LEA Training Grant Scheme
LISC	Library and Information Services Council
LMS	Local Management of Schools
MA	Master of Arts
M.Ed.	Master of Education
MENCAP	National Society for Mentally Handicapped Children and Adults
MESU	Microelectronics Education Support Unit
MLA	Modern Language Association
MLD	Moderate Learning Difficulties
M.Phil.	Master of Philosophy
MRO	Media Research Officer

MSC	Manpower Services Commission
M.Sc.	Master of Science
NACAE	National Advisory Council on Adult Education
NACESW	National Association of Chief Education Social Workers
NACGT	National Association of Careers and Guidance Teachers
NACYS	National Advisory Council for Youth Services
NAEIAC	National Association of Educational Inspectors, Advisers and Consultants
NAFE	Non-Advanced Further Education
NAGC	National Association for Gifted Children
NAGN	National Association of Governors and Managers
NAHT	National Association of Head Teachers
NAIEA	National Association of Inspectors and Educational Advisers
NAPE	National Association for Primary Education
NAS/UWT	National Association of Schoolmasters/Union of Women Teachers
NASMO	National Association of School Meals Organisers
NASEN	National Association for Special Educational Needs
NASWE	National Association of Social Workers in Education
NATE	National Association of Teachers of English
NATFHE	National Association of Teachers in Further and Higher Education
NATHE	National Association of Teachers of Home Economics and Technology
NAYCEO	National Association of Youth and Community Education Officers
NBL	National Book League
NCE	National Commission on Education
NCES	National Council for Educational Standards
NCET	National Council for Educational Technology
NCMA	National Child Minding Association
NCPTA	National Confederation of Parent-Teacher Associations
NCSS	National Council for Schools' Sports
NCVQ	National Council for Vocational Qualifications
NCVYS	National Council for Voluntary Youth Services
NEAB	Northern Examinations and Assessment Board
NEEDS	New Examinations-Evaluation and Development in Schools
NFAE	National Foundation for Arts Education

NFER	National Foundation for Educational Research (in England and Wales)
NFVLS	National Federation of Voluntary Literacy Schemes
NIACE	National Institute of Adult Continuing Education
NIECE	National Institute for Careers Education and Counselling
NJC	National Joint Committee
NNEB	National Nursery Examination Board
NPFA	National Playing Fields Association
NSEAD	National Society for Education in Art and Design
NSSA	National School Sailing Association
NUS	National Union of Students
NUSS	National Union of School Students
NUT	National Union of Teachers
NVQ	National Vocational Qualification
NYB	National Youth Bureau
OAL	Office of Arts and Libraries
OFSTED	Office for Standards in Education
ONC	Ordinary National Certificate
OND	Ordinary National Diploma
OU	Open University
PA	Publishers' Association
PACE	Parent Alliance for Choice in Education
PANN	Professional Association of Nursery Nurses
PAT	Professional Association of Teachers
PCEF	Polytechnics and Colleges Employers Forum
PCFC	Polytechnics and Colleges Funding Council
PE	Physical education
PEA	Physical Education Association
PGCE	Postgraduate Certificate in Education
PH	Physically handicapped
PHAB	Physically handicapped and able-bodied
Ph.D.	Doctor of Philosophy
PIT	Pool of Inactive Teachers
PLEASE	Permanent Liaison of Educational Associations and Schools
PoS	Programmes of Study
PPA	Pre-school Playgroups Association
PS	Partially sighted
PSE	Personal/Social Education

PSI	Policy Studies Institute
PtHg	Partially hearing
PT	Part Time
PTA	Parent–Teacher Association
PTR	Pupil–teacher Ratio
QTS	Qualified Teacher Status
RANSC	Records of Achievement National Steering Committee
RC	Roman Catholic
R & D	Research and Development
RE	Religious Education
RSA	Royal Society of Arts
RSG	Rate support grant
SA	Special agreement
SACRE	Standing Advisory Council on Religious Education
SALT	Scottish Association for Language Teaching
SATs	Standard Assessment Tasks
SATIPS	Society of Assistants Teaching in Preparatory Schools
SATRO	Science and Technology Regional Organisations
SCAA	School Curriculum and Assessment Authority
SCALU	Scottish Adult Literacy Unit
SCDC	School Curriculum Development Council
SCEA	Service Children's Education Authority
SCEC	Scottish Community Education Council
SCENE	Rural Schools Curriculum Enhancement National Evaluation
SCETT	Standing Committee for the Education and Training of Teachers in the Public Sector
SCIA	Society of Chief Inspectors and Advisors
SCIP	School Curriculum Industry Partnership
SCOP	Standing Conference of Principals
SCOLA	Second Consortium of Local Authorities
SCOTVEC	Scottish Vocational Education Council
SCSST	Standing Conference on Schools' Science and Technology
SEA	Socialist Education Association
	Society for Education through Art
SEC	Secondary Examinations Council
SED	Scottish Education Department
SEFT	Society for Education in Film and Television
SEMERC	Special Education Microelectronic Resource Centres

SEO	Society of Education Officers
SERC	Science and Engineering Research Council
SGSS	Self Governing State School
SHA	Secondary Heads' Association
SHEFC	Scottish Higher Education Funding Council
SHMIS	Society of Headmasters of Independent Schools
SI	Staff Inspector
SI	Statutory Instruments
SLA	School Library Association
SLD	Secretarial Language Diploma
	Severe learning difficulties
SLS	School Library Service
SPACE	Satellite Project for Adult and Continuing Education
SRC	Science Research Council
SSA	Scottish Schoolteachers' Association
SSR	Staff–student ratio
STABIS	State Boarding Information Service
TACADE	Teachers Advisory Council on Alcohol and Drug Education
TASC	Teaching as a Career Unit
TCA	Tertiary College Association
TEC	Training and Enterprise Councils
TECHBAC	Technological Baccalaureate
TEFL	Teaching English as a Foreign Language
TES	*Times Educational Supplement*
THES	*Times Higher Educational Supplement*
UCAC	Undeb Canedlaethol Athrawon Cymru (National Association of Teachers of Wales)
UCCA	Universities Central Council on Admissions
UCET	Universities Council for the Education of Teachers
UFC	Universities Funding Council
UGC	University Grants Committee
ULEAC	University of London Examinations and Assessment Council
UNESCO	United Nations Educational, Scientific and Cultural Organisation
U3A	University of the Third Age
VA	Voluntary Aided (schools)
VC	Voluntary Controlled (schools)

Section 3 – Directory of Organizations

Carolle Kerry

ACTION FOR SICK CHILDREN (NATIONAL ASSOCIATION FOR THE WELFARE OF CHILDREN IN HOSPITAL)

Action for Sick Children joins parents and professionals in promoting high quality health care for sick children in hospital and at home. Formed in 1961, it successfully campaigned for open visiting for children by their families and for provision of accommodation for parents. Some of the current aims of the Association include:

- an end to the nursing of children on adult wards;
- the provision of more paediatric trained nurses;
- the provision of more education in hospitals;
- a greater sharing of care with and support of parents.

Action for Sick Children may be contacted at:
Argyle House, 29–31 Euston Road, London NW1 2SD
tel: 071 833 2041   fax: 071 837 2110
Membership is open to interested professionals or parents, corporate membership is available to Health Authorities.

ASSOCIATION FOR LANGUAGE LEARNING (ALL)

The Association for Language Learning is the major UK subject teaching association for all involved in the teaching and learning of modern foreign languages in all sectors of education and at all levels from 5–18 to Further, Higher and Adult Education and Training. Members' needs are met through branch meetings, INSET courses, the annual conference and materials exhibition Language World, and its newsletter, published four times a year. The Association is linked to language teaching organizations world-wide through its membership of international bodies. Membership is open to all involved in language teaching and learning.

The publications for the Association for Language Learning are specifically produced for teachers in all school sectors, lecturers, advisers, teacher trainers, business language trainers and interested students of modern languages. The Association publishes six journal titles. These are each produced twice a year and are available to libraries and teaching institutions on the basis of an annual subscription. *Language World* newsletter is published quarterly.

Further details about the Association may be obtained from:
Association for Language Learning, 16, Regent Place, Rugby CV21 2PN
tel: 0788 546443   fax: 0788 544149

ASSOCIATION FOR SCIENCE EDUCATION (ASE)

The Association is open to teachers, advisers, technicians, industrialists and others contributing to science education. The Association has a membership of over 24,000.

The Association is independent in its thinking and finance, and is a registered charity financed by members' contributions. ASE provides a forum for the views of members on science education issues through its regional and national committee structures. It promotes, supports and develops science education in schools and colleges from primary through to tertiary education.

ASE encourages, initiates and promotes curriculum development projects in science – for example, the growing range of SATIS (Science and Technology in Society) projects.

ASE offers support, advice and information to:

- individual teachers of science, schools, colleges and local education authorities;
- those involved in industry and commerce.

ASE organizes a wide range of meetings and conferences both nationally and regionally, and publishes a variety of journals, newsletters and occasional publications. Further details of these may be obtained from:
The General Secretary, ASE, College Lane, Hatfield, Herts AL10 9AA
tel: 0707 267411   fax: 0707 266532

ASSOCIATION OF GRANT MAINTAINED AND AIDED SCHOOLS (AGMAS)

The purpose of the Association of Grant Maintained and Aided schools is to:

- promote the interests and the well-being of member schools;
- represent the views of members on educational matters to the DFE;
- provide support and information for member schools.

The Association is non-political with a committee composed of heads, clerks or governors of member schools, who give their services free. There are no paid officers and the subscription is kept to a minimum. Membership is open to all primary and secondary Grant Maintained and Aided schools, and further details may be obtained from:
The Hon. Secretary, AGMAS, 1, St Margaret's Drive,
Twickenham TW1 1QL
tel: 081 892 3305

ASSOCIATION OF TEACHERS AND LECTURERS (ATL), FORMERLY THE ASSISTANT MASTERS AND MISTRESSES ASSOCIATION (AMMA)

The Association is open to teachers and lecturers in maintained and independent schools, sixth form, tertiary and further education colleges in England, Wales and Northern Ireland.
    The Association aims to:

- promote the cause of education generally in the United Kingdom and elsewhere;
- protect and improve the status, and to further the legitimate professional interests of teachers;
- render legal advice and assistance in professional matters to members.

The Association produces a variety of publications, ranging from general leaflets (e.g. Accidents to pupils; First Aid in schools) through to booklets, factsheets and reports (e.g. Education 16–19: Breaking the Barriers; Teachers as governors). These publications are free to members and an order form may be obtained from:
ATL, 7 Northumberland Street, London WC2N 5DA
tel: 071 930 6441   fax: 071 930 1359

ASSOCIATION OF TEACHERS OF MATHEMATICS (ATM)

The Association of Teachers of Mathematics brings together all those concerned with mathematical education in primary schools, secondary schools, colleges and universities.
    The aims of the Association are:

- to encourage and enable increased understanding of the learning process, especially in relation to mathematics and its applications;

- to encourage sharing of teaching and learning strategies and to promote the exploration of new ideas and possibilities;
- to elucidate the above aims and their practical implications, for the benefit of those who have working involvement with, or an interest in, mathematical education.

Membership is open, with options for personal, student or institutional membership. Members receive four issues of *Mathematics Teaching*, three issues of *Micromath*, newsletters and occasional free publications. For details of membership and publications (the Association has an extensive publications list), contact:
ATM, 7 Shaftesbury Street, Derby DE23 8YB
tel: 0332 46599   fax: 0332 204357

ASSOCIATION OF UNIVERSITY TEACHERS (AUT)

The objects of the Association are the advancement of University Education and Research, the regulation of relations between academic and related staffs in universities and analogous institutions and their employers, the promotion of common actions by those staffs, and the safeguarding of interests of the members.

Membership of the Association is open to all academic or similar staff in universities and equivalent or related institutions. Full or part-time staff are equally welcome, as are academic-related staff; that is, those whose occupation would normally require a degree or professional qualification. All members of the Universities Superannuation Scheme (or eligible members) may join the Association. Membership is also open to visiting members who are academics or academic-related staff. Postgraduate and retiree staff may also join.

Publications, which are free to members, include *AUT Bulletin*, a termly A4 journal, *AUT Update*, nine times per annum newsletter and *AUT Woman*, a termly newsletter. Details of publications and membership may be obtained from:
Association of University Teachers, United House, 9 Pembridge Road, London W11 3HJ
tel: 071 221 4370   fax: 071 727 6547

BRITISH EDUCATIONAL RESEARCH ASSOCIATION (BERA)

The British Educational Research Association is the major organization for educational research in the United Kingdom. It was formed in 1974 with 'the broad aim of encouraging the pursuit of educational research and its applications for the improvement of educational practice and the general benefit of the community'. The Association has about 600 members, most of whom are university or college lecturers, some are contract researchers and a small proportion are school teachers.

BERA is active in the UK Association of Learned Societies in the Social Sciences and regularly makes submissions to government and national bodies on educational research issues. Recently a set of ethical guidelines for educational research has been adopted and published.

The publications of BERA include: the *British Educational Research Journal*, *BERA Dialogues* and *BERA Research Intelligence*. *BERA Research Intelligence* is a quarterly newsletter which gives substantial reports on BERA activities, and accounts of issues affecting educational research nationally and internationally.

At the end of each summer BERA organizes a four-day residential conference which is the largest gathering of educational researchers in the UK. Recent venues have included London, Nottingham, Stirling, Liverpool and Oxford.

BERA sees educational research as attempts to advance educational knowledge and wisdom through systematic enquiry and critical debate, and governed by three ethical principles: respect for truth, respect for persons, and respect for democratic values. BERA takes a broad view of educational research to include any disciplined enquiry – empirical, reflective and creative – which serves educational judgements and decisions. This may be conducted in educational settings such as nursery, primary, secondary, further, higher, continuing and adult education; industrial, commercial and professional training; and local and national systems of education. The methods and techniques of enquiry may originate from a practical view of how knowledge is best generated and utilized by teachers, and educational policy makers and managers, or they may draw on the methodologies of other social science disciplines, such as sociology, psychology, anthropology, philosophy or economics.

Membership is open to all who are interested in educational research. In 1994 the subscription rate is £40, for which the member receives four issues of *BERJ* and three issues of *Research Intelligence*. He/she is entitled to attend BERA meetings at members' rates and to vote at general meetings. Reduced rates are available for retired persons and students, and for members joining during the calendar year.

Further information may be obtained from:
BERA Office, Scottish Council for Research in Education,
15 St John Street, Edinburgh, EH8 8JR
tel: 031 557 2944   fax: 031 556 9454

BUSINESS AND TECHNOLOGY EDUCATION COUNCIL (BTEC)

BTEC is an awarding body, and approves work-related programmes of study run by schools, colleges, universities and other training organizations in a wide range of subjects throughout England, Wales and Northern Ireland. It awards qualifications to students who successfully complete these programmes, which are recognized by employers, educationalists and professional bodies throughout the United Kingdom.

BTEC is working with NCVQ (the National Council for Vocational Qualifications) to develop the NVQ framework of vocational qualifications. BTEC qualifications give entry to over 100 professional bodies and in many cases give exemption from some of their examinations.

For further general information, contact:
BTEC Information Services, Central House, Upper Woburn Place, London WC1H 0HH
tel: 071 413 8400   fax: 071 387 6068
BTEC produces fact sheets on specific courses, general guides for students and employers, and annual reports. These, together with a full publications list, may be obtained from the address given above.

CHOIR SCHOOLS ASSOCIATION

The aim of the Association is to promote the welfare of Choir Schools, and to hold meetings to discuss and improve education and other matters relating to the life of choristers and the running of Choir Schools. Members of the Association are headmasters of preparatory, senior, independent and state Choir Schools. Associate members include headmasters of schools that provide education for some younger members of a cathedral, college or church choir. There are overseas members. The Association publishes an annual magazine '*Choir Schools Today*'; further details may be obtained from:
The Choir Schools Association, The Minster School, Deangate, York Y01 2JA
tel: 0904 625217   fax: 0904 632418

CITY AND GUILDS OF LONDON INSTITUTE (CGLI)

The City and Guilds of London Institute exists to encourage, assess and recognize achievement to the benefit of the individual and of industry, commerce and the community. It was founded in 1878 by the Corporation of London and sixteen of the City Livery Companies. It was granted a Royal Charter of Incorporation in 1900.

It is now one of the country's longest standing awarding bodies in the field of vocational education, with schemes in over 400 subjects in most occupational sectors. In addition, City and Guilds also offers certificates for technical and leisure activities, for general education and use in schools. Every year there are around 1.3 million entries for City and Guilds awards.

City and Guilds awards Certificates and Diplomas to candidates who have been successful in all elements of the assessment at a given level and RECORDS OF ACHIEVEMENT for success in a unit or component of an assessment.

City and Guilds has five different grades of membership from Founder members (the Corporation of London and the livery companies) through Corporate Ordinary Members, Fellows of the City and Guilds of London Institute, members by qualification and honorary members. The Institute publishes a City and Guilds Handbook and a Directory of Assessment of Awards. Further information may be obtained from:

The Secretary to the Institute, 76 Portland Place, London W1N 4AA
tel: 071 278 2468   071 436 7630

CITY TECHNOLOGY COLLEGES TRUST

Founded in 1987, the City Technology Colleges Trust is a registered charity, and is funded through a combination of private sector sponsorship and government grant.

During its early years the Trust played an important role in establishing the fifteen City Technology Colleges. This included both helping to raise £35 million in sponsorship from industry as well as finding the sites. Between 1990 and 1993 the Trust carried out a major curriculum project which provided support for City Technology Colleges (CTCs) and schools associated with the Trust. The main thrust of this development covered the curriculum areas of Information Technology, Design and Technology, Science, Business Education, Modern Languages for Business and Post-16 provision.

The Trust's current projects include the following:

The new Technology Colleges programme – The 1993 Education Act makes provision for the establishment of Technology Colleges, building on the success and popularity of the fifteen CTCs and enabling existing schools to adopt the characteristics of a CTC style education. The CTC Trust is the lead non-governmental body with a remit to promote and support the Technology Colleges Programme.

Affiliation Scheme – schools which support the CTC style of education may apply for affiliation to the CTC Trust.

Identification and dissemination of best practice – The CTC Trust, through its publications and conferences, helps to disseminate the good practice developed in CTCs and affiliated schools.

The Royal College of Art Schools Technology project – A three-year programme of curriculum and assessment development to support Technology Education, organized in association with the Royal College of Art and Imperial College, London.

The Technological Baccalaureate (TechBac) – The TechBac is an initiative of the CTC Trust and the City and Guilds of London Institute. It is a new advanced level qualification and is designed to bridge current academic and vocational routes with a technical focus for all students.

Further information about the CTC Trust and details of its publications may be obtained from:
CTC Trust, 15 Young Street, London W8 5EH
tel: 071 376 2511   fax: 071 938 1961
Information supplied by CTC Trust

COPYRIGHT LICENSING AGENCY LTD (CLA)

The Copyright Licensing Agency was formed in 1982 by the Authors' Licensing and Collecting Society (ALCS) and the Publishers' Licensing Society (PLS). CLA administers collectively photocopying and other copying rights that it is uneconomic for writers and publishers to administer for themselves. The Agency issues collective and transactional licences, and the fees it collects, after the deduction of costs, are distributed at regular intervals to authors and publishers via their respective societies. Since 1987 CLA has distributed £15.6 million.

CLArion is a newsletter which CLA publishes twice yearly. Further information may be obtained from:
The Chief Executive, CLA, 90 Tottenham Court Road, London W1P 9HE
tel: 071 436 5931   fax: 071 436 3986

COUNCIL FOR THE ACCREDITATION OF TEACHER EDUCATION (CATE)

CATE was established in 1984 by the then Secretary of State for Education and Science to review existing courses of INITIAL TEACHER TRAINING (ITT) in

England and Wales (and, subsequently, Northern Ireland) to ensure that they met his newly-published criteria for accreditation and to advise him on the approval of new courses. The Council completed this task by 1989. It was reconstituted in 1990 and given the additional tasks of reviewing the criteria and of identifying and disseminating good practice. Its role in the accrediting process was adjusted to take account of the more substantial contribution to the process required from local committees under Circular 24/89.

The accrediting procedure and the criteria for secondary phase courses for all providers of initial teacher training were reviewed in 1991. The Department of Education's Circular 9/92 abolished local committees and substituted institutional accreditation for the process of course approval. At the same time the Circular signalled a marked increase in the amount of time which students on secondary phase courses should spend in schools and in the share of responsibility for training entrants to the teaching profession which should be undertaken by schools.

CATE had offered advice on both this major procedural development in England and Wales in accrediting institutions for their ITT provision and re-shaping the criteria in which the professional competences of those seeking QUALIFIED TEACHER STATUS (QTS) would be the clearly stated focus of training. The Council was invited by the Secretary of State to offer guidance to higher education institutions and schools on the implementation of Circular 9/92. CATE has issued a corresponding Note of Guidance for Circular 14/93 (England) and 62/93 (Wales) for the primary phase of initial training.

As well as making recommendations to the Secretary of State on the accreditation of ITT, CATE has undertaken an enquiry into training for the teaching of reading and has responded to Ministers' requests to advise them on the development of primary phase training and a range of recent developments including the option for a post-CATE accrediting procedure. Before its work is brought to an end in August 1994, the Council will be advising the Secretary of State in two other areas:

(a) statements of competence and records of achievements for new teachers;

(b) the content and structure of courses designed specifically to prepare classroom assistants in primary schools to offer greater support to qualified teachers in the teaching and learning of basic skills.

Information supplied by CATE

DYSLEXIA INSTITUTE, THE

The Dyslexia Institute was founded in 1972 as an educational charity for assessing and teaching dyslexic students and for training their teachers. In 1993 the Institute operates centres throughout Britain and has become the national educational organization for those who experience specific difficulties with learning. The aim of the Institute is to continue to set and maintain standards of education for dyslexic people by:

- identifying the needs of each individual;
- teaching him/her in the way in which he/she can learn;
- developing his/her abilities;
- equipping him/her to overcome his/her difficulties using strategies and information technology.

Membership of the Institute is available to teachers trained by the Institute, and there is also a Friends' Association. *As we see it* is published by the Dyslexia Institute twice-yearly, and further details, for both membership and information generally, may be obtained from:
The General Secretary, 133 Gresham Road, Staines TW18 2AJ
tel: 0784 463851   fax: 0784 460747

EDUCATIONAL RECORDING AGENCY (ERA)

An Educational Recording Agency licence enables educational establishments to record legally from radio and television virtually any programme which is deemed for use for education purposes. The licence allows unlimited copies to be made, with no restriction on the length of time they can be kept. At the moment, Open University programmes are subject to a separate licence and are not covered by the ERA licence. Only establishments as defined by the Secretary of State in the Act and Statutory Instruments Nos 1067 and 1068 are able to take out an ERA licence. These include schools (both maintained and independent), colleges of further and higher education, universities and colleges of nursing.
As well as issuing the initial licence, ERA:

- offers advice on aspects of its Licensing scheme;
- issues publicity material free of charge;
- makes presentations at seminars and conferences;
- exhibits at education shows;
- operates a sampling exercise and visits selected institutions.

ERA licence fees are divided in agreed shares between the various rights owners, and each category of rights owners handles their fees in their own ways.

Further information about the legal position and what may, or may not, be recorded, may be obtained from:

ERA, 33–34 Alfred Place, London WC1E 7DP
tel: 071 436 4883   fax: 071 323 0486

FURTHER EDUCATION FUNDING COUNCIL (FEFC)

The Further Education Funding Council is a statutory body set up under the Further and Higher Education Act 1992 and is the funding mechanism for (English) Colleges of Further Education and Sixth Form Colleges freed from the ties of the LEA in April 1993. For the first year following their newly acquired independence, College funding levels from the FEFC were similar to that which may have been expected from the LEA had the Colleges stayed within that system. The FEFC has signalled, however, that with the pressure on to reduce unit costs, future extra student numbers will have to be accommodated with less than a pro rata increase in the funding.

The FEFC produces an Annual Report, and further information may be obtained from:

FEFC, Cheylesmore House, Quinton Road, Coventry CV1 2WT
tel: 0203 863000   fax: 0203 863100

GEOGRAPHICAL ASSOCIATION, THE

The Geographical Association aims to further the study and teaching of geography. Its Council and committees are all active in working to safeguard and extend recognition of geography's contribution to education at all levels and in supporting teachers of the subject, in particular with the introduction of the National Curriculum. In addition to the journals *Geography*, *Teaching Geography*, and *Primary Geographer*, a range of handbooks and shorter booklets is published for teachers. A catalogue is available on request. A conference is held annually before or after Easter with lectures and workshops, as well as an extensive exhibition of new books, visual aids, computer software and other materials for geography and related areas. Branches across the country offer varied programmes to meet local needs.

Membership is open to any person who is interested in the objects of the Association. Membership categories depend on whether personal or

corporate membership and which journals are taken. Full details of membership, together with publications information, may be obtained from: The Geographical Association, 343 Fulwood Road, Sheffield S10 3BP
tel: 0742 670666   fax: 0742 670688

GOVERNING BODIES ASSOCIATION (GBA)

Membership is restricted to the Governing Bodies of independent secondary schools for boys (and co-educational schools) which are constituted as educational charities. There are minimum requirements as to the number of pupils and academic achievement. There are 92 schools in membership. Overseas schools are considered for membership provided that they follow a similar pattern of education and that at least one-third of the pupils are of British nationality, most of whom anticipate proceeding to higher education in the UK.

The objects of the Association are:

- to advance education in independent schools;
- to discuss matters concerning the policy and administration of independent schools, and to encourage co-operation between their governing bodies;
- to consider the relationship of such schools to the general educational interests of the community;
- to express the views of governing bodies on the foregoing matters, and to take such action as may be expedient.

The Association produces an Annual Report and periodic papers which are available to members. Further details of these and membership may be obtained from:
The Secretary, Windleshaw Lodge, Withyham, Nr Hartfield, East Sussex
tel: 0892 770 879   fax: 0892 770 879

HIGHER EDUCATION FUNDING COUNCIL FOR ENGLAND (HEFCE)

The Higher Education Funding Council for England (HEFCE) was established on 2 June 1992 under the Further and Higher Education Act 1992. The HEFCE is a non-departmental public body operating within a policy and funding context set by the Government.

The Council's principal task is to distribute funds made available by the Secretary of State for Education for the provision of education and the undertaking of research by higher education institutions in England. The HEFCE works closely with the Higher Education Funding Councils for Scotland (SHEFC) and Wales (HEFCW) and the Department of Education for Northern Ireland (DENI).

The HEFCE, SHEFC and HEFCW assumed responsibility from 1 April 1993 for the funding of higher education institutions in England, Scotland and Wales respectively. Before then the Universities Funding Council (UFC) had responsibility for funding universities in Great Britain and the Polytechnics and Colleges Funding Council (PCFC) for funding the former polytechnics and higher education colleges in England.

The new arrangements, which were proposed in the Government's White Paper 'Higher education – a New Framework' (Cm 1541) published in May 1991, created a single funding structure for universities, polytechnics and colleges of higher education. The Further and Higher Education Act 1992 also removed the distinction between polytechnics and universities and allowed polytechnics to adopt a university title.

The Council funds education, research and associated activities at a total of 129 institutions of higher education – seventy-two universities, the eight directly funded schools of the University of London and fifty colleges of higher education. The Act brought into the sector three institutions which were previously funded directly by the Department for Education – the OPEN UNIVERSITY, the Royal College of Art and Cranfield Institute of Technology.

The HEFCE is also responsible for funding prescribed courses of higher education taught in seventy-seven further education colleges.

The HEFCE has established a number of committees and working groups including:

- a Quality Assessment Committee to advise on the Council's statutory duty to secure the provision for assessing the quality of education;
- a Joint Medical Advisory Committee with the SHEFC and HEFCW to advise on medical education and research;
- a Joint Information Systems Committee with the SHEFC and HEFCW to advise on the development of information systems, particularly networking.

The Council's Executive is based in Bristol and consists of the following divisions:

- Institutions and Programmes
- Finance
- Policy

- Quality Assessment
- Audit
- Analytical Services
- Information Systems
- Services.

The HEFCE's mission

The mission of the Higher Education Funding Council for England is to promote the quality and quantity of learning and research in higher education institutions, cost-effectively and with regard to national needs.

The Council's role is to advise the Secretary of State for Education on the funding needs of higher education institutions and to distribute available funds.

The Council in performing this role will:

- encourage institutions to meet the demand from students cost-effectively, while promoting and assessing quality in teaching and research;
- encourage diversity in the provision of higher education, a widening of access and greater opportunities;
- develop active partnerships with institutions, which recognize fully their autonomy;
- encourage institutions to build on their strengths and expand their local, regional, national and international roles;
- encourage institutions to support these aims and ensure the effective and efficient use of their funds and assets.

The Council produces a range of publications throughout the year including circulars, reports and a newsletter. Details are available from the external relations team:
Northavon House, Coldharbour Lane, Bristol BS16 1QD
tel: 0272 317317   fax: 0272 317203
Information supplied by the HEFCE

HIGHER EDUCATION QUALITY COUNCIL (HEQC)

The stated mission of the HEQC is to contribute to the maintenance and improvement of quality, at all levels, in institutions of higher education in the United Kingdom. Through its activities it assures the public, the funding councils and the Government of the quality of higher education

provision. HEQC was established in May 1992 as a company limited by guarantee, and is funded by subscriptions from individual universities and colleges of higher education. HEQC is divided into three divisions, which cover the principal services of quality audit, credit and access and quality enhancement. The Division of Quality Audit undertakes academic quality audits of institutes of higher education; the Division of Credit and Access works with colleges, universities and other organizations to facilitate credit transfer by the development of systems for assuring the quality of portable credits, and to assure the quality of access arrangements to higher education, and the Division of Quality Enhancement helps institutions to maintain and enhance the quality of their educational provision. Further details of HEQC may be obtained from their London office:
HEQC, 344–354 Gray's Inn Road, London WC1X 8BP
tel: 071 837 2223   fax: 071 278 1676

HISTORICAL ASSOCIATION, THE

The Historical Association, founded in 1906, is the only organization in the United Kingdom to be concerned with the history of all periods and places and at all levels – from primary to post-doctoral. It brings together people who share an interest in, and love for, the past. Members receive *The Historian*, a fully illustrated quarterly magazine, and can subscribe to *History, Teaching History, Primary History* and the *Annual Bulletin of Historical Literature* as well as buy Historical Association pamphlets all at substantial discounts. The Historical Association organizes education conferences for primary, secondary and A level and has over 70 local branches.

Membership is open to all, and further information may be obtained from:
The Historical Association, 59a Kennington Park Road, London SE11 4JH
tel: 071 735 3901   fax: 071 582 4989

INDEPENDENT SCHOOLS INFORMATION SERVICE (ISIS)

The Independent Schools Information Service was founded in 1965 and became a national organization in 1972. It has two aims:

1. To answer parents' questions about independent schools and help them with their educational problems; and
2. To ensure that the general public has an accurate image of independent schools and appreciates their contribution to the nation.

National ISIS is part of the Independent Schools Joint Council and receives most of its funds from four bodies:

The Governing Bodies Association;
The Governing Bodies of Girls' Schools Association;
The Incorporated Association of Preparatory Schools; and
The Independent Schools Association Incorporated.

ISIS produces an annual directory 'Choosing Your Independent School', which is available from:
ISIS, 56 Buckingham Gate, London SW1E 6AG
tel: 071 630 8793   fax: 071 630 5013

ISLAMIC ACADEMY, THE

The Islamic Academy, Cambridge, was established in 1983 as a religious charity. The aims of the Academy are:

(a) to provide the Muslim educationalists of the world with a central forum through which they may communicate with one another and also with non-Muslim educationalists;

(b) to establish Islamic schools of thought in all branches of knowledge, most particularly in the fields of natural sciences, humanities and social sciences;

(c) to promote research in earlier Muslim classics, especially on education and related subjects, and find out their relevance for life today;

(d) to take steps to make education in Muslim minority countries grounded in an explicit commitment to those essential values of life that religion teaches mankind;

(e) to carry on dialogues with non-Muslim communities for mutual knowledge, understanding and good relationships;

(f) to establish effective means of communications among scholars, thinkers, writers and educationalists, through publication of journals, periodicals, bulletins and books, and the holding of conferences, seminars and dialogues.

Membership of the Islamic Academy is in two grades, with the Fellowship open to Muslim educationalists and scholars and the Associateship open to postgraduate students. Further details of the Academy, together with details of its publications, may be obtained from:
The Islamic Academy, 23 Metcalfe Road, Cambridge CB4 2DB
tel: 0223 350976   fax: 0223 350976

LIBRARY ASSOCIATION

Since 1876, the Library Association has been promoting and defending libraries, both for those working in them and for the people who use them. At a time when economic, political and social change may have far-reaching implications, the Library Association is alert to the challenge and the need to make representations at all levels of influence. 25,000 members work to preserve and improve the services, and because the Association represents everyone working in library and information services, it can speak with one voice to government, external agencies and decision makers.

The Library Association is able, through the energy and commitment of its members, to influence key people in local and central government by their professional input and consultation. The Library Association has been active in Copyright Law, the National Curriculum, working with academic institutions on library qualifications, British Standards, protecting school libraries and the SCHOOL LIBRARIES SERVICE.

The Library Association comprises both decision-making and consultative bodies that determine policy and action. The six lead committees deal with specific services: Information Technology, education, employment, membership services, library and information services, and international matters.

Membership is available to everyone who works in any branch of the library or information services. There are seven categories of membership, chartered, ordinary, student, affiliated, supporting, overseas and institutional. Full details of membership may be obtained from:
The Library Association, 7 Ridgmount Street, London WC1E 7BR
tel: 071 636 7543   fax: 071 436 7218

NATIONAL ASSOCIATION FOR GIFTED CHILDREN (NAGC)

The NAGC is a national charity committed to the belief that all children have the right to develop their talents and abilities to the full, and as such, subscribe to Article 29 of the United Nations Convention on the Rights of the Child:

> ... the education of the child shall be directed to the development of the child's personality, talents and mental and physical abilities to their fullest potential.

NAGC's particular work is to support the ablest children, who can suffer particular deprivation and unhappiness if their needs are not met. NAGC is very involved in raising national awareness of the needs of gifted children by means of the media, lobbying of Parliament, liaising with Government departments and through the quarterly journals – and striving to ensure that these needs are met.

NAGC provides direct help to gifted children and their families through:

- online telephone help to parents – a listening ear and a chance to talk through a problem with an understanding staff member;
- a counselling service for the children and their families;
- some thirty local self-help branches which offer a forum for parents to share concerns and work out solutions;
- local Explorer Clubs where children have the chance to meet like-minded children and pursue planned activities together.

NAGC also provides a consultancy service for teachers, health visitors, nursery nurses and all who are concerned with the education or welfare of gifted children. NAGC also organizes regular in-service courses for schools.

Membership is available as follows:

Family membership – where the family identifies the 'gifted' child, membership is open to siblings and parents.

Individual membership – friends who wish to support NAGC and receive information.

Establishment membership – for schools, colleges etc.

NAGC publishes *Looking to the Future* and a newsletter twice yearly. For further details of publications or membership details:
NAGC, Park Campus, Boughton Green Road, Northampton NN2 7AL
tel: 0604 792300   fax: 0604 720636

NATIONAL ASSOCIATION FOR PRIMARY EDUCATION (NAPE)

The National Association for Primary Education is a registered charity, non-aligned and non partisan. Its aims include:

- access to full educational opportunity for all chlldren;
- equal resourcing per pupil in the primary phase as in every other phase of compulsory schooling.

NAPE recognizes that the education of children is a partnership between parents, schools and other concerned groups and that good practice is a matter for continual debate which NAPE is concerned to foster.

NAPE promotes:

- national conferences;
- national NAPE week (National Primary Education Week);
- national Festivals of Voices (children singing together).

NAPE lobbies:

- Parliament;
- Government quangos.

Membership of NAPE is open to school groups, members of the public, parents, governors and teachers. Its publications include a three times a year journal and *Newsbrief*, which is published six times a year. Further details of both publications and membership may be obtained from:
NAPE, Queens Building, University of Leicester Annexe, Barrack Road, Northampton NN2 6AF
tel: 0604 36326

NATIONAL ASSOCIATION FOR SPECIAL EDUCATIONAL NEEDS (NASEN)

The National Association for Special Educational Needs was formed in January 1992 following the decision of members of the National Association for Remedial Education (NARE) and the National Council for Special Education (NCSE) to abandon their separate identities and form a single, more powerful association that might speak for children and young people with special educational needs. NASEN is the largest voluntary, charitable, educationally based organization for special educational needs in the United Kingdom.
The Association aims:

- to promote the development of children and young people with SEN, wherever they are located, and to support those who work with them;
- to influence the quality of provision through strong and cohesive policies and strategies;
- to promote the education, welfare, treatment, rehabilitation and equal opportunities of people with SEN as presented in the recommendations of the Warnock report.

NASEN achieves these aims by being active at governmental, national and local levels, able to advise and influence decision-making processes.
NASEN provides specialist advice and support to those involved in meeting special educational needs, and organizes conferences, courses and

meetings, both locally and nationally, to extend members' professional development.

Every member of NASEN is associated with one of the 60 or so local branches, with each branch having an elected representative to the General Assembly of NASEN.

Membership is open to teachers, lecturers, and all those involved in education with an interest in SEN. Parents of a child experiencing SEN may also join; subscription rates and benefits vary, but full details may be obtained from:

NASEN, York House, Exhall Grange, Wheelwright Lane,
Coventry CV7 9HP
tel: 0203 362414   fax: 0203 362414

NASEN provides the rapidly-growing membership with a range of services, including the publication of two journals *The British Journal of Special Education* and *Support for Learning*. *The British Journal* is a quarterly journal and is open for material on pre-school, school or post-school needs of those with special educational needs, whatever the degree of learning difficulty or disability. The readership of the journal is drawn mainly from teachers in both main stream and special schools, special units and classes, including those who have taken advanced courses of study as well as students in training. The journal is read by a wide range of other professional workers: teacher trainers, educational psychologists, researchers, lecturers, therapists, medical, administrative and social workers, and parents. The journal aims to contain articles which are presented in an interesting way, and one which provides accessibility to those who may not be working in the precise field covered by the article. *Support for Learning* is directed at the publication of research-based articles on any aspect of work with children and students who have special educational needs. It covers the whole range of pupil and student ages, and the broad spectrum of curriculum. Articles are printed with an abstract, and consist of relatively short reports of researched activity and development. The journal also covers issues in the initial and in-service training fields as they relate to special educational needs. Further information and details of these, and the termly magazine called *Special!*, are available from NASEN Enterprises Ltd, 2 Lichfield Road, Stafford ST17 4JX.

NATIONAL ASSOCIATION OF EDUCATIONAL INSPECTORS, ADVISERS AND CONSULTANTS (NAEIAC)

NAEIAC is the only Association exclusively serving the interests of those engaged in educational inspection and advice. Full membership is open to people employed to provide or manage the provision of educational advice, inspection or consultancy in an organization with educational objectives compatible with those of the Association or who have relevant qualifications and experience acceptable to the Executive Committee. There is also an associate membership.

The Association offers the following services to its members:

- specialist legal help as well as professional advice and support on such matters as salaries, superannuation, conditions of service, taxation, redeployment and professional indemnity;
- representation of members in dispute with their employers over salary and conditions of service;
- access to a 24-hour advice service on legal problems;
- a means of keeping members in touch with colleagues in their regions and across the country;
- enrolment on a register of members who wish to collaborate with or employ people in undertakings relating to inspection, advice and support;
- organization of a wide range of courses and conferences for its members;
- maintains and develops links with other professional bodies representing senior managers in local authorities, schools and colleges at both national and regional levels;
- representation of members' opinion through the Association's representation on over thirty national educational bodies.

The Association produces the journal *Perspective*, which is provided free to all members four times a year, and an information bulletin approximately once a month. Further details of the Association may be obtained from: NAEIAC, 1 Heath Square, Boltro Road, Haywards Heath, West Sussex RH16 1BL
tel: 0444 441279   fax: 0444 458178

NATIONAL ASSOCIATION OF GOVERNORS AND MANAGERS (NAGM)

The Association is open to individual governors, governing bodies and others with an interest in education.

The Association aims to:

- provide support to school governors;

- provide up-to-date information to school governors through publications.

The Association provides a variety of publications, details of which may be obtained from the secretary at the address below. On first joining, new individual members receive free copies of five assorted papers, group members fifteen copies. NAGM publishes a termly newsletter. Further details of both publications and membership may be obtained from:
The Secretary, NAGM, Suite 36/38, 21 Bennetts Hill,
Birmingham B2 5QP
tel: 021 643 5787   fax: 021 643 5787

NATIONAL ASSOCIATION OF HEAD TEACHERS (NAHT)

Further details may be obtained from:
1 Heath Square, Boltro Road, Haywards Heath, West Sussex RH16 1BL
tel: 0444 458133   fax: 0444 416326
Further information requested, but not supplied.

NATIONAL ASSOCIATION OF SCHOOL MASTERS AND UNION OF WOMEN TEACHERS (NASUWT)

The Association is open to teachers, lecturers and instructors, student teachers and retired teachers.
   The Association aims to:

- regulate relations between members and their employers; to regulate professional relations between members; and to regulate professional relations between members and other teachers and other employees in the education service;
- protect and promote the interests of its members generally and in particular to ensure that the salary scales encourage the recruitment to and retention in the teaching profession of career men and women teachers;
- promote and protect the interests of the education service;
- secure the representation of members' interests on public and private bodies concerned with education or related matters;
- afford the Government, the Local Education Authorities and other bodies with an interest in the education service, the advice and experience of the Association and its members;

- render legal advice and assistance in professional matters to members of the Association in accordance with the Association rules.

The Association produces a newspaper *'Career Teacher'* and a journal *Teacher Today*. Further details about these publications and the Association may be obtained from:
NASUWT, Hillscourt Education Centre, Rednal, Birmingham B45 5RS
tel: 021 453 6150   fax: 021 453 7224

NATIONAL ASSOCIATION OF TEACHERS IN FURTHER AND HIGHER EDUCATION (NATFHE)

Membership is open to lecturers, tutors and research staff in post-school education, teaching in colleges of further education, new universities, adult education, agricultural education, and penal education establishments. The Association is open to full-time and part-time hourly paid staff.

The Association aims to:

- promote the professional interests of members individually and collectively;
- advance further and higher education and vocational training and promote research into educational development;
- put forward members' views before various educational authorities, other bodies and the public;
- offer a range of services – including legal services – to its members;
- offer comment on government and parliamentary matters.

The Association produces a variety of publications which include *The Lecturer*, a 16-pp tabloid newspaper; the *NATFHE Journal*, and the *Journal of Further and Higher Education*, an academic journal produced three times a year. Further details of these may be obtained from:
The General Secretary, 27 Britannia Street, London WC1X 9JP
tel: 071 837 3636   fax: 071 837 4403

NATIONAL ASSOCIATION OF TEACHERS OF HOME ECONOMICS AND TECHNOLOGY (NATHE)

NATHE seeks to represent the interests of all teachers of Home Economics/food and textiles Technology. Particular attention is paid to achieving high status and resourcing for HE specialisms, and NATHE has been active throughout the recent technology review. NATHE is represented on local and national examination bodies.

NATHE members not only receive subject-specific support, but also obtain legal and professional cover. As part of their membership teachers receive NATHE's journal *Modus* eight times per year.

Membership is open to all teachers of Home Economics/Technology at all key stages and into further and higher education. Young teacher, full, part-time and associate grades of membership are available.

The Association's journal *Modus* and its associated supplements are available to non-members (a charge is made); further details of these may be obtained from:

NATHE, Hamilton House, Mabledon Place, London WC1H 9BJ
tel: 071 387 1441   fax: 071 383 7230

NATIONAL CONFEDERATION OF PARENT–TEACHER ASSOCIATIONS (NCPTA)

NCPTA is the national organization for over 10,000 PTAs in England and Wales. It is the largest organization of its kind in Europe and has contact with over 8 million or so parents. NCPTA's main aim is to develop the partnership between home and school, between children, parents and teachers and between everyone else responsible for the education and welfare of children. As well as offering parents and associations support, guidance and information on education and the changes, NCPTA liaises with government departments, teacher representatives, charity commissioners on all matters where support is needed for parents and schools. Full membership is available to any school association, and individuals may become affiliated members. Details of publications, together with further information about NCPTA may be obtained from:

The Public Relations Officer, 2 Ebbsfleet Industrial Estate, Stonebridge Road, Gravesend, Kent DA11 9DZ
tel: 0474 560618   fax: 0749 564418

NATIONAL COUNCIL FOR EDUCATIONAL TECHNOLOGY (NCET)

The National Council for Educational Technology is a registered charity funded by the Department for Education to be the national focus of expertise in educational technology.

NCET develops and promotes the use of technology in every area of education and training.

The Council produces an Annual Report and a resources catalogue. Further details may be obtained from:

NCET, 3 Devonshire Street, London W1N 2BA
tel: 071 636 4186   fax: 071 636 2163
or
NCET, Sir William Lyons Road, Science Park, Coventry CV4 7EZ
tel: 0203 416994   fax: 0203 411418

NATIONAL COUNCIL FOR VOCATIONAL QUALIFICATIONS (NCVQ)

The National Council for Vocational Qualifications (NCVQ) was set up by the government in 1986, and was asked to 'hallmark' qualifications which met the needs of employment – National Vocational Qualifications (NVQs) – and to locate them within a new structure which everyone could use and understand, i.e. the NVQ Framework.

NCVQ aims to:

- improve the value of vocational qualifications to employers and individuals alike;
- encourage individuals to develop their vocational competence by improving access to vocational qualifications and by clearly defining progression routes;
- encourage the provision of more and better vocational education and training through NVQs which meet the real needs of employment and prepare individuals for changes in technology, markets and employment patterns, thus contributing towards improved national economic performance.

The Council produces a quarterly update, *The NVQ Monitor. NVQ notes*, research and development reports, video-disc and VHS programmes, form part of the council's publications programme. Details of these, together with further information about the work of the council may be obtained from:
NCVQ, 222 Euston Road, London NW1 2BZ
tel: 071 387 9898   fax: 071 387 0978

NATIONAL CURRICULUM COUNCIL (NCC)

The National Curriculum Council was established in August 1988 by the Secretary of State for Education and Science under the Education Reform Act. The aims of the NCC were:

- to keep all aspects for maintained schools under review;
- to advise the Secretary of State on such matters with the curriculum as he may refer to it or as the Council may see fit;
- to advise the Secretary of State on programmes of research and development connected with the curriculum and, if requested by him, to carry these out;
- to publish and disseminate information relating to the curriculum.

NCC replaced the Schools Curriculum Development Council, and worked closely with the Schools Examination and Assessment Council (SEAC). A new body, the *School Curriculum and Assessment Authority (SCAA)* replaced NCC and SEAC on 1 October 1993.

NATIONAL FOUNDATION FOR EDUCATIONAL RESEARCH (NFER)

The NFER, founded in 1946, is Britain's leading educational research institute. It is an independent body undertaking research and development projects on issues of current interest in all sectors of the public education system. Its approach is scientific, apolitical and non-partisan. It provides objective evidence on important educational issues for the policy-making needs of Government, teachers and administrators. Its membership includes all the local education authorities in England and Wales, the main teachers' associations, the Association of County Councils, the Armed Forces, examining boards and a large number of other major organizations with educational interests.

NFER's publications list is extensive, with the major findings of research generally published in-house. Publications cover every aspect of the education service of England and Wales, with about 30 research reports appearing each year. *Educational Research* is a journal published by the NFER to present new informed thinking and empirical evidence on issues of concern in education. The journal contains both substantial articles and short reports of research, as well as reviews of newly-published literature on educational research and its methodologies. Some articles cover topics from international perspectives. *Topic* is aimed mainly at teachers, and is one of the first resources to offer teachers easy access to the most up-to-date research materials. *Topic* is a collection of detailed and valuable research articles; all the items are photocopiable, and may be used for group discussions, staff meetings and INSET sessions. *Topic* is published twice a year. A full publications list, together with further details about NFER, may be obtained from:

The Publications Officer, NFER, The Mere, Upton Park, Slough, Berks SL1 2DQ
tel: 0753 574 123   fax: 0753 691 632

NATIONAL NURSERY EXAMINATION BOARD (NNEB)

Information may be obtained from:
NNEB, Argyll House, 29/31 Euston Road, London NW1 2SD
tel: 071 837 5458
Information requested, but not supplied

NATIONAL UNION OF STUDENTS (NUS)

Information may be obtained from:
National Union of Students, Nelson Mandela House, 461 Holloway Road, London N7
tel: 071 272 8900
Information requested, but not supplied

OFFICE FOR STANDARDS IN EDUCATION (OFSTED)

(See entry in Section 1 – A to Z Entries)

PROFESSIONAL ASSOCIATION OF NURSERY NURSES (PANN)

The Professional Association of Nursery Nurses was formed in 1982 by a group of nursery nurses disturbed at the way some unions took industrial action which harmed children in their care and damaged relationships within the community.
The objects of the Association are:

- to promote professional standards, particularly emphasizing the well-being of children and service to the community;
- to further the advancement of child care by study and research, by initiating proposals for reform and by resisting reduction of standards;
- to promote services to members including information and advice on employment opportunities and training facilities, provision of insurance cover and legal assistance;

- to protect members and negotiate improvements in pay and conditions of service;
- to help members to gain and deserve high status in the community.

The Association's Code of Practice provides advice for all practising professional nursery nurses in carrying out their duties and responsibilities; under the Code of Practice, members are not allowed to take strike action under any circumstances.

Membership of PANN is open to NNEB/BTEC/NAMCW or those who have a minimum of three years' experience. Students undertaking a course leading to a recognized child care qualification are welcomed as members; they receive all the benefits of full membership, including legal protection.

The Association produces *Nursery Nurse* three times a year. Details of the Association, together with membership information may be obtained from: PANN, 2 St James' Court, Friar Gate, Derby DE1 1BT
tel: 0332 343029   fax: 0332 290310

PROFESSIONAL ASSOCIATION OF TEACHERS (PAT)

The Professional Association of Teachers was founded in 1970. There are members in all parts of the United Kingdom and in all sectors of the education service.

PAT members never strike. They accept the right of others to strike, and trust that they accept their right not to do so. There is a growing recognition that action which damages the educational chances of young people also damages the reputation and standing of teachers in the community and society at large. PAT welcomes that growing recognition and seeks to extend it. PAT is strictly non-party political and firmly believes in teacher unions working co-operatively together as much as their individual policies and philosophies allow.

The fundamental ingredient of professionalism is service to those in receipt of education. Three elements are important in the delivery of that service. Firstly, the control of teacher quality. Career development, appraisal, membership of the profession, in-service and post-qualification courses should be a professional responsibility. PAT is concerned about recent government initiatives in this area, and is seeking to achieve a change of mind. Secondly, the profession should be self-governed, with appropriate machinery for ensuring accountability. PAT would approve the establishment of a General Teaching Council. The third element is the determination of salaries and conditions of service. PAT does not believe that market forces are a suitable determinant of either salary or conditions of service for teachers.

Membership is open to all practising heads, deputies, teachers and lecturers in the UK, and to student teachers. Associate and retired membership is also available.

Members benefit from legal protection and support provided by expert headquarters staff together with consultants and solicitors retained for their knowledge in educational matters. Field Officers support the professional staff.

Publications include the *Professional Teacher* (free to members, on subscription to non-members). Numerous advice booklets and various sectional newsletters are published for members. For further details about PAT, contact:

PAT, 2 St James' Court, Friar Gate, Derby DE1 1BT
tel: 0332 372337   fax: 0332 290310 or 0332 292431

ROYAL SOCIETY OF ARTS (RSA) EXAMINATIONS BOARD

RSA Examinations Board is one of the leading providers of vocational qualifications in the United Kingdom. One of the most respected names in education, RSA offers more than 200 qualifications, including a wide range of NVQs, through over 8,000 recognized centres. RSA provides schemes to assess candidates' competence against clearly defined criteria in a variety of occupational sectors. RSA was involved in pioneering work for the recently introduced 16+ GNVQ. Further details of courses and general information may be obtained from:

The Chief Executive, RSA Examinations Board, Westwood Way, Coventry CV4 8HS
tel: 0203 470033   fax: 0203 421944

SCHOOL CURRICULUM AND ASSESSMENT AUTHORITY (SCAA)

The School Curriculum and Assessment Authority was established under the Education Act 1993. It replaced the National Curriculum Council and the School Examinations and Assessment Council with effect from 1 October 1993. It has the statutory duty to advise the Secretary of State for Education on all aspects of the school curriculum and school tests/ examinations. The Chairman of SCAA is Sir Ron Dearing, CB.

The Authority produces a newsletter *Schools Update* termly; further details of this and other information may be obtained from:

Newcombe House, 45 Notting Hill Gate, London W11 3JB
tel: 071 229 1234   fax: 071 243 0542

SECONDARY HEADS' ASSOCIATION (SHA)

The Secondary Heads' Association is a professional association for Heads and Deputy Heads, Principals and Vice-Principals in secondary schools and colleges, offering support and advice to all members, including legal services when necessary. The Association offers professional development opportunities through Management and Professional Services (SHA) Ltd on a wide range of topics and provides professional publications and regular updates on all educational initiatives. Local support is given to members through area and branch meetings, convenors and area secretaries. A residential Annual Conference is held to which all members are invited.

Membership is open to all heads and deputies, principals and vice-principals in secondary schools and colleges. Publications include *Headlines* three times per year. Further details may be obtained from:
Secondary Heads' Association, 130 Regent Road, Leicester LE1 7PG
tel: 0533 471797   fax: 0533 471152

SERVICE CHILDREN'S EDUCATION AUTHORITY (SCEA)

The Service Children's Education Authority is responsible for the education of some 20,000 Service children overseas, in approximately 80 schools (the number is presently declining in line with the partial withdrawal of British forces from Germany). Apart from Germany, where a Defence Support Agency (Service Children's Schools North West Europe) has executive responsibility, SCEA has schools in Hong Kong, Brunei, Cyprus, Gibraltar, Italy, Norway, Denmark, Belize and the Falkland Islands. All these schools are regularly inspected by HMI/OFSTED and mirror the best of UK LEA practice. The NATIONAL CURRICULUM is fully in place. All SCEA teachers are qualified and experienced in the UK system.

Although SCEA does not run schools in the UK, it looks after the interests of the 90,000 Service children in LEA and GM schools, and the 15,000 in boarding schools by close and constant liaison with the DFE, LEAs and the various independent school associations. It has an advisory section which offers assistance to Service parents. It also has a Special Educational Needs (SEN) Section which looks after the interests of Service children with SEN. The provision of a youth service for Service children overseas through the British Forces Youth Service is also a SCEA responsibility.

Further information may be obtained from:
SCEA, HQ DGAGC, Worthy Down, Winchester SO21 2RG
tel: 0962 887965   fax: 0962 887963
Information supplied by SCEA

STATE BOARDING INFORMATION SERVICE (STABIS)

STABIS provides information for parents wishing to find boarding places for secondary age pupils. STABIS covers the full range of maintained secondary provision – comprehensive, selective, single-sex and co-educational schools – which can be found in all areas of England. Most STABIS members are day schools with boarding houses and were originally long established grammar or independent schools which offered residential accommodation. They provide boarding places for children from all social backgrounds.

STABIS aims to increase public awareness that the maintained sector provides boarding for children from all backgrounds and that parents have an entitlement to seek and, if accepted by the school, secure this kind of educational experience for their children. Under the terms of Education Acts the LEA is obliged to pay for tuition costs incurred by children receiving their schooling at establishments both within and outside of that LEA. Parents are responsible *only* for boarding costs unless support is forthcoming from the Armed Services, the parents' employers, and in a few cases, from local authorities and social services. Tuition fees are paid direct by the LEA. All STABIS schools are members of the Boarding Schools' Association.

STABIS publishes a directory, periodic newsletters and the Boarding Schools' Association magazine. Further details of these, and further information about current boarding provision may be obtained from:
The Secretary, Boarding Schools' Association, 'Westmorland',
43 Raglan Road, Reigate, Surrey RH2 0DU
tel: 0737 226450   fax: 0737 226775

UNIVERSITY OF THE THIRD AGE (U3A)

The University of the Third Age is a learning co-operative of older people which enables members to share many educational, creative and leisure activities. U3A members organize their own activities by drawing on the skills of one another. They share their knowledge and experience, and develop their own individual capabilities by learning from other members.

U3As all over the United Kingdom share the same philosophy, but each develops its own character according to its members and the resources of the community; their programmes of cultural, social and recreational activities grow out of their study groups and general meetings. There are more than 250 local U3As, with a total membership of some 32,000. Further details may be obtained from the National Office at:

University of the Third Age, 1 Stockwell Green, London SW9 9JF
tel: 071 737 2541

Section 4 – Legislation

Michael Farrell

ENGLAND AND WALES

This section gives a brief description in chronological order of reports and legislation concerned with education in England and Wales from the middle of the nineteenth century. Lawson and Silver (1973) in *A Social History of Education in England* give an account from Anglo-Saxon times to the 1970s, setting legislation and other developments in a social context.

Liell and Coleman (1993) concentrate on the law of education. Summaries of the major Acts are obtainable from the Advisory Centre for Education (ACE) who can provide a free publications list. Copies of specific Acts, Statutory Instruments and Regulations can be ordered from Her Majesty's Stationery Office.

Orders by post can be made to:

HMSO, PO Box 276, London SW8 5DT
tel: 071 622 3316   general enquiries: 071 211 5656
Copies of circulars are obtainable from the following address:

Department For Education, Publications Centre, PO Box 2193, London E15 2EU
tel: 081 533 2000

Newcastle Report (1861)

When, in 1839, the Committee of Privy Council was formed to administer government grants for education, schools were required, in order to receive money, to have boards of managers and to allow inspection. Perceived inequalities in these arrangements led to the setting up of the Newcastle Commission to consider measures needed, 'for the extension of sound and cheap elementary instruction to all classes of the people'.

The Commission recommended the abolition of existing grants which were paid directly to teachers in order to supplement their salary. These and certain other grants would be replaced by an overall grant paid to school managers, who would negotiate salaries with teachers individually. The amount of grant was to be influenced by pupil attendance and performance as established by Her Majesty's Inspectors who would test the pupils. The system amounted to payment by results. The Newcastle

Commission led to the widely abhorred Revised Code of 1862 which formalized the payment by results system.

Clarendon Report (1864)

The Clarendon Commission examined nine schools: Eton, Winchester, Westminster, Charterhouse, Harrow, Rugby, Shrewsbury, St Paul's and Merchant Taylors'. The administration, studies and methods of the nine schools were criticized and the report recommended the reform of the schools' governing bodies and the reform of curriculum and pedagogy. The report led to the Public Schools Act 1868.

Taunton Report (1868)

The government of endowed schools was the subject of the Taunton Report. The commission selected eight districts for each of which assistant commissioners inspected endowed, proprietary and private schools for boys and girls. It considered the extent to which parental demand for education was being met. The Report recommended the reform of the charities on which the schools were founded. While arguing for Latin to be retained on the curriculum, the Report conceded that Greek could be dropped in all but the top-grade schools. Political economy and mathematics should be extended in the curriculum and science should be included. The Report led to the Endowed Schools Act 1869.

Elementary Education Act 1870 (Forster Act)

Aiming to provide elementary schools throughout the country, the Forster Act mapped out school districts country-wide. In areas lacking the necessary resources for elementary education, the Education Department would cause a school board to be elected for that school district so that it could provide public elementary schools. Such schools should be open to inspection and parents had the right to withdraw their children. School boards could delegate some of the their tasks to boards of managers.

School boards could (although they did not have to) require pupils aged 5 to 13 years to attend school under local by-laws. Parents could be fined if they did not ensure that their children attended. However, exemptions could be made for a number of reasons, for example, if the child was shown to have reached a certain educational level.

The Education Department could agree to school boards requiring weekly fees although reductions could be made for the poor. Financial support was meant to come in equal measure from fees, local rates and grants, although grants could be increased if local rates were not enough to pay for schooling. School boards were to provide and maintain schools and ensure that they were efficient.

In brief, the Forster Act opened the door to a universal system of education and education as a right.

Education Act 1880

Seeking to make attendance at elementary school compulsory, the Education Act 1880 required school boards to enact by-laws making attendance at school necessary.

Cross Report (1888)

Considering the workings and implementation of the Education Act 1870, the Cross Commission foreshadowed the Education Act 1902, the Balfour Act.

The Report enquired into the conditions of elementary education in England and Wales. It compared conditions and standards in board schools and voluntary schools.

Religious issues split the committee, fifteen of whom signed the main Report while eight put their names to the minority Report.

Education Act 1890

Under the Act, central government paid a grant each year for each child in public elementary schools. This enabled most schools receiving such grants to waive fees to pupils. School boards were to have a duty to establish free schools in districts where there was insufficient free elementary education. Broadly speaking, the Act heralded free elementary education.

Bryce Report (1895)

Considering how the national secondary education system could best be formed, the Bryce Commission paved the way for the Education Act 1902, the Balfour Act.

One of its recommendations was the formation of a central authority for education to 'supervise the Secondary Education of the country', and to draw together and encourage co-operation among the agencies providing education.

Board of Education Act 1899

A Board of Education, able to inspect secondary schools, was formed to oversee the education system.

Education Act 1902 (Balfour Act)

The Balfour Act introduced local education authorities (LEAs) to control secular teaching in denominational schools and to enable state schools to fill gaps in existing secondary provision. The framework in which LEAs would operate had been established by the Local Government Act 1888.

LEAs were made from all the existing councils of counties and county boroughs. Non-county boroughs with over 10,000 inhabitants and urban districts exceeding 20,000 people were to become responsible for only elementary education in their areas. (As elementary education was dealt with in Part III of the Act these councils became known as Part III authorities.)

The new LEAs had a duty to consider their areas' needs with regard to education over and above elementary education. After consulting the Board of Education, the authorities were to supply such education themselves or help others to supply it. This was to be done by providing schools, awarding scholarships at those schools, giving aid to other schools and awarding grants for the attendance of pupils at schools other than LEA provided schools. The LEAs could raise rates and spend the funds to ensure that secondary education was provided.

In schools which the LEA did not provide, they could not require that denominational instruction was provided nor prevent it. Denominational instruction was to be provided in LEA schools. There was to be no religious discrimination in publicly provided schools.

LEAs assumed powers which had previously been awarded to school boards by the Education Acts 1870, 1880 and 1890. Also LEAs assumed responsibility for secular instruction in schools which they aided but had not originally provided.

Individual elementary schools or groups of elementary schools had to have managers. LEA provided schools were to have four managers representing the LEA, and two representing the minor authority. Non-provided schools required four foundation managers and two representing the LEA. Of these two LEA managers, one should be from the minor authority in counties or county boroughs.

LEAs were responsible for their schools' efficiency and maintenance. They were empowered to inspect schools and to provide for teacher training. Where teachers were appointed in non-provided schools, the LEA had to give approval but could only deny approval if there were educational reasons.

Procedures were laid out for the planning of new schools. Public notices were to be issued, arrangements were made to hear any objections and the Board of Education then had to come to a decision.

Arrangements for grant aid from government were set out. Aid was given according to the number of pupils. In non-provided elementary schools, fees were charged.

If an LEA was not discharging its duties, a public enquiry could be instituted after which the Board of Education could direct the LEA to rectify its shortcomings.

LEAs had to form education committees. Pupils could attend elementary school up to the age of 16. If there was no appropriate school for older pupils in the area, a pupil could attend elementary school even after the age of 16.

In summary, the Education Act 1902 focused on secondary education in a similar way to the manner in which the Education Act 1870 had focused on elementary education.

Education Act 1918

The post 'Great War' Fisher Act aimed to ensure that a national system of public education was provided. The Board of Education could compel local authorities 'to provide for the progressive development and comprehensive organization of education in respect of their area'.

In 1902, ceilings had been placed on educational expenditure except in the case of elementary education. These limits were now lifted. All fees for elementary education were abolished and local authorities were empowered to provide, or help to provide, nursery schools and classes. In 1914, some 40 per cent of children were leaving school before the age of 14, but under the Act of 1918, all children between the ages of 5 and 14 had to attend school without exception. LEAs had to ensure that central classes or schools were providing instruction in practical subjects. Also older or abler pupils had to have the opportunity of more advanced teaching in public elementary schools. LEAs had a responsibility for young people over the compulsory school leaving age who had become employed. These youngsters were to attend day continuation classes for a certain number of days a year.

Hadow Report (1926)

'The Education of the Adolescent', The Hadow Report which appeared in 1926, was concerned with the education of pupils up to the age of 15 years, except those in secondary schools. It recommended that the school-leaving age be raised to 15. Secondary education should be for all children and should take place in four types of schools:

- existing grammar schools;
- central schools, to be called 'modern schools', where the final two years of schooling would be mainly practical;
- central 'modern' schools catering for pupils of differing abilities;
- senior departments within existing elementary schools.

Education should be understood as occupying two stages, primary and secondary, with the break at about the age of 11.

Hadow Report (1931)

A second Report chaired by Hadow, and dealing with primary education, appeared in 1931. It considered courses of study appropriate for children up to the age of 11 (but not infants) and in particular the needs of children in rural areas.

The curriculum in primary schools was to be seen in terms of activity and experience rather than the acquisition of knowledge and the storage of facts. Primary classes were to be no larger than 40 pupils.

The transfer from primary to secondary school was to continue at eleven and transfer from infants at 7 plus. By the age of 10, pupils were to be streamed. Teachers were to be trained to teach 'backward' groups.

Spens Report (1938)

Concerned with grammar schools and technical schools, the Spens Report contributed to the tripartite approach of secondary modern, technical and grammar school education.

It focused on secondary schools (except for the senior classes in elementary schools) and particularly considered the education of pupils who did not stay on at school after 16. The Spens Report recommended that secondary education should take place in grammar, technical and secondary modern schools; the number of technical schools should be increased; vocational courses should be introduced and careers teachers appointed. Spens further recommended that a tutorial system should be implemented and the school leaving age should be raised to sixteen.

Norwood Report (1943)

Focusing on examinations, the Norwood Report contributed to the tripartite system of grammar, technical and modern schools for secondary education.

McNair Report (1944)

The McNair Report on the supply and training of teachers also considered youth workers. It recommended that teacher training courses be extended to three years (full-time) and that teachers' salaries should be increased. Youth leaders, similarly, should undergo three years of full-time training and should be paid salaries on a par with those of teachers.

Education Act 1944 (the Butler Act)

R. A. Butler's post-war Education Act, provided that public education be organized into the stages of primary, secondary and further education. Local authorities were required to provide free secondary education as well as free primary education. Schools would have to be 'sufficient in number, character, and equipment to afford for all pupils opportunities for education offering such variety of instruction and training as may be desirable in view of their different ages, abilities and aptitudes'.

The school-leaving age was raised to 15 and provision was made for it eventually to be raised to 16. The Board of Education became a ministry, with central government having a dynamic role. The Minister would arbitrate in disputes between LEAs, LEAs and the public, and LEAs and school managers. Local authorities were to provide school meals and free milk and regular medical inspection.

For children with mental or physical handicaps education by special methods was to be provided either in special schools or elsewhere. Children categorized as 'severely subnormal' were considered ineducable and excluded from these provisions.

Privately-owned schools had to be registered and inspected. Voluntary schools could choose to become 'controlled' or 'aided'. For voluntary controlled schools, the local authority would meet all the school's expenses. For voluntary-aided schools, the local authority would pay for the running of the school and half of the cost of adapting the school so that it met the Act's requirements.

Local authority schools called 'county schools' and voluntary schools were required to provide religious instruction and to hold daily an act of collective worship. Local authorities and religious bodies were to agree a syllabus for religious instruction in county schools. LEAs had a responsibility to consider the local cultural and recreational needs of children below compulsory school age and of people above it. 'Part III' authorities, as defined under the Education Act 1902, were abolished.

Percy Report (1945)

The Percy Report on higher technological education looked at what was needed in that sphere in England and Wales and at the roles of universities and colleges of technology. It recommended that selected technical colleges should offer degree standard full-time courses.

Barlow Report (1946)

The Barlow Report tried to forecast manpower needs and recommended that the output of scientific manpower be immediately doubled. This influenced the growth of scientific training in universities and further education.

Education Act 1946

This Act set out the circumstances in which the Minister for Education could direct an authority to pay the cost of enlarging a controlled school. It also set out provisions concerning the duties of LEAs and managers as to the maintenance of voluntary schools.

Gurney-Dixon Report (1954)

The Gurney-Dixon Report looked at the reasons why some pupils left secondary school as early as possible, and considered how more pupils could be encouraged to stay on until 18. It recommended that, for needy pupils who were staying on at school after the age of 15, better maintenance allowances should be introduced. Family allowances should be paid for all children at school and a higher percentage of grammar school places should be provided.

Crowther Report (1959)

The wide remit of the Crowther Report was the education of children and young people from 5 to 18 years. It examined the implications of social and economic change for the full and part-time education of those aged 5 to 18. The Report recommended that the school-leaving age should be raised to 16. Also a target should be agreed so that by 1980, half of the young people in the country should be in full-time education until the age of 18. Earlier, the Education Act 1944 had described the role of county colleges, and Crowther argued for the policy of county colleges to be implemented.

Albemarle Report (1960)

Reviewing the youth service (14 to 20 year olds), Albemarle recommended that its framework of statutory and voluntary provision should be kept. It also argued for a Youth Service Development Council and ten-year development plans (national and local).

Youth clubs, the Report said, should provide opportunity for association, training and challenge.

Anderson Report (1960)

The Anderson Report looked into the administration of students' grants, recommending that a student should be entitled to a grant from public funds when he or she was given a place on a first degree course at a university. Other recommendations were that state scholarships of all types should cease, parents should no longer have to contribute to the student grant (or if the practice continued the amount of contribution should be greatly reduced for about 40 per cent of parents and abolished for the remaining 60 per cent).

Education Act 1962

This Act reduced the number of dates on which a pupil could leave school from three to two. It specified the dates in relation to the pupil's sixteenth birthday (the age at which a pupil ceased to be of compulsory school age).

The Act also made it mandatory upon LEAs to give awards for first degree university courses or comparable courses. It enabled LEAs to give discretionary awards to students who were over the compulsory school age and attending courses of further education either full or part-time. The Secretary of State could give awards to post-graduate students and students above a prescribed age.

Newsom Report (1963)

The Newsom Report, 'Half Our Future', considered the education of pupils aged 13 to 16 years who were of average ability or below. It recommended that the school-leaving age be increased to 16 years. The school day should be longer so as to encompass extra-curricular activities, which would be part of the school's provision rather than being voluntary. There ought to be more broadly-based courses for pupils not studying for the General Certificate of Education. Schools should offer more broadly-based courses for less able pupils. Methods ought to include enquiry approaches which began with the modern world and the child's own experience. The courses for older pupils should be reviewed, particularly when the school-leaving age was raised. Teacher training should keep both academic and professional aspects running concurrently. In deprived areas, a joint working party on social services was necessary.

Robbins Report (1963)

The Robbins committee was set up to look at future demand in full-time higher education in Britain, in universities, training colleges and advanced work in colleges of further education. Its Report recommended that the percentage of people receiving full-time higher education should be increased from approximately 8 per cent to 17 per cent by 1980. Growth in the university sector was required. A new body (the Council for National Academic Awards) would be founded to award degrees in approved non-university colleges. A new Ministry of Arts and Sciences should be founded. Local Authorities should no longer be responsible for teacher training, which should be fitted into the same administrative structure as universities, giving a higher status.

Plowden Report (1967)

Every aspect of primary education and the transition to secondary education was the broad remit of 'Children and their Primary Schools', the Plowden Report. The importance of home and social background to a child's education was vital. The Report recommended that deprived areas be designated educational priority areas (EPAs) and that deprived schools within these areas be recognized as EPA schools. In such schools, class sizes should be reduced to 40 and teachers working there should receive extra payment.

Part-time nursery provision should be expanded and in EPAs up to half the children should receive full-time nursery education. Corporal punishment should be abolished. Teachers should receive in-service training every five years.

A broader curriculum and child-centred education should be encouraged.

Gittins Report (1968)

Considering primary education in Wales, the Gittins Report recommended that the teaching of Welsh should be encouraged but that the statutory requirement for religious education should be eased. Teachers should receive sixty hours of in-service training within each five-year period. Very small schools for 5 to 12 year olds where there were only one to three teachers should be replaced by larger schools serving a wider area. For 8 to 12 year olds, middle schools should be established. Universal part-time education should be provided for children of 3 years old and above. For the 15 per cent of deprived children, full-time nursery education should be provided.

Newsom Report (1968)

The Newsom Committee considered the integration of public schools with the maintained sector. It recommended that suitable independent boarding schools which wished to integrate should initially admit assisted pupils from the maintained sector so that after seven years at least half of the school's places would be occupied by assisted pupils. Legislation should enable a Boarding Schools Corporation to be set up under which an integrated sector would develop. If a school's refusal to enter such an integrated sector inhibited the implementation of integration policy, the Education Secretary would have the power to compel the school to comply.

Education (No. 2) Act 1968

This Act concerned the government of colleges of education and other further education colleges. It set out the framework and rules relating to the governance of these colleges.

Haslegrave Report (1969)

Considering technicians' courses and examinations, the Haslegrave Report recommended the formation of a Technician Education Council and a Business Education Council. These councils were to be responsible for planning, co-ordinating and administering technical courses and examinations.

On leaving school, a trainee technician would pursue a Technician Certificate course enabling the successful student to follow a Higher Technician Certificate course and later, if desired, a Higher Technician Diploma. The system of certificate and diploma courses in business studies was to remain unchanged.

Donnison Report (1970)

The Donnison Committee recommended ways of integrating independent day schools and direct grant schools into the maintained system of education. Day schools which received grants from central government or local authorities should play their part in the movement towards comprehensive reorganization. The legal right of direct grant schools to become independent should be recognized.

Education (Handicapped Children) Act 1970

Under this Act the concept of ineducability categorized as 'severe subnormal' in the Education Act 1944 was abolished. The education of all children became the responsibility of the LEA.

James Report (1972)

Considering the existing arrangements for the education, training and probation of teachers in England and Wales, the James Report recommended that three consecutive stages should exist for teacher training:

1. A two-year diploma or degree course of a general nature giving a Diploma in Higher Education (Dip.H.E.).
2. A year of professional studies culminating in an appointment as a 'licensed teacher'. This would be followed by a year based in school with a minimum of one day per week spent at a professional centre. Successful completion of these two years would give 'registered teacher' status and a B.A. (Education) degree.
3. Regular in-service training courses equalling a full term of training every seven years.

All entrants to the teaching profession would be graduates.

Russell Report (1973)

The Russell Report considered non-vocational adult education in England and Wales and recommended expansion. A national development council and regional advisory councils should be set up. Development councils should be established in all LEAs, which should also establish area organizations each having a management committee and a full-time head.

In the case of some adult education, the DES should continue to award a direct grant. Rather than Workers' Education Association districts being paid a grant separately, the central organization should be paid a single grant. Small fees should be charged.

All new secondary schools and buildings for further education should be designed bearing in mind adult education requirements.

Houghton Report (1974)

Considering the pay of non-university teachers in Great Britain, the committee recommended an average 30 per cent increase for all teachers, a common scale for all further education teachers including those in Colleges of Education, and other amendments to pay and scales of seniority.

Bullock Report (1975)

In 1973, the National Foundation for Educational Research (NFER) published 'The Trends of Reading Standards', a Report which led to the appointment of the Bullock Committee by the then Secretary of State for Education, Margaret Thatcher.

The Bullock Report 'A Language for Life' reviewed all aspects of teaching the use of English in schools. This encompassed reading, writing, speaking and listening. The committee considered how current practice could be improved and how initial teacher training and in-service training could help. It examined how the monitoring of general level of attainment could be introduced or improved.

The Report recommended the introduction of a system of monitoring to assess a wide range of attainment. Children's language ability should be developed in the years before school and in nursery and infant years and teachers' aides with some language training should be employed to help in this. All school teachers should be involved in developing a school language and reading policy with a teacher in each school being responsible for language and the teaching of reading.

Each LEA should have an English adviser and an advisory team. Records should be transferred from school to school with a pupil. Early screening ought to be introduced by schools and LEAs, and there should be a reading clinic or remedial centre. Tuition should be provided for adults who could not read. Immigrant children should receive more tuition in English. A standing working party ought to examine school capitation allowances and the level of provision of books. A national centre for language in education should be established. Initial teacher training for all primary and secondary school teachers should feature language education including the teaching of reading.

Education Act 1975

One of the provisions of the 1975 Act concerned contributions and grants which the Secretary of State paid to aided and special agreement schools. These were to go towards meeting expenses which governors incurred in:

- establishing aided schools;
- maintaining aided and special agreement schools.

By the Act, these contributions and grants were raised from levels set by previous Acts to 85 per cent of the total.

Earlier, the Education Act 1962 provided for the Secretary of State to give awards respecting post graduate courses and to students above a prescribed age. The 1975 Act extended this provision to some students on courses at adult education colleges.

LEAs must give mandatory awards to full-time students on courses for the Diploma of Higher Education, Higher National Diploma or Higher

Diploma of BTEC. Similarly, students on initial teacher training courses have to be given this mandatory award.

Holland Report (1977)

The Manpower Services Commission set up a working party to consider ways of helping unemployed young people. It recommended setting up a programme of placements giving work opportunities. All unemployed people aged 16 to 18 should be eligible and would be paid a weekly allowance. The courses would be of two types; working experience and work preparation.

Taylor Report (1977)

Focusing on maintained primary and secondary schools in England and Wales, the Taylor Report considered their management and government. It recommended that governing bodies should have equal numbers of representatives from the LEA, school teachers (and non-teaching staff where the size of the school permits), parents and the local community. While the LEA would retain formal responsibility for the running of the school, governors would be given a range of duties and powers. LEAs would have to train governors. Headteachers would be accountable to governors for the management and conduct of the school.

Oakes Report (1978)

Looking at the control of maintained sector higher education in Britain, the Oakes Report considered how management and control could be improved. Any management system should be able to carry out the following:

- collect data on supply and demand;
- plan for development and change;
- determine provision and provide resources;
- oversee the whole management system.

A national body should be set up to advise the Secretary of State on how much in total should be given to capital expenditure and how this should be shared out to particular institutions. Higher Education should be financed in two ways. Most of the cost should be met from an annually determined fixed amount 'pool'. A smaller contribution would be made by the LEA which maintained each institution.

While LEAs and governing bodies should retain their responsibilities, their respective roles should be clarified. Governing bodies should have operational freedom regarding purchasing, contracts and appointments. Nine regional bodies should be set up to help plan, and inform, and to draw together LEAs with small higher education facilities, universities and industry.

Warnock Report (1978)

The Warnock Report, 'Special Educational Needs', considered education provision for children and young people handicapped by disabilities of body and mind. England, Scotland and Wales were included in the remit. The committee took account of medical aspects of these children's needs and considered arrangements to prepare them to enter employment.

In general, the Report recommended a wider concept of special need and greater parental involvement. Recognizing and assessing disability needs to involve progressive stages; three based in school and stages four and five involving a multi-disciplinary team of professionals.

The Warnock Report recommended that special education should start as early as possible, with a 'named person' professional as a contact person for parents when a child was identified as having special needs.

Considering the question of integrating pupils with special needs into mainstream schools and that of segregated special schools, the Report called for a reinterpretation of section 10 of the Education Act 1976 which concerned the integration of pupils with special needs in mainstream schools under certain conditions. The Report recommended that each LEA prepare a comprehensive, long-term plan for special education which would include mainstream and special schools.

The role of special schools needed to be broadened and their facilities be more available to mainstream schools. More effort was needed on behalf of disabled school leavers and further education should develop a co-ordinated regionally planned approach to handicapped young people.

Waddell Report (1978)

The Waddell Report recommended replacing the ordinary level General Certificate of Education examination and the Certificate of Secondary Education examinations by a common 16+ examination covering the same range of ability as both GCE and CSE. With the Schools Council co-ordinating, the new examinations should be regionally based and controlled by teachers.

Education Act 1980

Under the Act, the terms 'managers' of schools and 'managing bodies' would not be used but both primary and secondary schools would use the expressions 'governors' and 'governing bodies'.

Every school should have its own governing body with a few exceptions. All schools, county or voluntary, were required to have parent and teacher governors elected by their peers. Every headteacher would be a governor ex-officio unless (s)he elects otherwise.

Parents were given the right to express a preference for the school which they would like their child to attend. LEAs and governors of aided schools must accede to this choice unless there are grounds to refuse. The grounds for refusal are that to comply will:

- 'prejudice the provision of efficient education or the efficient use of resources';
- be incompatible with admission arrangements agreed between the LEA and the governors of a voluntary aided school;
- fail to take account of the fact that in a selective school the pupil must meet entry requirements.

An appeals committee would hear appeals from parents not offered their preferred school. For county and controlled schools, the committee would be set up by the LEA. In the case of voluntary schools, the LEA and governors would set up the committee. For aided schools, the committee would be set up by the governors.

Nursery schools and special schools were not included in the school preference arrangements.

Anomalies in previous legislation were cleared so that:

(a) parents involved in proceedings for the non-attendance of their child at school were allowed the same rights to appeal as other parents;
(b) parents could not tilt the parental preference procedures in their favour by keeping their child away from school.

The Act set out revised procedures for establishing new schools, closing schools and significantly changing the character of schools. It introduced a new procedure for reducing school intakes.

The Act had provisions concerning an assisted places scheme. The Secretary of State was required to initiate and operate a scheme to enable children to attend independent schools who would otherwise be unable to do so. Assistance would come from public funds. Participating schools would remit fees for an agreed number of pupils on a standard scale related to parental income and would be reimbursed by the Secretary of State. Tuition and examination fees but not boarding fees were covered by the scheme.

The Act removed an earlier requirement that LEAs provide school meals for all pupils and free meals for needy children. Instead, the LEA was able to provide meals if it wished and to charge whatever it deemed appropriate. However, the LEA must provide as appears 'requisite' for children entitled to a free lunch at midday. For pupils who bring meals from home, the LEA is, for the first time, under a statutory obligation to provide free facilities for eating it.

Regarding nursery education, all provision for under fives is at the discretion of the LEA. However, nursery schools cannot be closed without public notice.

LEAs were allowed automatically to recoup charges for pupils admitted to schools in other authorities. Also all independent schools were to be registered.

Rampton Report (1981)

The Rampton Committee considered the educational needs and attainment of ethnic minority children in relation to school. The committee was briefed to take into account, as necessary, external factors relating to school performance, including:

- early childhood factors;
- prospects for school leavers.

They considered the potential value of introducing arrangements to review the educational performance of different ethnic minority groups, and looked at possible ways of doing this.

The Interim Report considered West Indian children and recommended that the Home Office and the DES should review the operation of Section 11 of the Local Government Act 1966. This Act required LEAs to provide for New Commonwealth Immigrants whose language and customs were different from those of the rest of the community.

Other recommendations related to:

- pre-school provision;
- reading and language curriculum;
- teaching materials including books;
- examinations;
- pastoral arrangements;
- school and community links;
- special provision, including the ethnic mix of schools catering for what were then called schools for the educationally sub-normal (moderate);
- preparation for adult life in relation to the careers service;
- the need for teacher education and the recruitment and training of West Indian teachers;
- the necessity of appointing multicultural advisers;
- recording statistics of the ethnic origin of school pupils, student teachers and students in universities, polytechnics and colleges of higher education.

Education Act 1981

Following the 1978 Warnock Report 'Special Educational Needs', the Education Act 1981 substantially changed the law relating to special education. Previously, the focus was the 2 per cent of children classified as handicapped and who were taught in special schools, units or classes. Warnock estimated that up to one in five children at some time in their schooling, would have special educational needs. While most of these children would be in mainstream schools, some would need the safeguard of a 'statement' of special educational need for which the Act provided. The Act gives parents rights to consultation in the assessment process and access to the appeal committees set up under the Education Act 1980.

Subject to certain conditions, children with special educational needs could be integrated into mainstream schools.

Cockcroft Report (1982)

The Cockcroft Report, 'Mathematics counts', focused on mathematics teaching in primary and secondary schools in England and Wales. In particular, it considered the mathematics needed for further and higher education, employment and adult life in general.

The Report argued that the quality of mathematics teaching needed improving. It recommended that mathematics co-ordinators be established, training be improved and the provision of teaching facilities and equipment be increased.

Examinations should offer practical targets and reflect appropriate curricula. The importance of the future needs of students with regard to employment should be recognized. Implementing the recommendations would need to involve fully teachers, examination boards, central government, LEAs, training institutions and educational research agencies.

Swinnerton-Dyer Report (1982)

This Report looked at the extent to which the scale and nature of post graduate education provision matched manpower needs. It focused on the areas covered by the Science and Engineering Research Council (SERC), the Social Science Research Council (SSRC), and the Natural Environment Research Council (NERC) and the role of these councils in meeting manpower requirements.

The Report recommended that the DES should consider the provision of maintenance grants for conversion courses. Responsibility for identifying needs and for commissioning courses held jointly by the University Grants Committee, Research Councils, Training Boards and others, should be held by a single body. The DES should liaise with other government departments to establish such a body.

Both the SERC and the SSRC should keep statistics of rates of submission for the research students which they support. These figures should be published and analysed into particular universities. This would identify any university having unacceptable submission rates, enabling the SERC or SSRC to impose sanctions.

Swann Report (1985)

The Swann Committee received the same brief as the Rampton Committee (see Rampton Report 1981).

The Report recommended that central government, HMI, examination boards, LEAs and others should keep relevant ethnically based statistics. Pupils needing extra teaching in the English language should not be withdrawn but should be taught within the classroom. While a child's mother tongue and languages used in the community ought to be encouraged, they should not be part of the standard school curriculum. The Report questioned the continuing need for a daily act of worship as required by the Education Act 1944. In the view of most of the committee, schools for minority communities, if formed, could lead to a greater degree of rejection of minorities.

All courses of teacher training should prepare students to teach in a multicultural society. While more teachers from ethnic minorities should be employed, there should be no quota system of recruitment.

Lindop Report (1985)

The Lindop Report was concerned with the duties of those responsible for the academic validation of first and higher level degree courses in the public sector in Great Britain. In particular, it considered ways in which academic standards in this area could be maintained and improved. It took account of validation arrangements of higher education courses in the public sector which were below degree level.

The Report recommended that there should be a range of different kinds of validation. These should include the following:

- external validation of particular degree courses and groups of courses;
- accreditation of institutions and possibly subject areas;
- complete self validation.

A new advisory committee should be formed to process applications for validation. The Secretary of State needed powers to designate self validating institutions. A national body ought to be formed to co-ordinate the validation activities of individual universities in the public sector. Applications of students lacking conventional entry qualifications who will not reach degree standard should be better scrutinized.

The legal ties regulating the relationship between LEAs and the institute of higher education which they maintain needed to be examined. The external examiner system should be strengthened.

Education (No. 2) Act 1986

This Act gave school governing bodies more responsibilities. Governing bodies were to have an instrument of government and articles of government made by order of the LEA. The composition of the governing body and the election (or co-option) of members was laid down. The Act defined new powers for discipline and exclusion divided between heads and governing bodies.

Corporal punishment was abolished in state schools.

Higginson Report (1988)

The background to the brief which the Higginson Committee received was that the government intended to keep the General Certificate in Education Advanced Level Examinations (A levels). The aim was to maintain or improve the character and standards of A level. The Report was to recommend the principles which should apply to A level syllabuses and their assessment. This was in order to ensure consistency in the content and assessment of subjects.

The Report recommended streamlined and more difficult syllabuses. Normally, full-time students should follow a programme of three to five A level subjects and one Advance Supplementary (AS) level subject. There should be a compulsory common core for each subject. All A level syllabuses should be reviewed, then AS level syllabuses should be revised. The number of A level syllabuses should be reduced, saving resources. Explicit assessment criteria should be developed to give more accurate and uniform marking. In-course assesment should comprise 20 per cent of the total marks. The Schools' Examinations and Assessment Council (SEAC) should act as a central body to consider appeals and co-ordinate the work of the Examination Boards. Certificates ought to be modified for prospective employers to show a summary of the syllabus and more information about the candidate's achievements.

Kingman Report (1988)

The Kingman committee was asked to recommend a model of English language (spoken and written). The model would influence how teachers are taught to understand how the language works. It would also inform professional discussion of English teaching. The committee were asked to recommend principles to guide teachers about how the model should be made explicit for pupils to make them realize how language is used in different contexts. The brief was also to recommend what pupils need to know about how the English language works and therefore what they should have been taught at the ages of 7, 11 and 16.

The Report recommended that primary schools should make a member of staff a language consultant to give advice on language work. Prospective primary school teachers should undergo a language course with half of the time spent on being taught 'knowledge about language' (KAL). The nature of KAL was given in the model of language which the Report provided.

In secondary schools, all subject departments involved in language teaching needed a co-ordinated policy. Potential secondary school English teachers should follow a special course which was recommended in the model.

All English teachers ought to have a first degree in English. A National Language Project should be initiated under the School Curriculum Development Council.

Education Reform Act 1988

This major Act provided for a National Curriculum for schools to be set up. The National Curriculum (NC) would not apply to hospital schools, nursery classes, nursery schools, independent schools or city technology colleges. Every pupil in a maintained school (including special schools and Grant Maintained schools) is entitled to a curriculum which: 'promotes the spiritual, moral, cultural, mental and physical development of pupils at the school and of society', and which: 'prepares such pupils for the opportunities, responsibilities and experiences of adult life'.

The NC would comprise core subjects (English, mathematics and science, plus Welsh in Welsh speaking schools in Wales) and foundation subjects (technology, history, geography, music, art, physical education and a modern foreign language). These, plus religious education, constitute the 'basic curriculum'.

The 'whole' curriculum includes cross curricular themes, careers education and guidance; health education; personal and social education and citizenship; economic and industrial understanding; and environmental education.

A National Curriculum Council (NCC), a Curriculum Council for Wales and a School Examinations and Assessment Council (SEAC) were to be formed with members appointed by the Secretary of State. All pupils at maintained schools should attend an act of collective worship. Each LEA was required to constitute a standing advisory council on religious education (SACRE).

Concerning the local management of schools, LEAs are required to provide the Secretary of State with a scheme for financing county and voluntary schools. This should include provision for delegating the management of a school's budget to its governing body.

The ERA made provision for certain schools to apply for Grant Maintained status and leave LEA control. The governing body of such a school must be of a certain size and composition and their powers and the financial arrangements are set out in the Act. A secret postal ballot of parents must be held as a step towards Grant Maintained status. Once proposals for Grant Maintained status have been published initial governors can be elected.

The duty of LEAs to provide facilities for higher education was removed. Institutions involved would become separate legal entities.

The National Advisory Body for Public Sector Higher Education would be replaced by the Polytechnic and Colleges Funding Council. The Universities Grants Committee would be replaced by the Universities Funding Council.

Further education colleges would continue to be maintained by LEAs. However, at least half of their governors must represent employment interests.

The Inner London Education Authority (ILEA) would be abolished and the Act set out the arrangements necessary for reorganizing education in inner London.

Elton Report (1989)

The background to the Elton Report was the public concern about violence and indiscipline in schools, and problems faced by teachers. It considered what action could be taken to secure the orderly atmosphere necessary in schools for effective teaching and learning.

The Report recommended that initial teacher training should include practical training and the management of pupils' classroom behaviour.

National standards should be established on the amount of time teacher trainers must spend in school. In the LEA Training Grants scheme for 1990–91, the management of pupil behaviour should be a national priority. A two-year scheme should monitor procedures for excluding pupils from school. Two new Education Support Grants should tackle: (a) truancy; and (b) the problem of difficult pupils on site and off.

Management training programmes for headteachers and senior staff should emphasize the skills needed to motivate and lead staff and manage institutional change.

Education (Schools) Act 1992

The Act deals with Her Majesty's Inspectorate for Schools in England and in Wales and the functions and powers of the Chief Inspector for each country to arrange for inspections. It concerns the registration of inspectors, the provision of inspection services by LEAs and the power of LEAs to inspect maintained schools for a specific purpose.

Under the Act the Office of Her Majesty's Chief Inspector of Schools in England was set up. This office, known as the Office for Standards in Education (OFSTED), is a new non-ministerial government department. It has a duty (section 2 of the Act) to keep the Secretary of State informed about:

- the quality of education provided by schools in England;
- the educational standards achieved in these schools;
- whether these schools are efficiently managing their financial resources;
- the spiritual, moral, social and cultural development of pupils in those schools.

A comparable department was set up in Wales to fulfil similar duties.

The Further and Higher Education Act 1992

The Act established a new Further Education Funding Council for England with effect from 1993. The FEFC became responsible for part-time education for all those over school age and full-time education for designated categories of 19+ year olds. Further Education colleges and sixth-form colleges were withdrawn from LEA responsibility, and achieved a far greater degree of self-determination in a process described as incorporation. The conditions of incorporation were laid down in the Act. The Act laid down outline arrangements for the transfer of property, rights, liabilities and staff from LEA to institutional control. The Act allowed LEAs to retain control of sixth forms in LEA secondary schools. It did not remove all post-16 provision from LEAs nor for ensuring progression between sectors of education. The Act laid down a number of requirements relating to quality assurance, the role of Her Majesty's Chief Inspector, the governance of institutions, and grants and travel arrangements.

Education Act 1993

This wide-ranging Act made it easier and quicker for schools to become Grant Maintained (GM), so building on the Education Reform Act 1988. A new Funding Agency for Schools took over the payment of grants to GM schools and shared with LEAs, the planning responsibility for school places. Small primary schools would be able to apply jointly for GM status. The government would encourage LEA schools and GM schools to co-operate regarding school admissions and the Secretary of State would intervene if necessary. Both voluntary bodies and independent promoters could propose the establishment of new self-governing schools. The Government would encourage more schools to specialize in technology and to appoint sponsor governors; offer help with finance and management and develop strong school–industry links.

Extending the provisions of the Education (Schools) Act 1992, where schools appear to be at risk, the government would ask Her Majesty's Chief Inspector to arrange for their early inspection. If LEAs and governing bodies do not show evidence of being able to improve 'at risk' schools, then 'Education Associations' will be formed to manage the school. Similar arrangements will apply to GM schools which are 'at risk'.

Again building on the Education Reform Act 1988, the Education Act 1993 provides that the National Curriculum Council and the Schools' Examinations and Assessment Council is replaced by a new School Curriculum and Assessment Authority. All secondary schools must provide sex education but parents have the right to withdraw their child.

Regarding special educational needs, the Act substantially modified parts of the Education Act 1981. A new code of practice would set out the role of LEAs and schools in making arrangements for pupils with special educational needs. An independent tribunal would hear the appeals of parents against decisions of the LEA regarding special education for their child. Any LEA or GM school named in an SEN statement must admit the child. The Secretary of State would be able to make regulations to enable special schools to become GM.

Turning to exclusions and education otherwise than at school, a framework would encourage effective management and high standards of school behaviour and discipline. The number of pupils being excluded from school would be reduced and those who are excluded would be returned faster. The standard of education provided for children educated otherwise than in school would be improved.

Regarding the more effective use of resources, new arrangements were envisaged to speed up the removal of surplus school places and enable the money saved to be spent on children. The Secretary of State would be able to direct LEAs and the Funding Agency to submit plans to reduce surplus places. In cases where the Secretary of State sets out alternative proposals for rationalization, there would be a new public enquiry system.

In summary, the Act developed from the White Paper, 'Choice and Diversity: a new framework for schools', published in 1992. This aimed to develop the themes of quality, diversity, increasing parental choice, greater autonomy for schools and greater accountability.

Dearing Report (1993)

The brief to Sir Ron Dearing in April 1993, from the Secretary of State for Education, was to undertake a review of the National Curriculum (NC), including considering the scope for slimming down the curriculum.

The main recommendations of the Report 'The National Curriculum and its Assessments' were as follows:

- for 5 to 14 year olds, the NC should be reduced to 80 per cent to provide schools with the equivalent to one day per week to use at their discretion. The curriculum of 14 to 16 year olds should be reduced to 60 per cent;
- both attainment targets (ATs) and statements of attainment (SATs) should be reduced in number;
- English, mathematics and science should be left as intact as possible. Mastering information technology should have great importance at key stages (KS) 1 to 3. It should be the non-core subjects which should attract most of the slimming down;
- concerning 14 to 16 year olds, the only mandatory subjects should be English, mathematics, single science, physical education and short courses in a modern foreign language and technology. History and geography should be optional;
- General National Vocational Qualifications and NVQ options should be developed for KS4;
- the way in which free-standing courses can be accredited should be considered urgently;
- the 10-level scale should be kept but some modifications should be made. These include making the steps between the levels more even. The scale should not apply to KS4, where the GCSE grades A to G should be kept;
- moderated teacher assessment should underpin standards;
- a committee on special educational needs should be set up as part of the continuing review of the NC.

SCOTLAND

This section gives a brief description in chronological order of Reports and Education Acts which have helped shape Scottish education. The period covered is from the early 1960s to 1980.

Wheatley Report (1963)

The Wheatley Report led to the General Teaching Council for Scotland being formed in 1966. The Council's role is to keep under review standards of fitness to teach and make recommendations regarding teacher supply. It also has to be aware of the nature of instruction given in Colleges of Education. It must establish and maintain a register and decide whether registration is to be refused or withdrawn.

Brunton Report (1963)

The Brunton Report enquired into aims suitable for groups of different ability and the kind of curricula appropriate for the third and fourth years of secondary education.

It recommended that more able pupils follow an academic curriculum leading towards the Scottish Certificate of Education. It recommended that other pupils should pursue a vocational curriculum.

Primary Education in Scotland Memorandum (1965)

The memorandum gave an assessment of best practice in primary schools in Scotland and set out principles on which primary education should be founded.

The Teaching Council (Scotland) Act 1965

This Act established a General Teaching Council for Scotland. The Council registers teachers and regulates their professional training. In cases of misconduct, teachers can be struck off the register.

Before Five Report (1971)

This report gave an appraisal of best practice in nursery schools and classes and set out the principles on which pre-school education should be based.

Brunton Report (1972)

The 1972 Brunton Report reviewed arrangements for postgraduate teacher training for secondary education and proposed 'sandwich' courses.

Melville Report (1973)

The Melville Report was concerned with the training of staff instructors in junior occupational centres for the mentally handicapped. It recommended that these centres became schools and formed part of wider educational provision. In addition to existing instructors, teachers should be appointed.

Education (Mentally Handicapped Children) (Scotland) Act 1974

Following the 1973 Melville Report, this Act gave responsibility for junior occupational centres to education authorities. Mentally handicapped children, therefore, became the responsibility of the education service.

Alexander Report (1975)

Looking at adult education, the Alexander Report considered aims suitable to voluntary adult leisure time courses which were educational but not specifically vocational.

Ruthven Report (1976)

The Ruthven Report reviewed the services of ancillary staff in secondary schools; administrative, clerical, technicians and auxiliaries. The report recommended a new staff to pupil ratio.

Stimpson Report (1976)

The Stimpson Report considered non-teaching staff in secondary schools; youth and community workers, librarians and instructors. It recommended a new staff to pupil ratio.

Munn Report (1977)

The Munn Report considered the Scottish secondary school curriculum with reference to curriculum structure in the third and fourth years. It looked at how the curriculum could be structured to ensure that all pupils received a balanced education suited to their abilities and needs. The committee also considered implications for the stages of education before and after the third and fourth year.

Dunning Report (1977)

Since the introduction of the Ordinary Grade of the Scottish Certificate of Education social and educational changes had occurred. The Dunning Report was to identify aims and purposes of assessment and certification bearing these changes in mind. Like the Munn Report, its remit was the third and fourth years of secondary schooling. The Dunning Report looked at forms of examination or assessment likely to meet the needs of third and fourth year pupils of different academic ability. It considered also the effect of any changes on Higher Grade of the examination and the Certificate of Sixth Year Studies.

Pack Report (1977)

Whereas the Elton Report 1989 was to focus on public disquiet about violence and indiscipline in schools in England and Wales, the Pack Report considered truancy and indiscipline in Scottish schools some twelve years earlier. Its remit was primary and secondary schools. The report considered ways in which the problem might be reduced, the circumstance which would justify the suspension or expulsion of a pupil from school and how such pupils might be provided for.

Sneddon Report (1978)

'Learning to Teach', as the Sneddon Report was titled, considered student teaching practice and the induction of probationer teachers. The report evaluated experimental work and recent work in colleges of education and schools. This work was aimed at improving the quality of:

• student teaching practice; and
• arrangements for probationary teacher induction.

The Education of Pupils with Learning Difficulties (1978)

This HMI report considered the education of pupils with learning difficulties in Scottish primary and secondary schools. In parallel with some of the thinking which informed the Warnock Report 1978, the report recommended that pupils with learning difficulties who are appropriately placed in mainstream schools should be educated as part of the normal school provision. It also recommended that remedial specialists should not only work with pupils taken out of class for teaching but should act also as consultants to class teachers.

Glasgow Report (1980)

Scottish school councils were the subject of the Glasgow Report, which recommended that there should be:

- a school council for every school;
- a national information and training centre;
- a regional service and information unit.

Education (Scotland) Act 1980

This Act repealed many earlier Acts and consolidated earlier legislation. Its provisions included the duties and powers of education authorities, the rights and duties of parents, the Scottish Examination Board which is responsible for examinations leading to certificates of secondary education, and provision for children with special educational needs.

Classified List of A to Z Entries

Education: Concepts and Issues, Disciplines, Types and Phases

Accountability
Adult education
Alternative education
Authority
Autonomy
Child-centred education
Christian education
Citizenship
Comparative education
Competition in school
Conductive education
Continuing education (*see* Adult
  education)
Creativity
Day release
Democracy and schools
Deschooling
Discipline
Discovery (Guided discovery)
Distance education (*see* Open
  education)
Education
Egalitarianism
Elitism
Equal opportunities
Experience (education through
  experience)
Further education (FE)

History of education
Home education (*see* Alternative
  education)
Home–school relations
Humanist education (*see* Plato)
Indoctrination
Industrial training (*see* Vocational
  education)
Integration–segregation
Interests
International education
Knowledge (and the school
  curriculum)
Multicultural education
Needs
Nursery education
Open education
Part-time education
Pastoral care
Philosophy of education
Play
Psychology and education
Quaker education
Racial discrimination
Rationality
Readiness
Recurrent education (*see* Adult
  education)
Sandwich courses
Scotland: Education system
Selection according to ability
Sociology of education

Tertiary education
Theory and education
Traditionalist education
Understanding
Unemployment (and school leavers)
Wales
Youth work

Schools and Other Institutions and their Organization

Ability grouping
Aided schools (admission to)
Banding
Business and Technology Education
  Council (BTEC)
Business education (*see* National
  Vocational Qualifications)
Cathedral (choir) schools
Catholic schools
Choir schools (*see* Cathedral schools)
Church of England schools
City Technology Colleges
Colleges and Institutes of Higher
  Education
Colleges of Further Education
  (*see* Further Education Colleges)
Day nursery
Department for Education
  (background from 1833)
Effective schools
Ethos of school
Feeder Schools
First schools (*see* Primary schools)
Funding Agency for Schools (FAS)
Further Education Colleges
Grant Maintained schools (GM
  schools)
Grouping by ability (*see* Streaming)
Higher education (HE)
Hospital schools service
Independent schools
Intellectual climate

International schools
Islamic education
Jewish education
Learning environment
Local management of schools (LMS)
Management of schools and colleges
Management style
Middle schools (*see* Primary schools)
Mission statement
Mixed ability organization
Montessori schools
Nursery classes
Nursery schools
Office for Standards in Education
  (OFSTED)
Open plan schools
Open University
Pastoral management
Positive management of schools
Preparatory schools(*see* Primary
  schools)
Pre-preparatory schools (*see* Primary
  schools)
Primary schools
Prison service education
Public schools
School environment
School Library Service (SLS)
School management plan
School management task force
Schools of Science and Technology
Secondary schools/secondary
  education
Setting
Sixth form/Sixth-form colleges
Special schools
Special units
Steiner schools
Streaming
Teachers' centres
Teacher Training Agency
Training Enterprise Councils (TECs)
University
Vertical grouping

Instrument of government
Insurance
Opting out
Parental choice
Playground safety
Punishment
Record keeping
Road safety
Safety of playgrounds (*see* Playground safety)
School brochure
School meals
Special purpose grants
Starting school
Statementing
Statutory instruments (SI)
Student charter
Teacher appraisal
Transfer between schools
Transitional grant
Transport (school)
Truancy
White paper – Education and Training for the 21st Century
Years of schooling (nomenclature)

Individual Differences Among Learners

Able pupils – characteristics
Able pupils: managing learning of
Able pupils: needs of
Abused children
Acquired immune deficiency syndrome (AIDS)
Adolescence
Alcohol abuse (*see* Drug abuse)
Average pupils
Bilingual pupils
Bullying
Child development (*see* Adolescence)
Cognition
Curiosity
Drug abuse
Dyslexia

Emotional/behavioural difficulties(EBD)
Gender (*see* Equal opportunities)
Gifted
Hyperactivity
Intelligence and intelligence tests
Learning difficulties (*see* Special educational needs)
Literacy/adult literacy
Nutrition and intelligence
Overachievement
School phobia
Skills
Smoking (*see* Drug abuse)
Social influences (on education)
Special educational needs
Traveller children
Underachievement

Curriculum and Assessment

Academic awards
Accreditation of prior achievement (APA)
Accreditation of prior learning (APL)
Advanced levels (A-levels)
Advanced supplementary levels (A/S levels)
Apprenticeship
Art (in the National Curriculum)
Articled teachers
Assessment (in the National Curriculum)
Attainment target (AT) (in the National Curriculum)
Baccalaureate
Bachelor of Education
Bachelor's degrees
Basic curriculum (*see* National Curriculum)
Basic skills
Careers education and guidance
Combined/balanced science

Profile components (*see* Assessment in the National Curriculum)
Programmes of study (PoS) in the National Curriculum
Qualified teacher status (QTS)
Records of achievement
Religious education (and the basic curriculum)
Science (in the National Curriculum)
Sex education
Spelling
Sport
Standard test or tasks
Statements of attainment (*see* National Curriculum)
Teachers' certificate
Vocational education and training
Vocational guidance/vocational education
Welsh language
Whole curriculum
Work experience
Writing (pupils) (*see* English)

Pedagogy

Action research
Active learning
Affective education
Behaviour modification
Body language (*see* Communication in the classroom)
Class control (*see* Class management)
Class management
Class size
Classroom climate
Classroom language (*see* Communication in the classroom)
Classroom organization
Classroom tasks (*see* Tasks)
Communication in the classroom
Computer-assisted learning
Counselling
Dependent learner
Detention

Didactic teaching
Differentiation
Direct instruction
Discipline (teacher achieving/ maintaining)
Discussion
Effective teacher
English as a foreign language (EFL)
English as a second language (ESL)
Experiential learning
Explaining
Feedback
Flexible learning
Group tasks
Group work
Homework
Independent learner
Individual learning
Individualized learning
Ineffective lessons
Interaction analysis
Interviews (for posts)
Interviews (for research)
Intonation
Learning theory
Lesson
Lesson planning/structure
Lesson structure (*see* Lesson planning)
Listening
Look and say (*see* Reading)
Marking
Micro teaching
Mixed ability teaching
Open learning
Paired learning (*see* Peer group tutoring)
Participant observation
Peer group tutoring
Phonics (*see* Reading)
Programmed learning
Project work
Questioning: probing skills
Reading: methods of teaching

Reflective practitioner
Reflective practitioner model
Rewards (use of)
Role play
Rote learning
Silence (use of)
Speaking
Story reading
Storytelling
Stress (teacher and pupils)
Study skills
Task
Teacher effectiveness: the pupils' views
Teacher talk (see Communication in the classroom; explaining)
Teaching method
Teaching mode
Teaching skills
Team teaching
Thinking skills
Topic work
Topic work: criteria for success
Topic work: teacher preparations for

Tuition
Tutorial
Whole class teaching

Resources

Audio visual aids
Books
Buildings
Calculators
Camcorder
Computers
Display
Educational journals
Information technology
Overhead projector (OHP)
Schools' broadcasting
Tape recorder
Teacher as a resource
Times Educational Supplement (*TES*)
Times Higher Educational Supplement (*THES*)
Video recorder (see Tape recorder)